MARGARET MEAD:
THE COMPLETE BIBLIOGRAPHY 1925-1975

Margaret Mead:

The Complete Bibliography 1925-1975

edited by

Joan Gordan

1976
MOUTON
THE HAGUE - PARIS

ISBN 90 279 3026 0

Printed in the Netherlands

TABLE OF CONTENTS

INTRODUCTION

As my publishing choices have been so unorthodox, it seems worthwhile to preface this bibliography with some explanation of how these choices were made. In my first years of writing I followed quite conventional lines: I decided that I wanted to publish an article and looked for the most likely professional journal in which to place it; I then wrote the article, submitted it, and if it was refused I tried to place it elsewhere. The articles themselves were based on my research work at the time and designed for specific technical audiences. For example, when "An Ethnologist's Footnote to *Totem and Taboo*" (21) was rejected by *The International Journal of Psychoanalysis*, I sent it to the *Psychoanalytic Review*, which accepted it. While I was a graduate student, I completed a brief piece of research using a single West African informant and sent it to the *Journal of the Royal Anthropological Institute* in 1925; they held it and finally published it in 1937 as "A Twi Relationship System" (93), without giving me any chance to review it in the light of five intervening field trips during which the specific kinship problems involved were at the center of my field investigations and subsequent publications, such as *Social Organization of Manu'a* (25) and *Kinship in the Admiralty Islands* (66).

By 1928, journals such as *Natural History* (23, 36, 65, 70 etc.), *Parents Magazine* (26, 59), *The Nation* (31) and *The Thinker* (20) were beginning to ask me for articles. I was asked to review books, not only for appropriate technical journals, but also for the *New Freeman* (28) and *The Nation* (15). In 1930, two literary entrepreneurs, Calverton and Schmalhausen, introduced a style which was to continue to this day of asking a group of contributors to write like *The New Generation* on topical subjects (19). In addition to requests for articles for encyclopedias (32, 33, 69, 81 etc.), journals of various degrees of technicality, ranging from *The New York Times Magazine* (63) to *Publishers' Weekly* (38), to *Safety Education* (40), began to ask me for articles.

These requests were partly a reflection of the popularity of *Coming of Age in Samoa* (6). I had not designed that book to reach a popular audience, in the sense in which one writes for a general nonfiction audience, but I did take what was then a very unusual course. I was trying to write a book on a technical subject, in which ethnological and psychological jargon would have been expected, and to make it intelligible to specially concerned groups of people, particularly those who had to work with adolescents in our own society — secondary school teachers and social workers. I did not realize then that if a book were written in English, stripped of technical jargon — which in the ethnographic literature of those days meant the use of an enormous number of words in the native language — it would automatically become accessible to the educated world, be easy reading for beginners in college and easily translatable into other languages.

The decision to make the material accessible to those most concerned had been presaged by the articles which I intentionally placed in educational journals, giving the results of my first piece of research on the effect of language learned at home on the test scores of Italian-American children, published in *School and Society* in 1927 (4, 5). As I had chosen anthropology as a profession because I felt the research was urgent and the application to current social problems was visible and compelling, making my findings available to a larger, but specialized audience, was a matter of conscious choice from the very start of my career.

When Pliny E. Goddard, Curator of Ethnology at The American Museum of Natural History, asked me in 1925 to join the staff of the Museum, he had specifically indicated his hope that I would be able to make ethnology as familiar to a wide and supportive audience as previous curators had made the subject of archeology. I had by then published nothing but poetry and editorials in the *Barnard Bulletin*, which I edited in 1922, and the only writing I had done was my dissertation, *An Inquiry into the Question of Cultural Stability in Polynesia* (7), which was dry and formal enough in all conscience. Goddard's prescience, however, provided me with a mandate for responding to the requests from such journals as *The New York Times* (63, 124), *The Saturday Review of Literature* (82), *The Nation* (15) and *Natural History* (23, 36, 65, 70), the house organ of The American Museum of Natural History, through which we reached our worldwide circle of Museum members.

I think that my original hope of becoming a writer played its part, as I had successively thought about and tried out various mediums — poetry, essays, short stories, plays and pageants — during my secondary school and college years, and I had not entirely relinquished my aspirations to publish poetry even after my decision to become an anthropologist. However, when "Ab-

solute Benison" (51), a poem I submitted under a pseudonym, was first rejected and then accepted by the same poetry editor when I resubmitted it
under my own name in 1932, after I had published *Coming of Age in Samoa*
(6), I never again submitted a poem for publication. My fortunate association
in college with the noted American poet, Leonie Adams, had convinced me
that poetry was not a field in which I could make any major contribution.
Ruth Benedict and Edward Sapir, my close associates in the mid 1920's, had
both written a good deal of poetry which was published in the little poetry
journals of the period and both had books of poems rejected in 1928. So I
turned firmly away from further attempts at publication.

The short stories I wrote during my graduate school days were, I later
realized, all designed to solve problems that puzzled me, rather than as
literature per se. The pageants which I wrote and produced were related to an
interest in production which I was later able to express in directing and
constructing ethnographic films in the field. It was also quite clear to us, as
students, that writing was a very valuable tool and that the anthropologist
who could write like Malinowski, who was already reaching a wide audience,
had a tremendous edge over his less gifted contemporaries. Malinowski's
Argonauts of the Western Pacific (1922) contrasted with Radcliff-Brown's
The Andaman Islanders (1922). Franz Boas' *The Mind of Primitive Man*
(1911) seemed to us to lack the literary persuasiveness which its importance
and its subject matter deserved. Thus there was a mandate within the profession, stretching back to Frazer (1907-1925), Crawley (1927) and Marett
(1909), to write in literate English rather than in the heavy German style
which had already captured the American university dissertation field.

This mandate to write in ordinary English and as intelligibly as possible
did not, however, mean that I abandoned technical writing. After all the
success and acclaim accorded *Coming of Age in Samoa* (6), I found it very
pleasant to turn to a technical audience of my peers when I wrote *Social
Organization of Manu'a* (25) for the Bernice P. Bishop Museum series. But
here also I was acutely conscious of the need to write at different levels of
generalization. I gathered together a pile of the famous monographs of the
period – Rivers' *The Todas* (1906), Malinowski's *Argonauts of the Western
Pacific* (1922), Roscoe's *The Baganda* (1911) and Grinnell's *The Cheyenne
Indians* (1923) – and studied their arrangements. Franz Boas, under whose
direction my graduate work and first field work were done, had said: "The
trouble with a monograph is that you need the end at the beginning, and this
is true of every chapter – you need each chapter in all the others." I also
decided that there were three groups of colleagues to whom the monograph
would be useful: scholars interested in the dynamics of social structure who
would have little familiarity with Oceanic ethnography, scholars interested

specifically in Oceania and scholars who were specializing in Polynesian ethnology, for whom details of Manu'an social organization would be important. This established, I organized the monograph into three levels of decreasing generality. Making this provision for readers with different types of expectations and capacities was echoed many years later when I worked on the discussion of the same set of ideas in *People and Places* (557), a book for children, a chapter for Lyman Bryson's book, *An Outline of Man's Knowledge of the Modern World* (592), for an adult audience and my most systematic theoretical book, *Continuities in Cultural Evolution* (771).

Experimentation with different levels and kinds of writing really went on until 1935 when I wrote *Sex and Temperament in Three Primitive Societies* (79), which I felt was a satisfactory combination of aesthetic requirements and a way of presenting difficult theoretical and unfamiliar ethnographic materials to the literate public. After that I stopped writing poetry. I do at times expend more craftsmanship on an essay designed for a more specifically literary audience like that of *The American Scholar* (470) or *Daedalus* (543), but on the whole I am not pursued by the type of regrets that haunt many of those who have learned to write in some other genre than the one to which they originally aspired. So I was spared the frustrations of so many scientists who write with pleasure but with a persistent hope that someday a great novel will emerge. Once I had satisfied myself that human cultures were far more complex and interesting than anything I could create and that in my attempts to write fiction I had actually been trying to understand real situations that I had encountered as a child, I had no further desire to write fiction.

But I kept an interest in form and I find each novel request — to narrate a film (*28, 29*), write a script to accompany photographs (832), a narration to be used on an audiograph in The American Museum of Natural History Hall of the Peoples of the Pacific (1146, 1151), for example, or to write for a foreign audience (360), to lecture in a combination of English and Pidgin English to a New Guinea audience with varying degrees of competence in English (160) — challenging and exciting.

By the time I had been writing professionally for about five years, there was a marked contrast between the way I planned my books and large scale monographs and the way I wrote articles, reviews and books which were more on the periphery of my central interest, especially books which I co-authored or edited. Thus for all of my major publications on my own field work — *Coming of Age in Samoa* (6), *Social Organization of Manu'a* (25), *Growing Up in New Guinea* (22), *Kinship in the Admiralty Islands* (66), *Sex and Temperament in Three Primitive Societies* (79), *The Mountain Arapesh* (94, 107, 269, 313), *Male and Female* (312), *New Lives for Old* (467),

Continuities in Cultural Evolution (771) and *Culture and Commitment* (1063) — I decided what I wanted to write; the input of editors and publishers was relatively slight. My first publisher, William Morrow, suggested that I add the last two chapters to *Coming of Age in Samoa*, discussing the relevance of the Samoan findings to American culture — a topic which I had already been discussing in lectures and teaching. Theyer Hobson, my editor at William Morrow complained that the central chapter on the Mundugumor in *Sex and Temperament in Three Primitive Societies* was too difficult, so I tore it up and rewrote it. He also suggested the title for *New Lives for Old*. The title for *Growing Up in New Guinea* was an unfortunate echo of the title of *Coming of Age in Samoa*, and the words *New Guinea* — quite accurate for the territory within which the Manus were situated — were used because my publisher complained that no one would know where Manus was. I had received an honorary appointment to the staff of the Bernice P. Bishop Museum and my monograph, *Social Organization of Manu'a*, fitted into their publication series on Polynesia. *Kinship in the Admiralty Islands* was my response to a review of *Growing Up in New Guinea*, inspired by Malinowski, who claimed I knew nothing about the kinship system; I postponed a planned field trip for four months to write it for The American Museum of Natural History series. The long papers on the Mountain Arapesh for the Museum series were planned first as a division of labor between Reo Fortune and myself and then revised because of the increased expense of production which made it necessary to abandon one entire section for which all of the preparatory art work had been done.

Since my Samoan trip, all my field work has been done in collaboration with others, resulting in numerous publications including: *Balinese Character*, with Gregory Bateson (140); "The Cult as a Condensed Social Process" (607) and a paper on "Micro- and Macro-Cultural Models for Cultural Evolution" (644) with Theodore Schwartz. In each case the publications were the result of various kinds of planning about what I would write and what my collaborators would write, the sequence in which books and papers were to be written and the extent to which our separate publications would rely on the other's field work.

In a second category are books which resulted from projects, the project itself having been originated by another person or institution. *The Changing Culture of an Indian Tribe* (53) was a report on a project which I had been asked to undertake by Clark Wissler, the Chairman of my department at The American Museum of Natural History, to discharge an obligation which he had assumed in accepting a $750 grant from Mrs. Leonard Elmhirst for a study of American Indian family life. Neither the problem nor the tribe selected, the Omaha (for whom I used the pseudonym, the "Antlers"), were my choice, but I did write and find a publisher for the book. Thirty-four years later, when there was a move to reprint some of the publications of the Columbia University Press, I write a new introduction on "The Consequences of Racial Guilt" for the paperback published by Capricorn Books, Putnam (866).

Cooperation and Competition among Primitive Peoples (89) was the end product of a project inaugurated by the Subcommittee on Competitive and Cooperative Habits of the Committee on Personality and Culture of the Social Science Research Council in the United States. I had assumed responsibility for preparing the section dealing with the possible contribution of ethnological material to the planning of research in competitive and cooperative societies. I had also developed a new method for using field workers as living primary sources to answer questions which had not been raised in the course of their own field work by setting them the task of reexamining in a seminar context their field materials plus, in a few cases, the unpublished work of other accessible field workers. This eventually became a book which I edited and then updated in 1961 for a Beacon Press paperback edition (634). The choice of publisher was made on the basis of a connection between the initiators of the project and the McGraw-Hill Publishing Company.

Balinese Character: A Photographic Study (140) was the outcome of careful consideration by Gregory Bateson and myself of what seemed to be the most methodologically innovative portion of our 1936-1939 field trip to Bali (99). In deciding to make a massive collection of over 25.000 still photographs, we had made a quantum leap from any previous use of still photography. In the design of the book we grouped widely disparate activities to show points of similarity on one page without disturbing the integrity of each event. This arrangement was itself an innovation in methods of presentation, followed nine years later by a related type of presentation in *Growth and Culture: A Photographic Study of Balinese Childhood* (363), which I undertook in response to Frances Macgregor's interest in developing her photographic experience in a social science context.

And Keep Your Powder Dry (142), written in the midst of World War II, was the result of a joint decision by Gregory Bateson and myself that it would be a good idea to make a "Penguin" out of the articles and lectures I had been giving during the first two years of the War. When I started assembling the materials, I decided it would be better instead to write a new book using the ideas from the earlier papers. This later did become a Penguin, coming out first in paperback in England in 1944 under the title, *The American Character* (142).

Cultural Patterns and Technical Change (399) was again a response to a project which went through a series of steps, in the first and last of which

I was involved. As Executive Secretary of the National Research Council, Committee on Food Habits during World War II (1941-1945), chaired in its final stages by Lawrence K. Frank, I had held a few sessions on living habits. These initial discussions were amplified in a memorandum prepared by Lawrence Frank through the National Association for Mental Health (of the United States) for the World Federation for Mental Health; this plan was brought to the attention of the Division of the Social Sciences in UNESCO. UNESCO offered the World Federation for Mental Health a contract with certain rather severe restrictions on the selection of an editor. I was faced in the midst of many other obligations with the danger that the WFMH would lose the UNESCO grant, which was desperately needed to meet a matching grant, unless I undertook the editorship. This became *Cultural Patterns and Technical Change*, again carefully written in ordinary English because it was designed for specialists of different sorts — nutritionists, public health workers, agriculturalists, etc. After an initial unenterprising publication in the UNESCO-Tensions and Technology Series, Mentor Books (399) published it as a paperback in 1955 and it became a longtime best seller.

Often planning a book like this involved simultaneously planning for and relating to other projects. *Cultural Patterns and Technical Change*, for example, was designed to deal with multilateral technical assistance to fit together with a proposed volume edited by Arensberg and Niehoff (1971) on the United States Bilateral Aid Program and a volume edited by Spicer (1952) dealing with United States domestic technical assistance.

Similarly, I participated in planning for a series of volumes dealing with personality and culture: *Readings in Social Psychology*, edited by T. M. Newcomb and E. L. Hartley (1958), *Personal Character and Cultural Milieu*, edited by D.S. Haring (1956), and *Personality in Nature, Society and Culture*, edited by C. Kluckhohn and H.A. Murray (1962). In these I combined placing my own articles with an advisory, editorial role.

Another category of writing involved preparing original research review chapters for specialized books; three chapters on primitive children for manuals of child psychology (39, 109, 243), a chapter on "Cultural Determinants of Sexual Behavior" (624) and on adolescence (75), articles for various encyclopedias, including *The Encyclopedia of Psychology* (241), *The Encyclopedia of the Social Sciences* (32, 33), the *International Encyclopedia of the Social Sciences* (953), *The Encyclopedia of Mental Health* (719, 725), and *The Encyclopedia of Photography* (713), for several of which I also had advisory, editorial responsibilities.

An Anthropologist at Work: Writings of Ruth Benedict (537) was prepared in response to the request of Ruth Benedict's publisher, Paul Brooks of Houghton Mifflin, for a posthumous collection of Ruth Benedict's papers.

As she wrote very sparingly, some of her most important papers had already been reprinted many times. So in conversations with Paul Brooks, I developed the idea of a book which would involve a sort of four-sided conversation between Ruth Benedict, Franz Boas, Edward Sapir and myself. While working on the book I became interested in an anthropological style of biography which would present materials in large, cohesive chunks. Ruth Benedict's diaries from 1923 to 1926, her unpublished poems, letters from Sapir to Benedict were all presented as material whose internal integrity was not violated by the usual biographical style of using bits and pieces of quotations. The second book on Ruth Benedict (1291) was written with students in mind as part of a Columbia University series on anthropologists edited by Charles Wagley and included a new selection of her shorter papers.

Another type of external stimulus came for the children's book, *People and Places* (557), when a gifted and imaginative children's book editor, Velma Varner, asked me to do a book on anthropology for children. I realized that because children's books are expected to be lavishly illustrated and yet inexpensive, I could make the book suit a double purpose, as a text for children as well as a history of the evolution of techniques for the presentation and recording of other cultures – from the fanciful reconstructions of and artist illustrator, through the careful drawings of museum artifacts, early paintings, still photography and finally color photography.

Family (832), with photographs by Ken Heyman, was planned after Ken Heyman and I had made several photographic expeditions together, in response to his desire to do a collaborative book on the subject of family. After the theme of kinship roles – mothers, fathers, brothers, and sisters – was established, Ken searched the world and his files for photographs and I then wrote the text to fit them. The same procedure has been followed in our recent collaboration, *World Enough: Rethinking the Future* (1395).

There were three books which I co-edited as the result of big projects: *The Study of Culture at a Distance*, with Rhoda Metraux (412), *Childhood in Contemporary Cultures*, with Martha Wolfenstein (440), and *Soviet Attitudes toward Authority* (359), which I wrote with the help of the entire project staff of The American Museum of Natural History project: Studies in Soviet Culture. All of these were the results of large scale studies on contemporary cultures inaugurated by Ruth Benedict, who died before they were completed.

The anthology, *Primitive Heritage* (411), which I did with Nicolas Calas, owed its origin to a suggestion by Leo Rosten to Bennett Cerf at Random House. It was designed as a collaboration between a surrealist critic and an anthropologist, but was ruined by a jacket blurb which described Calas as an anthropologist.

The Small Conference (971) was the result of a long cooperation with Paul Byers. After the death of a collaborator with whom Byers had planned a description of a single conference, Wilton Dillon suggested that Byers and I rescue some of the original material and do a general book on conferences.

Occasionally requests would involve writing in a foreign language or for a foreign compendium, including a chapter on "Ethnology and Psychiatry" for a German encyclopedia (635), a chapter for *The Policy Sciences*, edited by Lasswell and Lerner (360), originally published in French (so that I had to adjust the references in terms of their availability in the library of the Musée de l'Homme), a chapter on the "Cross-Cultural Approach to the Study of Personality" (466), which was designed for translation into Spanish — which never occurred — in which both references and illustrations were adapted to a Spanish audience, and a chapter I wrote in 1975 with Walter Fairservis for a German book on the environment (1356).

When I knew beforehand that I was writing for a foreign publication I consulted with those who understood both languages and something about the cultural and theoretical points involved. On the other hand, with very few exceptions, foreign translations of my books have been done without any consultation, including two almost simultaneous translations, one in Germany in 1946 and one in Austria in 1947, of *And Keep Your Powder Dry* (142).

There were always amusing episodes in working with the French. An original plan to publish all three of my pre-World War II books on the South Seas — *Coming of Age in Samoa* (6), *Growing Up in New Guinea* (22) and *Sex and Temperament in Three Primitive Societies* (79) — was abandoned because the French publisher disliked *Growing Up in New Guinea*. But later the first and third books were published, leaving in the photographs which had been selected to illustrate *Growing Up in New Guinea* plus a number of irrelevant photographs from other Melanesian peoples which French anthropological consultants had inserted without consulting me. The publication of *Male and Female* (312) was delayed because a French publisher wanted to omit the chapter, "Each Family in a Home of Its Own," because it was about America and therefore did not apply to France! However, it was finally published in French as *L'Un et L'Autre Sexe* in 1966. Very often where something was being written expressly for a French audience, I would be asked to change the phrasing or even the actual idea because it was untranslatable into French. There were serious difficulties, for example, with words like *cultural patterns*, where the difficulty was not in the word *pattern*, for which there are many French equivalents, but with the pluralizing "s", as it was unacceptable to think of more than one real pattern of culture — the French, with its classical precursors.

Italian translations presented different problems. The editions are beautiful, but the enthusiastic editors disregard such details as matching pictures and text. For instance, in the Italian translation of *Childhood and Contemporary Cultures* (453), in 1963, the photographic illustrations of an East European shtetl are scattered throughout the other sections of the book.

English editions have also presented various problems. For *Growing Up in New Guinea* (22), I had to change words (*overalls* to *jeans*, for example) and to use references to English rather than to American books. When *And Keep Your Powder Dry* (142) was published in England (1967), I wrote an introduction in "English" English. At other times I simply had the American edition put into English spelling so that it could be easily transferred to the English edition. (While Americans read English spelling without even noticing the difference, the English would still have complained about American spelling. This ould not, of course, be true today.) After World War II I felt it was important to write as an American using American spelling. In fact, when I published *New Lives for Old* (467), in which I reproduced some parts of *Growing Up in New Guinea*, published twenty-seven years earlier, endless confusion resulted in the various stages of editing, copy-editing and proof-reading.

The publications of scientists are normally somewhat geared to the meetings of the scientific societies which they attend and at which they present papers. The form of these papers often depends on the requirements of the publication in which they are subsequently placed. This can be an exceedingly capricious process. The abstracts of the contributions to the meeting of the Seventh International Congress of Anthropological and Ethnological Sciences, held in Moscow in 1964, were not published until 1970 (1054). On the other hand, of my contributions to the Ninth International Congress of Anthropological and Ethnological Sciences, held in Chicago in 1973, one has already been published by Mouton (1352), while one "A Re-examination of Major Themes of the Sepik Area, Papua, New Guinea" is not yet in press.

However, as such a large part of my publishing has been stimulated in other ways, I have been less dependent than many scientists on such formal publications. On the other hand, other sorts of international congresses and symposiums represent a different kind of publication in which individual contributions are simply a part of the proceedings: the ten meetings of the Delos Symposium, accounts of which appeared in *Ekistics* (1963-1972), the proceedings of the various study group reports of the World Federation for Mental Health (853, 935) and publications of the World Council of Churches (867). This is also true of the conference type developed by the Josiah Macy, Jr. Foundation which includes a mixture of discussions and presentations: *Cybernetics*, edited by H. von Foerster (1951-1955), *Problems of Consciousness*, edited by H. A. Abramson (1951-1955), *Group Processes*, edited by

B. Schaffner (1955-1960), and *Discussions on Child Development*, edited by
J.M. Tanner and B. Inhelder (1957-1960).

Another type of stimulus to the preparation of material has come from requests to give an address to such unlikely groups as the National Association
of Deans of Women (118), the Western Personnel Service (220), or the Middle
States Association of Colleges and Secondary Schools (105). Although I
would very often introduce new ideas in such lectures, their subsequent
publication in some journal which my colleagues never saw was likely to
mean the article got lost entirely. I tried to make up for this obscurity of
publication by publishing the articles in volumes of reprints, such as *Anthropology: A Human Science* (1964); *A Way of Seeing*, by Rhoda Metraux
and myself (1970) and *Twentieth Century Faith*, edited by Ruth N. Anshen
(1972).

From 1943 to the early 1960's the Institute for Intercultural Studies sent
out selected reprints pertinent to the field of culture and personality and the
application of anthropological methods to contemporary problems. This
provided for some systematic distribution of articles published in unorthodox
places. However, it was found that the turnover of addresses was so great that
this distribution became unfeasible. I now distribute a list of my publications
periodically to about 450 of my colleagues, asking them to request any re-
print they would like to see, as the burden of receiving reprints has now
become so great that I myself tend only to read reprints that I have requested
or that have been sent to me with a personal letter.

The development of new electronic media has also made a tremendous
difference in the kind of publication requests one receives. Beginning with
stenotyping, the audiograph, wire and then tape recording, it has been possible
for organizations or conferences to transcribe one's words, usually in a highly
garbled form, and then request that the speaker edit the transcript for publication. These requests take various forms: an obligation entered into beforehand and carried out under extremely difficult conditions — lost tapes,
incoherent transcripts,etc.; transcripts from lectures or discussions which had
no previous provision for publication and which involve various kinds of
pressures, including the possibility of reproduction without permission, as
was done with the paper I presented for the Conference on the Pill (919), and
the pleas of worthy causes, fund-raising attempts, annual reports, etc. These
practices result in an enormous number of publications, the content of which
overlaps with other publications and the quality of which varies depending
upon deadlines and accessibility. It seems to be an inseparable accompani-
ment of the contemporary world, with its plethora of publication. Every
organization and institution attempts to individualize its activities and tends
to lionize a few well-known individuals while failing to develop second and

third groups of people who can take their place.

We have very few adequate means of introducing into symposiums, conferences and public occasions younger people who, if given the opportunity, might become real resources. I have used every method available to me — refusal to participate in a conference or discussion unless younger people were included, referral of conference organizers to younger people — but with very little success. I have also tried various other devices. After the 1950 White House Conference on Children (in the United States), I proposed that no one who had played a prominent role in that conference be permitted to participate prominently in the forthcoming 1960 Conference on Children, but that instead a younger age group be tapped. Despite my efforts, the same age group was used again with very unsatisfactory results. In the end I had to do an article for the series to supplement the original papers (597). Similarly, after the conference convened by the late C.H. Waddington in Chichen Itza, Mexico (1216), where I complained about the absence of young people, a great deal of time was wasted trying to get retrospective participation by young people in the proposed publication which was ultimately dropped. Later, partly as a sequel to the Waddington conference, a conference of young people nominated by outstanding scientists and scholars was convened in Sweden just prior to the Nobel Symposium 14 (1067). The students convened were given the papers of the distinguished participants to read; their major response was to cut them up and paste the cutout paragraphs at angles to one another — an activity responsive to the mood of the middle and late 1960's, which contributed very little to the deliberations of the conference.

I have reluctantly come to the conclusion that the only feasible way to elicit the participation of very young people is to involve the children of those who have won a reputation in the same field. This has two advantages: their participation is more likely to be welcomed because of their names and as they have known their distinguished parents all their lives, they are neither intimidated nor do they need to display hostility to cover a sense of the overburdening demands made upon them. So, while I regard the discovery and encouragement of younger or lesser known colleagues as very important, I have not found it easy in practice. I try to take telephone requests myself so that I can explore the possibilities of suggesting other people and I read letters asking me to go to conferences (even when the date is impossible) so as to think about and suggest suitable substitutes. I encourage others to ask busy people to do things they will most probably refuse and then to ask for the suggestion of an alternate. But one of the real difficulties of the present day world is the cumulative nature of reputation; the more one publishes, the more requests one receives.

Another problem today is the amplifier effect of the sheer number of cheap, reduplicative media and the insatiability of a throw-away society. Collections pile up on collections, articles are reprinted with different titles or parts are used as excerpts for museum exhibits, in catalogues, in books of sayings collected for all sorts of purposes, as bedtime stories and for calendars. In turn, other collectors and exploiters pick up quotations from the press and write earnestly asking to what publication the saying is to be attributed. Books published years ago, in which I had a chapter, are suddenly resuscitated, like the recently revised *While You Were Gone* (251), published in 1946 and out of print for years. This amplifier effect combines with the recent trend of editing endless volumes on special subjects for classroom use, consisting of reprints especially provided for a particular teacher's curriculum. The company which prints the collection by some cheap offset process then tries to use the opportunity to obtain permanent rights to the reprints included. All of these procedures require correspondence, checking, permissions, refusals of permission, and result in a situation where, as a recent critic said, "People can quote you on almost any subject out of context to prove anything they want to prove, and they are often wrong."

This pervasive, diffuse effect of repetitive publication is further amplified by the use of radio. Speeches made years ago and recorded for some "educational" purpose lie around in archives and suddenly appear on the air years later, containing strange anachronisms that the listener cannot explain. For example, the tone of voice I would have used in referring to "the President" in the original broadcast might be very different if I were talking about "the President" at the time the program is rebroadcasted. I try to control this by stipulating that time and place must be given whenever a tape is replayed, but here again, this is virtually impossible to enforce. The existence of taped records of broadcast series does make it possible to check up on false accusations of what one has said, but on the whole radio remains an insidious medium, and it is on radio that one is more often unfairly attacked and misquoted. No one can be sure just who said what or when and the rumors survive.

There are also other aspects of the changes in technology. In the reproduction of photographs, for example, it is now possible to bring up old, faded photographs to quite respectable levels, as was done with the old snapshots used in my autobiography, *Blackberry Winter* (1178). Illustrations need no longer be bunched in one part of a book as in *New Lives for Old* (467) but can now be interleaved where they are appropriate. But in some other ways we have suffered. There is no comparison between the beauty of the first edition of *Balinese Character* in 1942 (140), where 2,000 copies were produced by the photogelatine process, and the reissue, in 1962, reproduced from the same prints in Gregory Bateson's collection. These were also used in my book with Frances C. Macgregor, *Growth and Culture* (363). Modern methods of reproduction allow for much more flexibility, but at the same time the demand for color is increasing with costs that are still very high for any kind of scientific work. I postponed publishing the last part of my Arapesh enthnography, "The Bark Paintings of the Mountain Arapesh of New Guinea" (715) until colored reproduction was available and was then told that I could only have one illustration in color.

I have only listed in this volume the tapes that have been made specifically for sale and that have a catalogue number and a source from which they can be purchased. This represents only a very small fraction of the tapes that exist in the tape archives of universities, local educational radio stations and other institutions.

There are many curious consequences of a long publishing life. The books one writes have to remain as permanent records of research that cannot be done again, while the theory based on one's own later work and the work of others in the discipline is continually changing. When an anthropologist dies, it is possible to reproduce his published work in continuing editions for many years, usually adding a new preface or introduction which places it in historical and contemporary contexts. I had the opportunity to write such a preface and to provide a new photographic appendix to Darwin's *Expression of the Emotions in Man and Animals* (456) which reflected the most recent work in the study of kinesics from the Louisville University Conference on Culture and Communication in 1954. The publishers had wanted me to insert new photographs in the text, which would of course have been a violation of the integrity of the book.

I have had to reject suggestions by critics that I rewrite *Coming of Age in Samoa* because it no longer applies to Samoan custom today. They have no idea that I could not "rewrite" it without doing a careful restudy and then possibly incorporating selections from the first book in a second, as I was able to do in *New Lives for Old*, a study done twenty-five years after *Growing Up in New Guinea*. The constant shift in editions, paperbacks, editions with limited life, expensive paperbacks, special overseas editions, etc., presents the possibility of writing new prefaces or new introductions, as I have done for *Coming of Age in Samoa* (6) which has appeared in six editions and for which I have done three new prefaces. *Growing Up in New Guinea* (22) has appeared in four editions with two new prefaces, *Sex and Temperament in Three Primitive Societies* (79) in three editions with two new prefaces, and *Male and Female* (312) in four editions with four new prefaces and one new appendix.

This makes it possible to introduce new insights, place a book in perspective, repudiate past over- and under-emphases, and in some measure introduce, by changes in terminology, a sense of the changing climate of opinion in the world. It has been especially important for a book like *Coming of Age in Samoa* which was written with identities carefully disguised, but without considering the possibility that young Samoans would be going to college where their classmates would have to read about the goings on, fifty years before, of their fellow students' grandmothers. These embarrassments are partly due to the fact that the titles were more general when English-speaking readers knew too little geography for me to write of coming of age in Manu'a or growing up in Manus. Today, like young Samoans from other parts of Samoa, young people from some other one of the over six hundred different linguistic groups of Papua New Guinea object because their own special version of "New Guinea," which they believe to be representative, is different from that which I described for the Manus in the 1920's. They angrily quote a sentence from *Growing Up in New Guinea* and say that I have misrepresented them as modern people today. In the summer of 1975 I spoke at the Lorengau High School on Manus Island where the young poet, Kumalau Tawali (1970) was teaching. A student stood up and said: "In your book, *Growing Up in New Guinea*, you said the Manus children lacked creative imagination. On what criteria did you base that statement?" To which I was able to answer: "On a collection of 35,000 children's drawings" (56) and I added, "But now you have a Manus poet teaching you and a chance to develop some creativity."

There have been other difficulties associated with the passage of time. When I started writing, the word *savage* was used interchangeably with *primitive*, in reference to preliterate peoples. I did not object to journalistic titles like *Savage Masters of the Sea* (40), although I always used *primitive* by choice. Today many members of emerging nations object to the word *primitive* and all sorts of euphemisms have been created to take the assumed stigma out of some words; *native* has now become *local* or *indigenous*; *Pidgin English* was renamed *Neo-Melanesian* after World War II (see *New Lives for Old*), but today the term *Pidgin English* can again be used. In the United States, *Negro*, with a compulsory capital "N" signaling minority status, was replaced by *Black* and occasionally *Afro-American*. When I write a new introduction or preface or an additional chapter for a later edition, I use the contemporary euphemisms: *humankind* for *mankind* or *chairperson* for the perfectly satisfactory *chairman* (if appropriately prefixed by *Mister* or *Madame*). But I am shocked by the lack of historical sense which makes younger anthropologists object to the use of outdated terms in works written years earlier. For example, Malinowski's diary (1967) was berated for its use in 1914 of a Polish word which was rendered in English as *nigger*, to refer to the Trobriand Islanders whom his work made immortal.

But even the use of later introductions which carefully emphasize dates does not help very much. When the omnibus volume *From the South Seas* (96), containing my first three books, was issued in 1939, I wrote a new introduction discussing what we had not known in 1925 when I did my first field work. Students responded by saying pejoratively, "Miss Mead herself admits..." and went on to say that I should have used methods that had not yet been developed at the time I did my field work. So while publishing and republishing over such a long time span makes it possible sometimes to contribute to a historical perspective, it also introduces new kinds of embarrassments and perplexities into the work of anthropologists, who are generally particularly susceptible to attacks on their earlier works.

I myself feel that only when people accept the full chronicle of their past can they behave with full integrity in the present. My records of earlier phases of New Guinea cultures stand as a record of how amazingly far the people have come in one generation, making the fastest progress the world has ever seen — from a state of stone-age isolation to participation in the post-atomic age. They can take pride in the record if they face it squarely; but if they fabricate a fictitious past, they will become prisoners of their fabrications. Today the people of Manus can read the most technical accounts of what I have written about them (22, 66, 467) as well as the published works of others, such as Reo Fortune (1935) and Theodore Schwartz (1962), who have written about them during the last forty-seven years — the best record that any people like themselves have of their past.

This need to face the past squarely is a recurrent problem in which anthropologists become involved. It was James Baldwin's willingness to claim his own past as an American who had no direct genealogical ties with Africa that made me happy to write *A Rap on Race* with him (1144). A review in *The New York Times* severely criticized the format of the book, saying that using a tape-recorded conversation was too easy and degraded the art of writing. But the tape recorder makes possible the kind of interchange which is rarely possible in discussions of race and, when the discussion is printed, the reader cannot help but read both sides of the issues involved.

In choosing the books that I have reviewed, at first I, of course, agreed to review whatever books were sent to me — a very odd lot indeed. Later I did a good deal of reviewing for the *Annals of the American Academy of Political and Social Science* (30, 48, 83, 659, 941, 990) because they only required short reviews and I was able to review books I really wanted to read carefully. As time went on I developed a policy of only reviewing books that I thought were important enough to read from cover to cover, and that I expected to find worthwhile. Occasionally I reviewed a book that I thought was dangerously misguided, like Wayne Dennis's *The Hopi Child* (134) or Kardiner's *The Individual and His Society* (137). I value a few of these reviews as cases where I myself developed some theoretical point: the review of Geoffrey Gorer's *Himalayan Village* (101), Z.S. Harris's *Methods in Structural Linguistics* (395), Roheim's *Riddle of the Sphinx* (84), and Edgerton's *The Individual in Cultural Adaptation* (1975). The size of the book has become a greater and greater consideration; carrying around a massive volume, like Simone de Beauvoir's *Coming of Age* (1271), as I travel about the country has become too much of a burden.

I accept requests to write prefaces and introductions as a part of my personal obligations to a student, a colleague or a young friend in whose work I have been interested. In the past I have written a few prefaces for books with which I have had no previous association (568), but I have received too many such requests, especially from publishers or promotional agents, to honor all of them. In the last ten years I have made it a practice to refuse to write a preface for any book with which I have not had some close personal association, either by reading and criticizing the manuscript before it was published, or as a teacher, a colleague or a friend. Through the years this has nevertheless added up to a good many prefaces and introductions.

I have also written autobiographical statements, articles, chapters or books in response to someone else's initiative. *An Anthropologist at Work: Writings of Ruth Benedict* (537) and *Ruth Benedict: A Biography* (1291) both contain a good deal of autobiographical material about my graduate student years and my later cooperation with Ruth Benedict, as do "Apprenticeship under Boas" (538), and *Blackberry Winter: My Earlier Years* (1178), a personal autobiography which emphasizes my upbringing as the daughter of social scientists and my preparation for marriage with fellow anthropologists. The chapter in the volume edited by Gardiner Lindzey (1287) discusses the way in which my training in psychology contributed to my field work. Various shorter pieces – my letters in Peggy Golde's *Women in the Field* (1069), "A Bread and Butter Letter from a Lecturer" (193), "Out of the Things I Read" (378), "Weaver of the Border" (601), "Field Work in High Cultures" (1186), "Retrospects and Prospects" (681), the introduction to *From the South Seas* (96), and the prefaces to the different volumes of *The Mountain Arapesh* (986, 1113, 1164a) – have combined discussions of method with specific statements about field work. I plan to publish a volume of *Letters from the Field: 1925–1975* based on the bulletin letters which I wrote for family, friends and colleagues, supplemented by some professional correspondence. There have also been more formal accounts of specific pieces of work: the introductions to *The Study of Culture at a Distance*

(412), *Soviet Attitudes toward Authority* (359), and *Childhood in Contemporary Cultures* (453), "The Committee on Food Habits" (166), "The Anthropology of Human Conflict" (834), "The Vicissitudes of the Study of the Total Communication of Process" (783), and three films (*35, 37, 41*).

Because I began my scientific work very early — I believe I was the first American anthropologist to begin my anthropological career as an undergraduate — I have had the good fortune to work with many older people on whose inspiration I drew and with colleagues who have since died: Lawrence K. Frank (1008, 1351), Ruth Benedict (319, 320), Robet Lamb (429), and Margaret Lowenfeld (1342). I have had to help finish the work of Jane Belo (1112), Colin McPhee (1966), Edith Cobb (in press) and Margaret Lowenfeld (in press).

The completion of my own field work falls into three parts: (1) the publications on my six field trips — alone in Samoa, and with Reo Fortune among the Omaha Indians, the Manus, the Arapesh, the Mundugumor and the Tchambuli — four of which I have completed. Of these early ethnographic studies, only the publication on the Mundugumor people (Reo Fortune and I abandoned our work on this culture because it was so broken) remains to be written. I returned there in 1973 and satisfied myself that no further work on the old culture could profitably be done, so I am at work on a monograph which will illustrate the first stages of an uncompleted piece of field work; (2) the two field trips with Gregory Bateson to Bali and to the Iatmul of New Guinea, during which photography and moving pictures were used for the first time, yielding a mass of material sufficient for an almost unlimited number of later studies, and on which subsequent publications have necessarily been partial, including my own (91, 99, 100, 103, 104, 105, 110, 118, 145, 149, 170, 260, 363, 440, 539, 624, *28, 29*), Gregory Bateson's (1937, 1941, 1942, 1946, 1949, 1975), and our work together (140); (3) the ongoing restudies developed since World War II in cooperation with younger colleagues — Theodore Schwartz (433, 607, 644, *33*), Lenora Schwartz (*33*), Lola Romanucci-Ross (1335), Jane Belo (1112), Ken Heyman (832, 1395), Barbara Heath, Rhoda Metraux. It can be said that these studies will never be completed and will be a continuing involvement for the rest of my life.

I have made seven expeditions to Manus, covering forty-seven years and four generations. I revisited the Iatmul twice while Rhoda Metraux was in the field, revisited the Arapesh village of Alitoa, relocated on Hoskins Bay on the island of New Britain, and I revisited Samoa in 1971. The fact that I began my work with children while I was very young, during a period when the world underwent the most rapid change in history, has been particularly fortunate for it has made possible these ongoing studies of change and the establishment of successorships among younger anthropologists.

About half my time has been devoted to the application of anthropological experience, data and theory to problems of nutrition and food habits (165, 773), technical change (399), mental health, family life and child-rearing practices. Today these interests have broadened to include studies of planetary problems (732, 824, 1063, 1131, 1194, 1247, 1286, 1395) as we are able to use our experience with small, easily encompassable, isolated whole societies to study the development of a world-wide society.

REFERENCES

Abramson, Harold, A., ed.
   1951-1955 *Problems of Consciousness*, 5 vols. New York: Josiah Macy, Jr. Foundation.
Anshen, Ruth N., ed.
   1972 *Twentieth Century Faith*. New York: Harper & Row.
Arensberg, C.M., and Niehoff, A.H.
   1971 *Introducing Social Change: A Manual for Community Development*. Aldine: Chicago.
Bateson, Gregory
   1937 "An Old Temple and a New Myth," *Djawa*, 17, No. 5-6, 1-17.
   1941 "The Frustration-Aggression Hypothesis," *Psychological Review*, 48, No. 4, 350-355.
   1942 "Bali: The Human Problem of Reoccupation," New York: Museum of Modern Art. (Mimeographed)
   1946 Arts of the South Seas," *Art Bulletin*, 28, No. 2, 119-123.
   1949 "Bali: The Value System of a Steady State," In *Social Structure: Essays Presented to A. R. Radcliffe-Brown*, ed. Meyer Fortes. Oxford: Clarendon Press, 25-53.
   1975 "Some Components of Socialization for Trance," *Ethos*, 3, No. 2, 143-155.
Boas, Franz
   1911 *The Mind of Primitive Man*. New York: Macmillan.
Crawley, Ernest
   1927 *The Mystic Rose*, 2 vols., 2nd rev. ed. London: Methuen.
Ekistics
   1972 "Delos Ten: The 1972 Athens Ekistics Month," *Ekistics*, 34, No. 203, 224-303.
von Foerster, H., ed.
   1951-1955 *Cybernetics*, 5 vols. New York: Josiah Macy, Jr. Foundation.
Fortune, Reo F.
   1935 *Manus Religion*. ("Memoirs of the Philadelphia Society," vol. 3) Philadelphia: American Philosophical Society.
Frazer, J.G.
   1907-1925 *The Golden Bough*, 3rd rev. ed. London: Macmillan.
Grinnell, G.B.
   1923 *The Cheyenne Indians*, 2 vols. New Haven: Yale University Press.
Haring, Douglas, ed.
   1956 *Personal Character and Cultural Milieu*, 3rd rev. ed. New York: Syracuse University Press.
Josiah Macy Jr. Foundation
   1955 *A Review of Activities, 1930-1955*. New York: Josiah Macy, Jr. Foundation.

Kluckhohn, Clyde, and Murray, Henry A.
   1962 *Personality in Nature, Society, and Culture*, 2nd rev. ed. New York: Knopf.
McPhee, Colin
   1966 *Music in Bali*. New Haven and London: Yale Universtity Press.
Malinowski, Bronislaw
   1922 *Argonauts of the Western Pacific*. London: Routledge.
   1967 *A Diary in the Strict Sense of the Term*. New York: Harcourt, Brace.
Marett, R.R.
   1909 *The Threshold of Religion*. London: Methuen.
Mead, Margaret
   1964 *Anthropology, a Human Science: Selected Papers, 1939-1960*. Insight Books,
      22. Princeton: Van Nostrand.
Mead, Margaret, and Metraux, Rhoda
   1970 *A Way of Seeing*. New York: McCall.
Newcomb, Theodore M., and Hartley, Eugene L.
   1958 *Readings in Social Psychology*, 3rd ed. New York: Holt.
Radcliffe-Brown, A.R.
   1922 *The Andaman Islanders*. Cambridge: Columbia University Press.
Rivers, William H.
   1906 *The Todas*. London: Macmillan.
Roscoe, John
   1911 *The Baganda*. (London: Macmillan).
Schaffner, B., ed.
   1955-1960 *Group Processes*, 5 vols. New York: Josiah Macy, Jr. Foundation.
Schwartz, Theodore
   1962 "The Paliau Movement in the Admiralty Islands, 1946-1954," *Anthropo-
      logical Papers of The American Museum of Natural History*, 49, Part 2, New
      York.
Spicer, Edward H., ed.
   1952 *Human Problems in Technological Change: A Casebook*. New York: Russell
      Sage Foundation.
Tanner, J.M., and Inhelder, B., eds.
   1957-1960 *Discussions on Child Development*, 4 vols. London: Tavistock, 1956-
      1960; New York: International Universities Press.
Tawali, Kumalau
   1970 *Signs in the Sky*. Port Moresby: Papua Pocket Poets.

INTRODUCTION

Mon choix d'éditeurs a été si peu orthodoxe qu'il semble utile de faire précéder cette bibliographie d'une préface qui explique comment ce choix a été fait. Les premières années de ma carrière d'écrivain, j'ai suivi des voies tout à fait conventionnelles: je décidais que je voudrais publier un article et me mettais en quête de la revue professionnelle où j'avais le plus de chance de le faire accepter; puis j'écrivais l'article, le soumettais et, si on me le refusait, essayais de le placer ailleurs. Les articles eux-mêmes s'appuyaient sur mes recherches du moment et étaient conçus pour divers publics de spécialistes. Par example, quand "An Ethnologist's Footnote to *Totem and Taboo*" (21) a été rejeté par *The International Journal of Psychoanalysis*, je l'ai envoyé à la *Psychoanalytic Review* qui l'accepte. Pendant mes études à l'Université je me suis livrée à une petite recherche en utilisant un seul informateur d'Afrique Occidentale. J'en ai envoyé les résultats au *Journal of the Royal Anthropological Institute* en 1925. Ils ont retenu l'article et l'on finalement publié en 1937 sous le titre: "A Twi Relationship System" (93), sans me donner le temps de le réviser à la lumière des cinq voyages que j'avais accomplis entre-temps sur le terrain et au cours desquels les problèmes de parenté dont traitait cet article étaient au centre de mes recherches et de publications ultérieures telles que *Social Organization of Manu'a* (25) et *Kinship in the Admiralty Islands* (66).

Vers 1928, des revues telles que *Natural History* (23, 36, 65, 70, etc.), *Parents Magazine* (26, 59), *The Nation* (31) et *The Thinker* (20) commencèrent à me demander des articles. On me demandait de faire des comptes rendus de livres, non seulement pour des revues techniques appropriées, mais aussi pour le *New Freeman* (28) et *The Nation* (15). En 1930, deux éditeurs dynamiques, Calverton et Schmalhausen, introduisirent un nouveau style qui devait continuer jusqu'à ce jour: celui qui consiste à demander à un groupe de contributeurs d'écrire sur des sujets d'actualité, en l'occurrence comme par exemple *The New Generation*. Outre des demandes d'articles venant d'encyclopédies (32, 33, 69, 81, etc...), des revues plus ou moins techniques, allant de *The New York Times Magazine* (63), au *Publishers' Weekly* (38) ou au *Safety Education* (40), commencèrent à m'en demander aussi.

Ces demandes venaient en partie du succès remporté par *Coming of Age in Samoa* (6). Je n'avais pas conçus ce livre pour atteindre un grand public pour un livre qui n'était pas un roman, mais j'ai pris, il est vrai, une voie plutôt rare à l'époque. En effet, vu le sujet technique du livre, on aurait pu s'attendre à y trouver le jargon de l'ethnologie et de la psychologie. J'ai essayé au contraire, de le rendre intelligible à des groupes de gens avec des interêts très spécialisés, notamment ceux qui avaient à travailler avec des adolescents de notre propre société − les professeurs d'enseignement secondaire et les assistants sociales. Je ne me rendais pas compte alors que si un livre était écrit en anglais, dépouillé de tout jargon technique − ce qui, dans la littérature ethnographique de l'époque, signifiait l'utilisation d'un nombre considérable de mots en langue indigène − ce livre deviendrait automatiquement accessible au monde éduqué, serait facile à lire pour de jeunes étudiants et facilement traduisible dans d'autres langues.

Ma décision de rendre les matériaux accessibles à ceux qu'ils concernaient le plus, a été préparée par les articles que j'avais présentés intentionnellement à des revues d'enseignement en donnant, par exemple, en 1927, dans *School and Society* (4, 5), les résultats de mes premières recherches sur les effets de la langue apprise à la maison, d'après les notes de tests des enfants italo-américains. J'avais choisi l'anthropologie comme profession, parce que je sentais que la recherche dans ce domaine était urgente et que son application à des problèmes sociaux d'actualité s'imposait de façon évidente. Ainsi, le fait de rendre mes découvertes accessibles à un public plus large mais spécialisé, a été, dès le début de ma carrière, l'effet d'un choix délibéré.

En 1925, quand Pliny E. Goddard, conservateur d'ethnologie au Musée d'histoire naturelle de New York, m'a demandé de travailler pour le Musée, il avait très précisément manifesté son espoir que je pourrais rendre l'ethnologie aussi familière au vaste public des adhérents du Musée, que l'avaient fait des conservateurs précédents dans le domaine de l'archéologie. Je n'avais alors écrit que de la poésie et des éditoriaux dans le *Barnard Bulletin* où je tenais un poste de rédactrice en 1922 et ma seule oeuvre était ma thèse de doctorat *An Inquiry into the Question of Cultural Stability in Polynesia* (7) qui, en toute conscience, était sèche et conventionnelle. Pourtant, la prévoyance de Goddard, m'a poussée de façon impérative à répondre aux demandes de journaux et de revues tels que *The New York Times* (63, 124), *The Saturday Review of Literature* (82), *The Nation* (15) et *Natural History* (23, 36, 65, 70), l'organe du Musée Américain d'Histoire Naturelle, par lequel nous atteignions notre cercle mondial de membres du Musée.

Je crois que mon espoir très ancien de devenir écrivain a joué son rôle, à mesure que je réfléchissais et m'essayais à plusieurs genres littéraires — poésie, essais, nouvelles, pièces de théâtre et spectacles — pendant mes années d'école secondaire et d'université. Même après ma décision de devenir ethnologue, je n'avais pas complètement abandonné mes aspirations de publier de la poésie. Pourtant, lorsque "Absolute Benison" (51), poème que j'ai soumis sous un pseudonyme, a été d'abord rejeté puis accepté par le même éditeur quand je l'ai présenté une seconde fois sous mon vrai nom en 1932, après la parution de *Coming of Age in Samoa* (6), je n'ai jamais essayé de publier de poèmes. A l'université, mon association avec la poétesse américaine distinguée, Léonie Adams, m'a heureusement convaincue que la poésie n'était pas un domaine que je pouvais beaucoup enrichir. Ruth Benedict et Edward Sapir qui ont été mes très proches collaborateurs dans les années 20, avaient tous deux écrit bon nombre de poèmes qui furent publiés dans les petites revues poétiques de l'époque et tous deux eurent des recueils de poèmes refusés en 1928. Aussi me suis-je fermement écartée de toute autre tentative de publier dans ce domaine.

Les nouvelles que j'ai écrites durant mes années de préparation au doctorat, furent toutes conçues, je m'en suis rendue compte plus tard, pour résoudre des problèmes qui m'intriguaient plutôt que comme de la littérature en soi. Les spectacles que j'ai réalisés et portés à la scène, se rattachaient à mon intérêt que j'ai pu exprimer ensuite en dirigeant et construisant des films ethnographiques sur le terrain. Il nous paraissait évident, étant étudiants, que l'écriture constituait un outil précieux et que l'ethnologue capable d'écrire comme Malinowski — lequel avait déjà atteint un large public —, possédait un atout considérable sur ses contemporains moins doués. *Argonauts of the Western Pacific* (1922) de Malinowski contrastait avec *The Andaman Islanders* (1922) de Radcliffe-Brown. *The Mind of Primitive Man* (1911) de Franz Boas nous paraissait manquer de la persuasion littéraire que méritaient son importance et son sujet. Ainsi, à l'intérieur de la profession, il y avait une obligation qui remontait à Frazer (1907–1925), Crawley (1927) et Marett (1909), d'écrire en anglais littéraire plutôt que dans le lourd style germanique qui avait déjà envahi le domaine des thèses universitaires en Amérique.

Cette obligation d'écrire en anglais courant et de façon aussi intelligible que possible, ne signifiait pourtant pas que je renonce à écrire des ouvrages techniques. Après le succès chaleureux accordé à *Coming of Age in Samoa* (6), je suis retournée avec plaisir à l'audience technique de mes pairs, en écrivant *Social Organization of Manu'a* (25) pour la série du Musée Bernice P. Bishop. Mais là encore, j'étais très consciente du besoin d'écrire à différents niveaux de généralisation. J'ai rassemblé un groupe de monographies célèbres de l'époque — *The Todas* (1906) de Rivers, *Argonauts of the Western Pacific*

(1922) de Malinowski, *The Baganda* (1911) de Roscoe et *The Cheyenne Indians* (1923) de Grinnell — et j'étudais leur composition. Franz Boas, sous la direction duquel j'ai fait mes études doctorales et mon premier terrain, a dit un jour: "Le problème des monographies, c'est qu'on a besoin de la fin au commencement et cela est vrai de chaque chapitre, on a besoin de chaque chapitre dans tous les autres." J'étais aussi convaincue qu'il y avait trois groupes de collègues à qui cette monographie serait utile: ceux qui s'intéressaient à la dynamique de la structure sociale mais étaient peu versés dans l'ethnographie de l'Océanie; ceux que s'intéressaient tout spécialement à l'Océanie et les ethnologues spécialistes de la Polynésie, pour qui les détails de l'organisation sociale de Manu'a seraient importants. Cela posé, j'organisais la monographie sur trois plans de généralité décroissante. J'ai repris ce souci d'atteindre des lecteurs ayant différents types d'intérêts et de compétences, quelques années plus tard, au moment où je travaillais sur une discussion du même ensemble d'idées dans *People and Places* (557), livre pour enfants; dans un chapitre écrit pour le livre de Lyman Bryson, *An Outline of Man's Knowledge of the Modern World* (592) destiné à des adultes; et enfin, dans mon livre théorique le plus systématique, *Continuities in Cultural Evolution* (771).

Cette expérimentation avec l'écriture sur des niveaux et des genres différents d'écrivain s'est vraiment prolongé jusqu'au moment où, en 1935, j'écrivis *Sex and Temperament in Three Primitive Societies* (79) qui, à mon avis, joignait de façon satisfaisante, des exigences esthétiques à la présentation de matériaux ethnographiques théoriques nouveaux difficiles et peu familiers au public lettré. Après quoi, j'ai cessé d'écrire de la poésie. Il m'arrive parfois, il est vrai, de m'attacher davantage au style dans un essai destiné à un public particulièrement littéraire, comme celui de *The American Scholar* (470) ou bien de *Daedalus* (543), mais dans l'ensemble, je ne suis pas tourmentée par le type de regrets qui hante bien de ceux qui ont appris à écrire dans un autre genre que celui auquel ils aspiraient à l'origine. Aussi cela m'a-t-il épargné les frustrations de tant de savants qui, tout en écrivant avec plaisir, gardent toujours l'espoir de voir émerger un jour un grand roman. Une fois que j'ai eu compris que les cultures humaines étaient bien plus complexes et intéressantes que tout ce que je pouvais inventer et que dans mes tentatives d'écrire des contes, j'avais en fait, essayé de comprendre des situations réelles où je me suis trouvée dans mon enfance, je n'ai plus eu d'autre désir d'en écrire.

Mais j'ai conservé mon intérêt pour la forme et je trouve chaque demande innovateur, qu'il s'agisse d'être le narrateur d'un film (*28, 29*), d'écrire un script pour accompagner des photos (832) ou un commentaire pour un audiographe — comme par exemple, celui de l'exposition des peuples du Pacifique au Musée Américain d'Histoire Naturelle (1146, 1151) —, ou bien encore d'écrire pour un public étranger (360) ou de donner une conférence moitié en anglais, moitié en pidgin, devant un public de Nouvelle Guinée ayant une connaissance de l'anglais très inégale — toute nouvelle tâche me paraît un défi passionnant.

Après avoir écrit professionnellement pendant environ cinq ans, il y a eu un contraste marquant entre la manière dont je concevais mes livres et les grandes monographies d'une part et, de l'autre, ma manière d'écrire des articles, des comptes rendue et des livres qui se trouvaient un peu en marge de mon intérêt majeur, en particulier les livres écrits en collaboration. Ainsi, pour toutes les publications majeures sur mon travail de terrain — *Coming of Age in Samoa* (6), *Social Organization of Manu'a* (25), *Growing Up in New Guinea* (22), *Kinship in the Admiralty Islands* (66), *Sex and Temperament in Three Primitive Societies* (79), *The Mountain Arapesh* (94, 107, 269, 313), *Male and Female* (312), *New Lives for Old* (467), *Continuities in Cultural Evolution* (771) et *Culture and Commitment* (1063) — j'ai choisi ce que je voulais écrire; l'apport du personnel d'édition et des éditeurs a été relativement minime. Mon premier éditeur, William Morrow, m'a suggéré d'ajouter les deux derniers chapitres de *Coming of Age in Samoa*, dans lesquels je montre les implications de mes découvertes sur Samoa pour l'actualité de la culture américaine, sujet dont j'avais déjà traité dans des conférences et des cours. Theyer Hobson, mon éditeur chez Morrow, s'est plaint de ce que le chapitre central concernant les Mundugumor dans *Sex and Temperament in Three Primitive Societies* était trop difficile. Enfin, c'est lui qui a suggéré le titre de *New Lives for Old*. Le titre de *Growing Up in New Guinea* a été un écho malheureux de *Coming of Age in Samoa*. Si on a choisi le nom de Nouvelle-Guinée — qui convenait tout à fait au territoire dans lequel Manus est situé — c'est parce que mon éditeur s'est plaint que personne ne saurait où se trouve Manus. On m'avait accordé un poste honoraire au Musée Bernice P. Bishop et ma monographie *Social Organization of Manu'a*, convenait à leur série de publications sur la Polynésie. *Kinship in the Admiralty Islands* fut ma réponse à un compte rendu de *Growing Up in New Guinea* inspiré par Malinowski dans lequel il prétendait que je n'y connaissais rien en matière de système de parenté. Pour pouvoir l'écrire et le publier dans la série du Musée Américain d'Histoire Naturelle, je retardais un voyage sur le terrain que je projetais de mener pendant quatre mois. Quant aux longs monographies sur les Arapesh des montagnes, écrits pour la série du Musée, Reo Fortune et moi devions d'abord nous en partager la rédaction. Ils furent révisés par la suite à cause du coût accru de production qui nous a obligé à abondonner une section entière pour laquelle toute la documentation visuelle avait été préparée.

Depuis mon voyage à Samoa, tout mon travail de terrain a été accompli en collaboration et a abouti à de nombreuses publications parmi lesquelles:

Balinese Character, écrit en collaboration avec Gregory Bateson (140), "The Cult as a Condensed Social Process" (607), et un article sur "Micro- and Macro-Cultural Models for Cultural Evolution" (644) avec Theodore Schwartz. Dans chaque cas, les publications résultaient de divers arrangements en ce qui concerne le partage de la rédaction, l'ordre dans lequel livres et articles devaient être écrits et la proportion dans laquelle nos publications séparées s'appuieraient mutuellement sur le travail sur terrain de l'autre.

Dans une seconde catégorie, il faut compter les livres qui découlent de projet conçus à l'origine par une autre personne ou institution. *The Changing Culture of an Indian Tribe* (53), est le rapport d'un projet que m'avait demandé d'entreprendre Clark Wissler, mon chef de département au Musée Américain d'Histoire Naturelle, pour se libérer d'une obligation qu'il avait contractée en acceptant une donation de $ 750 de Mrs Leonard Elmshirst, donation destinée à financer une étude de la vie familiale des Indiens d'Amérique. Ni le choix du problème, ni celui de la tribu — les Omaha, pour lesquels j'utilisai le pseudonyme "Bois de cerfs" — n'étaient de moi, mais c'est moi qui ai rédigé le livre et trouvé un éditeur pour le publier. Quarante quatre ans plus tard, quand on a commencé à réimprimer certaines des publications des presses de l'Université de Columbia, j'ai écrit une nouvelle introduction sur "The Consequences of Racial Guilt" pour une édition de poche par Putnam dans la collection Capricorn (866).

Cooperation and Competition among Primitive Peoples (89) fut le résultat d'un projet conçu à l'instigation d'un des sous-comités de "Culture et Personnalité", organisé par le Conseil de la Recherche Sociale aux Etats-Unis, souscomité qui s'occupait des habitudes compétitives et coopératives. J'avais accepté la responsabilité de préparer la partie consacrée à l'apport éventuel de matériaux ethnographiques au plan de recherches sur les sociétés compétitives et coopératives. J'avais aussi mis au point une nouvelle méthode pour utiliser des ethnologues ayant fait du terrain, comme sources vivantes de première main, pour répondre à des questions qui n'avaient pas été soulevées pendant leur travail de terrain. Pour cela, ils devaient s'imposer la tâche d'examiner à nouveau leurs notes et même, en certains cas, de prendre connaissance du travail inédit d'autres collègues, dans le contexte d'un séminaire. Cette exprérience s'est achevée par un livre dont j'ai dirigé la publication et que j'ai mis à jour en 1961 pour une édition de poche, aux Presses Beacon (634). Le choix de l'éditeur s'est trouvé décidé par les relations qui existaient entre les initiateurs du projet et la compagnie d'édition McGraw-Hill.

Balinese Character: A Photographic Study (140) est sorti de notre choix, Gregory Bateson et moi, très attentive de ce qui nous paraissait être la partie la plus innovatrice, du point de vue de la méthode, dans notre terrain accompli à Bali entre 1936 et 1939. En décidant de constituer une collection massive de plus de 25.000 photos, nous avions fait un saut quantitatif par rapport à tout autre usage qui avait déjà été fait de la photographie. Dans la composition du livre, nous avons groupé des activités extrêmement disparates pour montrer des points de similarité sur une seule page, sans altérer l'intégrité de chaque événement. Cette disposition a été en elle-même une innovation dans les méthodes de présentations. Elle fut suivie neuf ans plus tard, par un type de présentation très proche, dans *Growth and Culture: A Photographic Study of Balinese Childhood* (363), que j'ai entrepris en réponse à l'intérêt que Frances MacGregor a manifesté, pour élargir son expérience dans le contexte des sciences sociales.

And Keep Your Powder Dry (142), écrit au milieu de la deuxième guerre mondiale, découle d'une décision commune, prise avec Gregory Bateson. Nous avons pensé que ce serait une bonne idée de publier en "Penguin" les articles et les conférences que j'avais donnés pendant les deux premières années de la guerre. Quand je me suis mise à rassembler les matériaux, je me suis aperçue qu'il vaudrait mieux écrire un nouveau livre en utilisant les idées des articles antérieurs. Il en est effectivement sorti un "Penguin", publié d'abord en livre de poche en Angleterre en 1944, sous le titre *The American Character* (142).

Cultural Patterns and Technical Change (399) fut aussi une réponse à un projet qui passa par une série d'étapes dont la première et la dernière seules m'ont occupée. En tant que secrétaire générale du "Comité sur les Habitudes Nutritives" pendant la deuxième guerre mondiale (1941-1945), comité présidé dans sa dernière période par Lawrence K. Frank, j'avais tenu plusieurs sessions sur les modes de vie. Ces discussions initiales furent développées dans un memorandum préparé par Lawrence Frank par le canal de l'Association Nationale de la Santé Mentale (les Etats Unis) pour la Fédération Mondiale de la Santé Mentale; ce plan fut porté à l'attention de la division des Sciences Sociales à l'UNESCO. L'UNESCO offrit un contrat à la Fédération Mondiale de la Santé Mentale avec certaines restrictions très sévères sur la sélection du rédacteur. Entre autres obligations, je devais faire face au danger que la FMSM perde la subvention de l'UNESCO, à moins de prendre moi-même la direction du volume. Or, nous avions absolument besoin de cette subvention pour pouvoir en recevoir une autre qui nous était promise sous conditions d'une subvention complémentaires. C'est ce qui est devenu *Cultural Patterns and Technical Change*, livre encore écrit, à dessein, en anglais non-technique, puisqu'il était destiné à des spécialistes de diverse domains – nutritionistes, agents de la Santé Publique, agriculteurs, etc... Après une première édition publiée timidement dans la série "Technology and Tensions" de l'UNESCO, les livres Mentor le publièrent dans une édition de poche en 1955 et il devint pour longtemps un "bestseller".

Bien souvent, un tel projet de livres en impliquait simultanément d'autres en relation avec lui. Par exemple, le problème de l'aide matériel multilatéral dont traite *Cultural Patterns and Technical Change* a été choisi en vue de faire pendant à un volume édité par Arensberg et Niehof (1951) sur le programme d'aide bilatéral offert par les Etats-Unis et à un autre ayant trait à l'aide technique à l'intérieur des Etats-Unis.

De façon analogue, j'ai participé à la création d'une série de volumes traitant du problèmes de "Culture et Personnalité": *Readings in Social Psychology*, dirigé par T.M. Newcomb et E.L. Hartley (1958); *Personal Character and Cultural Milieu*, dirigé par D.S. Haring (1956), et *Personality in Nature, Society and Culture*, dirigé par C. Kluckhohn et H.A. Murray (1962). Je contribuai à ces livres à la fois par des articles qui y étaient publiés et en jouant un rôle de lectrice et de conseillère de rédaction.

Il faut placer dans une autre catégorie les écrits qui consistaient à préparer des chapitres résumant des recherches originales pour des livres specialisés: trois chapitres sur les enfants dans les sociétés primitives pour des manuels de psychologie de l'enfant (39, 109, 243); un chapitre sur "Cultural Determinants of Sexual Behavior" (624) et sur l'adolescence (75); des articles rédigés pour plusieurs encyclopédies pour certaines desquelles j'assumais aussi des responsabilités de rédactrice conseillère, notamment, *The Encyclopedia of Psychology* (241), *The Encyclopedia of the Social Sciences* (32, 33), *International Encyclopedia of the Social Sciences* (953), *The Encyclopedia of Mental Health* (719, 725) et *The Encyclopedia of Photography* (713).

An Anthropologist at Work: Writings of Ruth Benedict (537) fut préparé en réponse à une demande de Paul Brooks, l'éditeur de Ruth Benedict aux éditions Houghton Mifflin, pour un recueil d'articles posthume. Puis qu'elle ai peu écrit, quelques-uns de ses articles les plus importants ont été republiés plusieurs fois. C'est donc au cours de conversations avec Paul Brooks, que l'idée m'est venue d'écrire un livre qui comprendrait une sorte de conversation à quatre entre Ruth Benedict, Franz Boas, Edward Sapir et moi-même. Tout en travaillant à ce livre, je commençai à m'intéresser à un style anthropologique de la biographie, capable de présenter des matériaux par grands morceaux, intégralement. C'est ainsi que je présentai les journaux de Ruth Benedict allant de 1923 à 1926, ses poèmes inédits, des lettres de Sapir à Benedict, sans violer l'intégrité interne de ces textes par le style biographique d'usage qui consiste à utiliser des bribes de citations. Le deuxième livre sur Ruth Benedict (1291) a été écrit en pensant aux étudiants dans le cadre d'une série publiée par l'Université de Columbia et consacrée aux anthropologues, série dirigée par Charles Wagley. Ce deuxième livre compensait une nouvelle sélection d'articles plus courts.

Un autre type d'encouragement extérieur m'est venu quand j'ai écrit un livre pour enfants *People and Places* (557). Velma Varner, qui dirige une collection de livres pour enfants avec beaucoup de talent et d'imagination, m'a demandé d'écrire un livre d'anthropologie pour les enfants. Je me rendis compte qu'on attendait des livres d'enfants qu'ils soient à la fois abondamment illustrés et bon marché et que, par conséquent, je pourrais, avec ce livre, faire d'une pierre deux coups: un texte pour enfants en même temps qu'une histoire des techniques dans la présentation et la description d'autres cultures, depuis les reconstructions fantaisistes d'un illustrateur, jusqu'aux soigneux dessins d'objets de musée, en passant par les premiers peintres, la photo en noir et blanc, puis en couleur.

Le project d'écrire *Family* (832), illustré de photographies de Ken Heyman, m'est venu après plusieurs expéditions photographiques que nous avons faites ensemble, pour répondre à son désir de collaborer à un livre sur la famille. Quand le thème des rôles de parenté (mère, père, frères et soeurs) a été établi, Ken a fouillé le monde et ses dossiers pour trouver des photographies et moi, j'écrivis ensuite un texte qui leur convienne. Nous avons suivi la même procédure dans notre récente oeuvre commune: *World Enough: Rethinking the Future* (1395).

Il y a trois livres dont j'ai dirigé la publication en collaboration, dans le cadre de grands projets: *The Study of Culture at a Distance*, avec Rhoda Métraux (412), *Childhood in Contemporary Cultures*, avec Martha Wolfenstein (440) et *Soviet Attitudes toward Authority* (359) que j'ai écrit avec l'aide de tout le personnel du Musée Américain d'Histoire Naturelle qui participait au projet d'études de la culture soviétique. Tous ces projets ont été le résultat d'études faites à grande échelle sur les cultures contemporaines à l'instigation de Ruth Benedict qui mourut avant qu'elles aient été achevées.

L'anthologie, *Primitive Heritage* (411) que j'ai constituée avec Nicolas Calas, doit son origine à une suggestion de Leo Rosten à Bennet Cerf aux éditions Random House. L'idée initiale d'y réunir une critique surréaliste et une ethnologue a été réduite à néant par un texte de la couverture qui décrivait Calas comme un ethnologue.

The Small Conference (971) est le fruit d'une longue association avec Paul Byers. Après la mort d'un collaborateur avec lequel Byers avait l'intention de faire la description d'une seule conférence, Wilton Dillon nous suggéra à Byers et à moi, de sauver une partie des matériaux originaux et d'en faire un livre général sur les conférences.

De temps à autre on me demandait d'écrire dans une langue étrangère ou pour une encyclopédie étrangère, notamment un chapitre sur "Ethnologie et Psychiatrie" pour une encyclopédie allemande (635); un chapitre pour *The Policy Sciences*, dirigé par Lasswell et Lerner (360), publié d'abord en français (de sorte qu'il m'a fallu revoir les références pour tenir compte du fichier du Musée de l'Homme); un chapitre sur "l'approche intercuturelle dans l'étude de la personnalité" (466) qui devait être traduite en espagnol, mais ne l'a jamais été, et dans lequel à la fois les références et les illustrations étaient adaptées à des lecteurs espagnols; enfin un chapitre que j'ai écrit en 1975 avec Walter Fairservis pour un livre allemand sur l'écologie (1356).

Quand je savais à l'avance que j'écrivais pour une publication étrangère, je consultais ceux qui comprenaient les deux langues et quelque chose aux questions culturelles et théoriques dont je traitais. D'autre part, à quelques exceptions près, les traductions de mes oeuvres ont été faites sans qu'on me consulte, y compris deux traductions presque simultanées, l'un d'abord en Allemagne en 1946, l'autre en Autriche en 1947 de *And Keep Your Powder Dry* (142).

Français. Un premier plan de publier mes trois livres d'avant-guerre sur les mers du Sud – *Coming of Age in Samoa* (6), *Growing Up in New Guinea* (22) et *Sex and Temperament in Three Primitive Societies* (79), a été abandonné parce que l'éditeur français n'aimait pas le second. Mais plus tard, le premier et le dernier des trois volumes furent publiés, en gardant les photographies qui avaient été choisies pour illustrer *Growing Up in New Guinea*, plus un certain nombre de photos d'autres peuples de Mélanésie qui n'avaient rien à voir avec le texte et que les Français anthropologues consultés pour l'édition, avaient insérées sans me demander mon avis. La publication de *Male and Female* (312) a été retardée parce qu'un éditeur français voulait supprimer le chapitre intitulé "chaque famille dans sa propre maison"; le chapitre ayant trait à l'Amérique, cela ne s'appliquait donc pas à la France! Le livre a fini tout de même par être publiée en français sous le titre: *L'un et l'autre sexe* en 1966. Très souvent quand quelque chose était écrit expressément pour un public français, on de demandait de changer la formulation ou même les idées elles-mêmes, parce que c'était intraduisible en français. Il y a eu de sérieuses difficultés, par exemple, avec des mots tels que "cultural patterns" la difficulté n'étant pas dans le mot "pattern" pour lequel il y a bien des équivalents français, mais dans le pluriel, comme s'il était impensable d'imaginer plus d'un vrai type de culture, la française, avec ses précurseurs classiques.

Les traductions italiennes présentèrent des problèmes différents. Les éditions sont magnifiques, mais les éditeurs enthousiastes ne s'occupent absolument pas de détails tels que ceux d'accorder des images à un texte. Par exemple, dans la traduction de *Childhood and Contemporary Cultures* (453), en 1963, les illustrations photographiques d'un "shtetl" d'Europe orientale sont dispersés dans toutes les autres sections du livre.

Les éditions anglaises ont aussi présenté de divers problèmes. Pour *Growing Up in New Guinea* (22), il m'a fallu changer les mots, ("overalls" pour "jeans", par exemple) et utiliser des références à des livres anglais plutôt qu'américains. Quand *And Keep Your Powder Dry* (142) a été publié en Angleterre (1967), j'ai écrit une introduction en anglais britannique. D'autres fois, je faisais simplement imprimer l'édition américaine avec l'orthographe anglaise, de sorte qu'elle pouvait être aisément transformée en édition anglaise (alors que les Américains lisent l'orthographe anglaise, sans même s'en apercevoir, les Anglais ne seraient plaints alors de l'orthographe américaine. Ceci, bien sûr, ne serait plus vrai maintenant). Après la deuxième guerre mondiale, j'ai senti qu'il était important d'écrire comme une Américaine, selon l'orthographe américaine. En effet, quand j'ai publié *New Lives for Old* (467) dans lequel je reproduisais certaines parties de *Growing Up in New Guinea*, publiée vingt sept ans plus tôt, une suite sans fin de malentendus s'est produite au cours des différentes étapes de l'édition du texte.

Les publications des savants s'adressent toujours quelque peu aux congrès des sociétés scientifiques auxquels ils assistent et présentent des communications. La forme de celles-ci dépend souvent de critères imposés par la publication dans laquelle elles doivent paraître ensuite. Ceci peut être un procédé extrêmement capricieux. Par exemple, au VIIème Congrès International de Sciences Anthropologiques et Ethnologiques qui s'est tenu à Moscou en 1964, le résumé des interventions n'a pas été publié avant 1970 (1054). D'autre part, les deux communications que j'ai présentées à la neuvième session de ce même congrès, tenu cette fois à Chicago en 1973, une a déjà paru chez Mouton (1975), tandis que "A Re-examination of Major Themes of the Sepik Area, Papua, New Guinea" n'est pas encore sous presse.

Cependant, puisqu'une si grande partie de mes publications a été suscitée par d'autres voies, j'ai moins été dépendante de telles publications officielles que beaucoup de savants. Par ailleurs, il existe d'autres sortes de congrès et de symposiums internationaux qui représentent un type différent de publications. Les contributions individuelles y font simplement partie des actes du congrès: les dix sessions du symposium de Delos, dont le compte rendu a paru dans *Ekistics* (1963-1972), le rapport des différents groupes d'études de la Fédération Mondiale de la Santé Mentale (853, 935) et les publications du Conseil Mondiale des Eglises (867). Ceci est vrai également du type de conférences organisées par la fondation Josiah Macy Jr. qui contient un mélange de débats et de communications: *Cybernetics*, dirigé par H. von Foerster (1951-1955), *Problems of Consciousness*, dirigé par H.A. Abramson (1951-1955), *Group Processes*, par B. Schaffner (1955-1960) et *Discussions on Child Development*, par J.M. Tanner et B. Inhelder (1957-1960).

Par ailleurs, on me demande de m'adresser à des groupes aussi disparates que l'Association des Universités et des Ecoles Secondaires des Etats du Centre des Etats-Unis (105), l'Association Nationale des Doyennes (118) ou la Compagnie "Western Personnel Service" (220) et cela m'aussi stimulée dans la préparation des matériaux. Bien que très souvent j'ai introduit des idées nouvelles dans ce genre de conférences, elles étaient ensuite publiées dans un journal que mes collègues ne lisaient jamais, de sorte qu'en fait, l'article avait toutes chances d'être entièrement perdu. J'essayais de compenser l'obscurité des ces publications en faisant paraître les articles dans des volumes consacrés à des réimpressions comme *Anthropology: A Human Science* (1964), *A Way of Seeing*, dirigé par Rhoda Métraux et moi-même (1970) et *Twentieth Century Faith*, dirigé par Ruth N. Anshen (1972).

Depuis 1943 jusqu'au début des années 60, l'institut d'Etudes Interculturelles envoya un choix d'articles réimprimés, se rapportant au domaine de "Personnalité et Culture" et à l'application des méthodes anthropologiques aux problèmes contemporains. Ceci a donné lieu à une distribution systématique d'articles publiés dans des endroits peu orthodoxes. Cependant, le nombre d'adresses changés s'est révélé si grand que cette distribution devint infaisable. Maintenant, je distribue périodiquement une liste de mes publications à environ 450 collègues, en leur demandant de mentionner les articles qu'ils voudraient recevoir, car le nombre des réimpressions que l'on reçoit maintenant est devenu si pesant que j'ai moi-même tendance à ne lire que celles que j'ai demandées expressément ou qui m'ont été envoyées avec une lettre personnelle.

Le développement de nouveaux moyens électroniques a aussi considérablement changé le genre de demandes de publication qu'on peut recevoir. Grâce à la sténotypie puis à l'audiographe et au magnétophone, il est devenu possible d'enregistrer ce qui se dit aux réunions et colloques, en général de façon très dénaturée et de demander ensuite aux participants de revoir la transcription pour l'éditer. Ces demandes prennent des formes très variées: obligation à laquelle on vous a fait souscrire à l'avance et qu'on doit satisfaire dans des conditions extrêmement difficiles (bandes magnétiques perdues, transcription incohérente etc.); transcriptions de colloques ou de discussions pour lesquelles aucune publication n'avait été prévue et qui sont accompagnées de toutes sortes de pressions, y compris l'éventuelle reproduction sans permission, ce qui m'est arrivé avec la communication que j'ai présentée à un colloque sur la "pilule" (919), sans compter les appels pour les bonnes causes, les tentatives pour lever des fonds pour une oeuvre, les rapports annuels, etc... Ces pratiques aboutissent à un nombre considérable de publications dont le contenu se recoupe et la qualité varie selon la possibilité et le temps laissés à l'auteur de réviser le texte. Ce procédé semble inséparable du monde contemporain avec sa pléthore de publications; chaque organisation ou institutions s'efforce d'individualiser ses activités et a tendance à s'attacher à quelques célébrités, sans permettre la formation de groupes moins prestigieux, capables de prendre la relève.

Nous manquons de moyens adéquats pour introduire dans les symposiums, colloques et occasions publiques, des jeunes qui, si on leur en donnait l'occasion, pourraient devenir une véritable ressource. J'ai utilisé tous les moyens à ma disposition — refus de participer à un colloque ou à un débat à moins que des jeunes y participent, recommandation de jeunes aux organisateurs de colloques — mais tout cela avec très peu de succès. J'ai aussi utilisé divers autres stratagèmes. Après "The White House Conference on Children" (colloque sur les enfants aux Etats-Unis qui a eu lieu en 1950 à la Maison Blanche), j'ai proposé que quiconque aurait tenu un rôle de premier plan cette fois-ci ne pourrait participer au colloque suivant en 1960 au même titre et qu'à la place on puise des participants dans des couches plus jeunes. Malgré mes efforts, on a encore fait appel à des conférenciers du même âge avec des résultats très insatisfaisants. A la fin, j'ai dû écrire un article pour supplémenter les contributions originales qui devaient être publiés dans cette série (597). De même, après un colloque réuni par le défunt C.H. Waddington à Chichen Itza, au Mexique (1216), comme je m'étais plainte de l'absence de jeunes, on a perdu un temps considérable à chercher la participation rétrospective de jeunes pour la publication proposée et qu'on a finalement abandonnée. Plus tard, en partie comme suite au colloque Waddington, un colloque de jeunes, choisis par des savants et érudits éminents, s'est réunie en Suède juste avant le Symposium Nobel 14 (1067). Les étudiants ainsi réunis eurent à lire les communications des participants distingués; leur principale réaction a été alors de les découper en morceaux et d'en faire des collages — activité qui correspond bien à l'atmosphère du centre et fin des années 60 qui n'a d'ailleurs pas eu grand effet sur les délibérations du colloque.

J'en suis venue, à regret, à la conclusion que le seul moyen viable d'obtenir la participation des très jeunes est d'entraîner les enfants de ceux qui ont acquis une réputation dans le même domaine. J'y vois deux avantages: leur participation a plus de chance d'être bien accueillie à cause de leur nom, et, comme ils ont connu leurs éminents parents toute leur vie, ils ne sont pas intimidés et n'ont pas besoin non plus de faire montre d'hostilité à leur égard pour cacher leur sentiment d'accablement devant eux. Ainsi, tout en considérant la découverte et l'encouragement des jeunes comme une tâche très importante, j'ai trouvé la pratique peu facile.

J'essaie de prendre moi-même les demandes par téléphone, de façon à pouvoir explorer les possibilités de recommander d'autres gens. Je lis le courrier m'invitant à des colloques (même lorsque le date est impossible), de façon à penser à qui je pourrais recommander à ma place. J'encourage les autres à solliciter les gens occupés à faire des choses qu'en toute vraisemblance, ils vont refuser pour ensuite leur demander de suggérer quelqu'un d'autre à leur place. Mais une des difficultés réelle du monde moderne est la nature cumulative de la renommée. Plus on publie et plus on est sollicité.

Le nombre croissant des moyens de reproduction bon marché et la multiplication qu'ils provoquent dans l'édition, ainsi que l'insatiabilité d'une société de gaspillage, sont un autre problème actuel. Les collections s'ajoutent aux collections; les articles sont réimprimés sous des titres différents ou bien des extraits en sont tirés pour des expositions de musée, des catalogues, des livres de citations compilés dans les buts les plus divers, des contes d'enfants aux calendriers. En retour, d'autres collectionneurs et exploiteurs prennent des citations à la presse et écrivent avec le plus grand sérieux pour demander à quelle publication le texte doit être attribué. Des livres publiés il y a des années, qui contenaient un chapitre de moi sont tout d'un coup ressuscités, tel que le livre récemment réédité dans une édition révisée, *While You Were Gone* (251), publié d'abord en 1946 et épuisé depuis des années.

A ces facteurs de prolifération s'ajoute la nouvelle tendance qui consiste à éditer des volumes à n'en plus finir sur des sujets particuliers à usage scolaire. Ces volumes réimpriment des textes réunis pour les besoins particuliers d'un cours. La maison qui a fait imprimer le recueil par un procédé d'offset bon marché, essaie ensuite de saisir l'occasion pour obtenir des droits permanents sur les textes réimprimés. Toutes ces procédures exigent correspondance, vérifications, permissions, refus de permission, et aboutissent à une situation où, comme un critique le disait récemment: "Les gens peuvent vous citer sur à peu près n'importe quel sujet hors de contexte, pour prouver tout ce qu'ils veulent prouver, et ils se trompent souvent."

Cet effet diffus et envahissant des publications qui se répètent est aggravé par l'usage de la radio. Des propos tenus il y a des années et enregistrés pour quelque "usage éducatif", sont enfouis quelque part dans des archives jusqu'-au jour où ils reparaissent sur les ondes, des années plus tard, avec d'étranges anachronismes que l'auditeur ne peut s'expliquer. Par exemple, le ton de voix que j'aurais pris en parlant du "Président" dans une première émission, serait très différent si j'avais à parler du "Président" au moment où le programme est retransmis. J'essaie de dominer cette situation en stipulant que le temps et le lieu doivent être donnés chaque fois qu'un enregistrement est rejoué, mais là encore, il est pratiquement impossible de faire appliquer cette règle. L'existence d'archives sonores des émissions radiodiffusées ou télévisées donne la possibilité de vérifier les fausses accusations sur ce qu'on a dit ou pas dit, mais, en général, la radio reste un moyen insidieux et c'est à la radio qu'on est le plus souvent attaqué injustement et cité à tort. Personne ne sait au juste qui a parlé, ce qui a été dit et à quel moment et la rumeur persiste.

Il y a aussi d'autres aspects des changements technologiques. Dans la reproduction de la photographie, par exemple, il est maintenant possible de raviver de vieilles photos toutes passées à un niveau de clarté tout à fait respectable, comme cela a été fait avec les vieux clichés utiliés dans mon autobiographie, *Blackberry Winter* (1178). Ces illustrations n'ont pas besoin d'être groupées dans une partie du livre comme dans *New Lives for Old* (467), mais peuvent être intercalées dans le texte là où elles conviennent. Mais ce qu'on gagne d'une part, on le perd de l'autre. Il n'y a aucune comparaison entre la beauté de la première édition de *Balinese Character* en 1942 (140) où 2.000 exemplaires ont été tirés par le procédé de photo gélatine et la seconde de 1962, reproduite à partir des mêmes photos de la collection de Gregory Bateson. Ces photos ont été aussi utilisées dans mon livre fait en collaboration avec Frances Macgregor, *Growth and Culture* (363). Les méthodes modernes de reproduction permettent plus de souplesse mais en même temps, la demande de couleur s'accroît avec des prix de revient encore beucoup trop élevés pour un travail scientifique. J'ai retardé la parution de la dernière partie de mon ethnographie des Arapesh. "The Bark Paintings of the Mountain Arapesh of New Guinea" (715), jusqu'à ce qu'on puisse utiliser la reproduction en couleur et, à ce moment-là, on m'a appris qu'on ne pouvait en publier qu'une seule.

Dans ce volume, je me suis contentée de citer les bandes qui ont été enregistrées spécialement pour la vente et qui portent un numéro de catalogue et le nom de l'endroit où on peut les acheter. Elles ne représentent qu'une très petite fraction des enregistrements qui existent dans les archives sonores des universités, des postes radiophoniques locaux de programmes éducatifs et dans d'autres institutions.

Une longue liste de publications, toute une vie durant, a des conséquences curieuses. Les livres qu'on écrit doivent rester comme des documents de recherche qui ne peuvent être retouchés, alors que la théorie qui se dégage de nos oeuvres récentes et de celle de nos collègues dans la même discipline, est en perpétuel changement. A la mort d'un ethnologue, il est possible de continuer de rééditer ses oeuvres pendant plusieurs années, en y ajoutant en général une nouvelle préface ou une introduction qui replace le texte dans son contexte historique et contemporain. J'ai eu l'occasion d'écrire une telle préface et de fournir un nouvel appendice photographique au livre de Darwin, *Expression of the Emotions in Man and Animals* (456). Ce livre se fait l'écho du travail le plus récent dans l'étude de la kinésie d'après le colloque, organisé par l'université de Louisville sur le sujet "Culture et Communication", en 1954. Les éditeurs voulaient que j'insère de nouvelles photographies dans le texte, ce qui, bien entendu, aurait violé l'intégrité du livre.

J'ai dû rejeter la suggestion faite par certains critiques de réécrire *Coming of Age in Samoa* sous prétexte que le livre ne correspond plus aux coutumes des Samoans d'aujourd'hui. Il ne leur vient pas à l'idée que pour réécrire ce livre, il me faudrait refaire une étude minutieuse et peut-être incorporer des extraits du premier livre dans le second, comme j'ai pu le faire pour *New Lives for Old*, étude faite vingt cinq ans après *Growing Up in New Guinea*. Le changement constant d'éditions, livres de poche, éditions spéciales de courte durée, livres brochés coûteux, éditions spéciales hors d'Amérique, etc.... offre la possibilité d'écrire de nouvelles préfaces ou de nouvelles introductions, comme je l'ai fait pour *Coming of Age in Samoa* (6) qui a paru dans six éditions et pour lequel j'ai écrit trois nouvelles préfaces. *Growing Up in New Guinea* (22) a paru en quatre éditions, avec deux nouvelles préfaces, *Sex and Temperament in Three Primitive Societies* (79), en trois éditions, avec deux nouvelles préfaces, et *Male and Female* (312) en quatre éditions, avec quatre nouvelles préfaces et un nouvel appendice.

Cela permet d'introduire de nouvelles idées, de replacer un livre dans son temps, de répudier des points auxquels on avait donné trop ou pas assez d'importance et, dans une certaine mesure, de faire pénétrer, par des changements de terminologie, un sens de l'évolution de l'opinion mondiale. Ce point a été particulièrement important pour un livre comme *Coming of Age in Samoa* que j'ai écrit en cachant soigneusement l'identité de mes informateurs, mais sans considérer la possibilité que les jeunes de Samoa iraient au collège où leurs condisciples auraient à lire les faits et gestes de leurs grandes-mères, cinquante ans auparavant. Cette source d'embarras est en partie due au fait qu'à l'époque les titres de livre étaient plus généraux, car les lecteurs de langue anglaise connaissaient trop peu de géographie pour qu'on puisse citer "Manu'a" ou "Manus" dans un titre. Aujourd'hui, comme l'ont fait de jeunes Samoans d'autres parties de l'île que celle que j'ai décrite, des jeunes d'une autre des quelques six cents différents groupes linguistiques de Papouasie-Nouvelle-Guinée, protestent, parce que leur propre version de la "Nouvelle Guinée" qu'ils pensent être la seule représentative, est différente de celle que j'ai décrite pour l'île de Manus dans les années 20. Ils citent avec colère une phrase de *Growing Up in New Guinea* en disant que je les ai grossièrement et faussement représentés comme un peuple moderne d'aujourd'hui. Au cours de l'été 75, j'ai parlé à l'école secondaire de Lorengau dans l'île de Manus où enseignant le jeune poète Kumalau Tawali (1970). Un élève s'est levé pour dire: "Dans votre livre *Growing Up in New Guinea* vous avez dit que les enfants de Manus manquaient d'imagination. Sur quel critère vous êtes-vous fondée pour porter ce jugement?" A quoi j'ai pu répondre: "Sur une collection de 35.000 dessins d'enfants." (56) et j'ajoutai: "mais maintenant, vous avez un poète de Manus comme professeur et la chance de développer votre créativité."

Le passage du temps a créé d'autres difficultés. Quand j'ai commencé à écrire, les mots "sauvages" et "primitifs" étaient interchangeables, en référence aux peuples sans écriture. Je ne voyais aucune objection alors, à des titres journalistiques tels que *Savage Masters of the Sea* (40), bien que, par goût personnel, j'aie toujours utilisé "primitif". Aujourd'hui, bien des membres des nouvelles nations contestent le terme "primitif" et on a créé toutes sortes d'euphémismes pour enlever le stigmate censé être attaché à certains mots. "Naturel" (native) est devenu "du pays" (local) ou "indigène" (indigenous). *Pidgin English* a été remplacé par *Neo-Melanesian* après la deuxième guerre mondiale (cf. *New Lives for Old*), mais aujourd'hui le terme de *Pidgin English* est redevenu acceptable. Aux Etats-Unis, *Negro*, avec majuscule obligatoire pour faire ressortir le statut de minorité, a été supplanté par *Black* et quelque fois par *Afro-American*. Quand j'écris une nouvelle introduction ou préface ou un chapitre supplémentaire pour une nouvelle édition, je me sers des euphémismes actuels: *Humankind* (genre humain) pour *Mankind* (humanité) ou *Chairperson* (président) à la place de *Chairman*[1], pourtant parfaitement acceptable à condition de le faire précéder de *Mister* ou de *Madame*. Mais je suis choquée par le manque de sens historique qui pousse de jeunes anthropologues à s'ériger contre l'usage de termes démodés dans des livres écrits des années plus tôt. Par exemple, le journal de Mali-nowski (1967) a été violemment attaqué pour avoir utilisé en 1914 un mot polonais traduit en anglais par "nigger" pour désigner les habitants des îles Trobriand que son oeuvre a rendus immortels.

Même l'usage d'introductions écrites ultérieurement et qui insistent sur les dates avec soin, est encore de peu de secours. Quand parut en 1939 *From the South Seas*, recueil de mes trois premiers livres, j'ai écrit une nouvelle introduction traitant de ce que nous ne savions pas en 1925 quand j'ai fait mon premier terrain. Les étudiants réagirent par des commentaires péjoratifs, tels que: "Mademoiselle Mead elle-même reconnaît ...", pour me reprocher ensuite de ne pas avoir utilisé des méthodes qui n'avaient pas encore été mises au point à l'époque de mon terrain. Si le fait de publier et de republier pendant une si longue période permet quelque fois d'apporter une perspective historique, il introduit aussi de nouvelles sources d'embarras et de perplexité dans les oeuvres d'ethnologues qui sont en général des gens particulièrement sensibles aux attaques visant leurs premières oeuvres.

En ce qui me concerne, je crois que c'est seulement en acceptant la chronique de son passé dans sa totalité qu'on peut affronter le présent dans son intégrité. Mes documents sur une phase révolue de la Nouvelle-Guinée té-moignent de l'étonnante distance parcourue par ce peuple en une seule géné-ration, ce qui constitue le progrès le plus rapide dont le monde ait jamais été témoin − de l'isolation dans l'age de pierre à la participation à l'âge post-atomique. Ses habitants peuvent être fiers de ce passé, s'ils le regardent avec franchise; mais s'ils se fabriquent un passé fictif, ils deviendront prisonniers de leurs propres fabrications. Aujourd'hui le peuple de Manus peut lire les comptes rendus les plus techniques de ce que j'ai écrit d'eux (22, 46, 467), ainsi que les oeuvres publiées par d'autres tels que Reo Fortune (1935) et Theodore Schwartz (1962) qui ont écrit sur eux pendant les quarante sept dernières années, période qui constitue la plus longue histoire qu'ait un peuple sans écriture.

heurtent constamment les ethnologues. Si j'ai été heureuse d'écrire *A Rap on Race* avec James Baldwin, c'est grâce à la bonne volonté qu'il a montrée à reconnaître son passé comme celui d'un Américain n'ayant aucun lien généalogique avec l'Afrique. Un compte rendu du *New York Times* a sévèrement critiqué la présentation du livre, en prétendant que d'utiliser des conversations enregistrées était un moyen trop facile et dégradait l'art d'écrire. Mais le magnétophone permet un genre d'échanges rarement possible dans des débats sur la race et dans lequel, lorsque le débat est imprimé, le lecteur ne peut pas ne pas lire les deux faces du problème.

Quant à mon choix de livres dont j'ai fait le compte rendu, j'ai, bien sûr, au début, accepté de faire celui de tous les livres qu'on m'envoyait dans ce but — en vérité, assemblage assez curieux. Plus tard, j'ai fait un bon nombre de comptes rendus pour les *Annals of the American Academy of Political and Social Science* (30, 48, 83, 659, 941, 990), parce qu'on n'y demandait que de très courts articles et je pouvais me limiter aux livres que j'avais vraiment envie de lire attentivement. Avec le temps, j'ai suivi la politique de ne faire la critique que des livres que je considérais assez importants pour les lire de bout en bout avec l'espoir de ne pas perdre mon temps. A l'occasion, j'ai fait des comptes rendus de livres dont je pensais qu'ils se fourvoyaient dangereusement, tel que le livre de Wayne Dennis, *The Hopi Child* (134) ou celui de Kardiner, *The Individual and His Society* (137). Je mis de valeur sur un petit nombre de ces critiques qui ont été pour moi l'occasion d'exprimer un point théorique: mon compte rendu du livre de Geoffrey Gorer, *Himalayan Village* (101), de celui de Z.S. Harris, *Methods in Structural Linguistics* (395), *Riddle of the Sphinx* (84) de Roheim et enfin *The Individual in Cultural Adaptation* (1975) d'Edgerton. La taille d'un livre est devenue de plus en plus un élément à considérer: emmener avec moi dans mes voyages à travers les Etats-Unis de pesants volumes comme *La Force de l'âge* de Simone de Beauvoir (1272), est devenu un trop grand fardeau.

J'accepte d'écrire une préface ou une introduction, si on me le demande, comme faisant partie de mes obligations personnelles à un étudiant, un collègue ou un jeune ami dont j'ai suivi le travail avec intérêt. Dans le passé, j'ai écrit un petit nombre de préfaces pour des livres avec lesquels je n'avais eu encore aucun rapport (568), mais j'en ai reçu trop d'invitations surtout venant d'éditeurs et d'agents de publicité, pour pouvoir tous les accepter.

Ces dix dernières années, j'ai refusé systématiquement d'écrire de préface pour tout livre avec lequel je n'ai eu aucune association antérieure personnelle, soit en lisant et critiquant le manuscrit avant qu'il soit publié, soit en tant que professeur, collègue ou amie. Avec les années, cette politique ne s'en est pas moins soldée par un bon nombre de préfaces et d'introductions.

J'ai aussi écrit des relations autobiographiques, des articles, des chapitres ou des livres en réponse à l'initiative de quelqu'un d'autre. Mes deux livres, *An Anthropologist at Work: Writings of Ruth Benedict* (537) et *Ruth Benedict: A Biography* (1291) contiennent une grande part de matériaux autobiographiques sur mes années d'études supérieures et sur ma collaboration ultérieure avec Ruth Benedict. C'est le cas également de "Apprenticeship under Boas" (538) et *Blackberry Winter: My Earlier Years* (1178), autobiographie personnelle qui met en relief mes années d'éducation par des parents sociologues et celles qui m'ont menées à des mariages successifs avec des collègues ethnologues. Le chapitre que j'ai écrit pour le volume dirigé par Gardiner Lindzay (1287), traite de l'influence que ma formation de psychologue a eue sur mon travail de terrain. D'autres petits textes contiennent un mélange de problèmes méthodologique et de détails précis sur mon terrain, en particulier mes lettres publiées dans *Women in the Field* (1069) de Peggy Golde, "A Bread and Butter Letter from a lecturer" (193), "Out of the Things I Read" (378), "Weaver of the Border" (601), "Field Work in High Cultures" (1186), "Retrospects and Prospects" (681), l'introduction à *From the South Seas* (96) et les préfaces des différents volumes de *The Mountain Arapesh* (986, 1113, 1164a). J'ai l'intention de publier un volume intitulé *Letters from the Field: 1925–1975*, d'après des lettres ronéotypées écrites sur le terrain pour ma famille, mes amis et collègues, accompagnées d'une correspondance professionnelle. Dans d'autres textes, je rends compte de façon plus formelle de travaux particuliers: l'introduction à *The Study of Culture at a Distance* (412), à *Soviet Attitudes toward Authority* (359) et à *Childhood in Contemporary Cultures* (453), "The Committee on Food Habits" (166), "The Anthropology of Human Conflict" (834), "The Vicissitudes of the Study of the Total Communication Process" (783) et trois films (*35, 37, 41*).

Du fait que j'ai commencé mon travail scientifique si jeune – je crois être la première parmi les ethnologues américains à avoir commencé ma carrière ethnologique dès mes premières années d'études universitaires – j'ai eu la chance de travailler avec beaucoup de gens plus âgés que moi dont j'ai tiré inspiration et avec des collègues maintenant disparus: Lawrence K. Frank (1008, 1351), Ruth Benedict (319, 320), Robert Lamb (429) et Margaret Lowenfeld (1342). J'ai eu la tâche d'aider à achever l'oeuvre de Jane Belo (1112), de Colin McPhee (1966), Edith Cobb (en préparation) et de Margaret

Lowenfeld (en préparation).

Mon travail de terrain complet se range en trois catégories: (1) les publications faites d'après mes six voyages sur le terrain — seule à Samoa et en compagnie de Reo Fortune chez les Indiens Omaha, les Manus, les Arapesh, les Mundugumor et les Tchambuli — publications dont quatre sont maintenant terminées. De ces premières études ethnographiques, seule la publication qui concerne les Mundugumor reste à écrire: Reo Fortune et moi avons abandonné notre travail sur cette culture, parce qu'elle était trop fragmentée. J'y suis retournée en 1973 et me suis convaincue qu'aucun travail plus approfondi sur l'ancienne culture pourrait être accompli avec profit. J'ai donc entrepris une monographie qui illustrera les premières étapes d'un terrain inachevé. (2) Les deux voyages accomplis avec Gregory Bateson à Bali et chez les Iatmul de Nouvelle-Guinée au cours desquels la photographie et le cinéma furent utilisés pour la première fois. Nous en avons rapporté une masse de matériaux suffisants pour en tirer ultérieurement un nombre presqu'illimité d'études. Celles qui ont été publiées n'en ont utilisé qu'une faible partie en comptant les miennes (91, 99, 100, 103, 104, 105, 110, 118, 145, 149, 170, 260, 363, 440, 539, 624, *28, 29*), celles de Gregory Bateson (1937, 1941, 1942, 1946, 1949, 1975) et notre oeuvre en commun (140); (3) les études nouvelles en progrès, refaites depuis la deuxième guerre mondiale en collaboration avec des collègues plus jeunes, Theodore Schwartz (433, 507, 644, *33*), Leonora Schwartz (33), Lola Romanucci-Ross (1335), Ken Heyman (832, 1395), Barbara Heath, Rhoda Métraux. On peut dire que ces études ne seront jamais achevées et continueront de m'occuper le restant de ma vie.

J'ai fait sept expéditions à Manus, pendant un total de quarante sept ans et quatre générations. J'ai revisité Iatmul deux fois quand Rhoda Métraux s'y trouvait; ainsi qu'au village arapesh d'Alitoa, transféré sur la baie d'Hoskins, sur l'île de la Nouvelle Bretagne; et à Samoa en 1971. Le fait d'avoir commencé mon travail avec des enfants quand j'étais très jeune, à une période où le monde a subi les changements les plus rapides de l'histoire, m'a été particulièrement favorable. C'est cela qui m'a permis de faires ces études toujours en course sur les changements sociaux et d'établir des successeurs parmi les jeunes ethnologues.

Près de la moitié de mon temps a été consacré à appliquer mon expérience d'ethnologue, les données que je récoltais et les théories que en découlaient, à des problèmes de nutrition et des modes de s'alimenter (165, 773), de changements techniques (399), de santé mentale, de vie familiale et de puériculture. Maintenant que nous sommes en mesure d'utiliser notre expérience des sociétés isolées, sur une petite échelle et faciles à cerner, pour étudier le développement de la société à l'échelle mondiale, ces champs d'intérêt se song élargis pour inclure des études des problèmes planétaires (732, 824, 1063, 1131, 1194, 1247, 1286, 1395).

NOTE

1. Note du traducteur: tous ces changements pour éviter des connotations "sexistes". "Mankind" et "chairman" sont formés sur "man" (homme), interprété par certains groupes féministes comme excluant la femme.

INTRODUCCIÓN

El conjunto de mis publicaciones revela poca ortodoxia en cuanto a las formas que escogí para expresarme, y por eso creo que vale la pena prologar esta bibliografía con una aclaración sobre las razones que me llevaron a escoger esas formas. En mis trabajos como escritora seguí una ruta bastante convencional: decidí publicar un artículo y luego busqué la revista profesional más adecuada para ofrecerlo. Los artículos se basaban en mis investigaciones del momento y se dirigían a cierto público especializado. Por ejemplo, cuando *The International Journal of Psychoanalysis* rachazó "An Ethnologist's Footnote to *Totem and Taboo*" (21), lo mandé a la *Psychoanalytic Review* donde lo aceptaron. Mientras hacía mis estudios graduados, trabajando con un solo informante del Africa del Oeste, llevé a cabo una breve investigación que mandé al *Journal of the Royal Anthropological Institute* en 1925; la guardaron y la publicaron por fin en 1937 bajo el título "A Twi Relationship System" (93). Ni siquiera me dieron la oportunidad de revisarla, a la luz de cinco viajes de campo que hice entre 1925 y 1937, durante los cuales los problemas de parentesco específicamente relacionadas con la investigación fueron también centrales para mi trabajo de campo y en mis publicaciones subsecuentes, tales como *Social Organization of Manu'a* (25) y *Kinship in the Admiralty Islands* (66).

Ya por 1928, revistas como *Natural History* (23, 26, 65, 70, etc.), *Parents Magazine* (26, 59), *The Nation* (31) y *The Thinker* (20) empezaron a solicitarme artículos. Me pedían reseñas, no sólo para revistas profesionales sino también para el *New Freeman* (28) y *The Nation* (15). En 1930, Calverton y Schmalhausen, dos empresarios literarios, iniciaron la costumbre – hasta hoy vigente – de invitar a algunos colaboradores a escribir sobre temas contemporáneos para *The New Generation* (19). Además de las peticiones de artículos para enciclopedias, algunas revistas de mayor o menor nivel técnico, desde *The New York Times Magazine* (63) hasta *Publishers' Weekly* (38) y *Safety Education* (40), comenzaron a pedirme escritos.

En parte esas peticiones reflejaban la creciente fama de *Adolescencia, sexo y cultura en Samoa* (6). Aunque no concebí ese libro para un público general, en el sentido de quien no se dirige a un público de literature de ficción, al escribirlo sí que incursioné en un camino hasta entonces poco frecuentado. Intentaba dar forma a un libro de tema técnico, en el cual habría sido de esperar la terminología etnológica y psicológica, y al mismo tiempo quería hacerlo comprensible a grupos mayores de individuos específicamente interesados, sobre todo a los que tenían que trabajar con adolescentes en nuestra propia sociedad — maestros de escuela secundaria y trabajadores sociales. No me daba encuenta todavía de que si se llegaba a escribir un libro en inglés sin jerga técnica (que en la literatura etnográfica de aquel entonces requería el use de un gran número de palabras en la lengua nativa), ese mismo libro resultaría asequible al mundo culto en general. Además sería fácil lectura para los nuevos universitarios, y podría ser traducido sin dificultad a otros idiomas.

Los artículos publicados a propósito en revistas pedagógicas ya me habían preparado el terreno para hacer la material asequible a las personas más interesadas. Esos artículos presentaron las conclusiones de mi primer trabajo de investigación, publicado en *School and Society* en 1927 (4,5), acerca de la influencia del aprendizaje del habla casera en niños Italo-Americanos y su efecto determinante en las calificaciones recibidas por estos mismos niños en el colegio. Puesto que yo había escogido la antropología como profesión y era evidente y necesaria su aplicación a los problemas actuales de la sociedad, el hecho de poner mis hallazgos a disposición de un público más amplio, aunque siempre especializado, fue intención consciente desde los comienzos mismos de mis carrera.

Cuando Pliny E. Goddard, conservador de Etnología del Museo Americano de Historia Natural, me invitó en 1925 a asociarme con el Museo, expresó concretamente la esperanza de que yo pudiera hacer de la etnología una material tan conocido y asequible a un público extenso y entusiasta como habían hecho los conservadores anteriores con la arquelogía. Para entonces, yo no había publicado más que algunos poemas y editoriales para el *Barnard Bulletin*, que redacté en 1922, y sólo había escrito mi tesis doctoral, *An* bastante solemne y árida para decir verdad. La fundada idea de Goddard, no obstante, me incitó a responder a las solicitudes de revistas y periódicos tales como *The New York Times* (63, 124), *The Saturday Review of Literature* (82), *The Nation* (15), y *Natural History* (23, 36, 65, 70), la publicación que corresponde al Museo Americano de Historia Natural, por medio de la cual hemos ampliado nuestro quehacer a un círculo mundial de socios.

También creo que mi esperanza inicial de hacerme escritora figuraba en todo esto, puesto que yo había contemplado y probado varios géneros sucesivamente: la poesía, el ensayo, el cuento, la comedia y el espectáculo público — durante los años del bachillerato y de la universidad, y no había abandonado del todo mi ambición de publicar poesía ni siquera después de mi resolución de hacerme antropóloga. Sin embargo, cuando "Absolute Benison" (51), poema que entregué bajo un seudónimo, fue al principio rechazado y luego aceptado por el mismo editor al proponerlo de nuevo bajo mi propio nombre en 1932, después de haber publicado *Adolescencia, sexo y cultura en Samoa* (6), decidí no volver a someter ningún otro poema para publicación. Mi feliz amistad durante los años universitarios con la ilustre poetisa norteamericana Leonie Adams, me había convencido que la poesía no era campo en que yo pudiera hacer ninguna contribución importante. Ruth Benedict y Edward Sapir, íntimos colegas míos a mediados de los año 1920, habían escrito bastantes poemas sueltos que llegaron a publicarse en las compilaciones de aquel entonces, pero a los dos les habían rechazado colecciones de poesía en 1928. De mode que abandoné sin vacilar toda otra tentativa de publicar mi poesía.

Tiempo después advertí que los cuentos que escribí durante mis días de escuela graduada surgieron de una necesidad de resolver cuestiones que me preocupaban, más que de un intento de hacer literatura. Las representaciones que escribí y monté se relacionaban con un interés en la representación teatral que pude expresar luego en el campo al componer y dirigir películas etno-gráficas. También era bien claro para nosotros, los estudiantes, que escribir constituía un ejercicio sumamente valioso y que el antropólogo que llegara a hacerlo como Malinowski (que ya tenía un vasto público), llevaba ventaje a sus compañeros menos dotados. Como ejemplo sólo hay que contrastar *The Andaman Islanders* (1922) de Radcliffe-Brown con *Argonauts of the Western Pacific* (1922), de Malinowski. Asimismo, *The Mind of Primitive Man* (1911) de Franz Boas, carecía para nosotros de la persuasión literaria que merecían su importancia y su tema. Por eso, una voluntad manifiesta dentro de la profesión, que remontaba a Frazer (1907–1925), Crawley (1927) y Marett (1900), nos animaba a escribir en un inglés claro y no en ese pesado estilo alemán que era predominante en el ámbito de las tesis doctorales norte-americanas.

Sin embargo, esta voluntad de escribir en un inglés corriente y lo más claro posible no me hizo abandonar la redacción científico-técnica. Después del amplio éxito de *Adolescencia, sexo y cultura en Samoa* (6) me resultó muy agradable dirigirme hacia el público especializado de mis colegas antropólo-gos, por ejemplo, cuando escribí *Social Organization of Manu'a* (25) para la colección de estudios monográficos del Museo de Bernice P. Bishop. Pero aún en este caso tenía plena conciencia de la necesidad de expresarme a múltiples niveles de generalización. Reuní, pues, varios de los más famosos estudios monográficos de la época – *The Todas* (1906) de Rivers, *Argonauts of the Western Pacific* (1922) de Malinowski, *The Baganda* (1911) de

Roscoe y *The Cheyenne Indians* (1923) de Grinell – y empecé a estudiar su estructura. Franz Boas, con quien yo había cursado los estudios graduados y realizado el primer trabajo de campo había dicho: "La dificultad al escribir un monografía estriba en la necesidad de incluir el final al principio, lo cual aplica a cada capítulo – la necesidad de incluir cada capítulo en todos los demás." Tambien llegué a la conclusión de que había tres grupos de colegas que podían valerse del estudio monográfico: investigadores interesados en la dinámica de la estructura social; investigadores interesados específicamente en Oceanía; e investigadores que se interesaban en la etnografía de Polinesia, para quienes serían importantes los detalles de la organización social de Manu'a. Una vez establecidos estos tres niveles decrecientes de generalización, organicé el estudio monográfico de acuerdo a ellos. Muchos años despues volvería a utilizar esta medida para dirigirme a lectores de ámbitos culturales y capacidades diferentes cuando redacté unos pasajes sobre la misma materia en *People and Places* (557), un libro para niños; un capítulo del libro de Lyman Bryson, *The Communication of Ideas* (228), para un público adulto; y mi obra teórica más sistemática, *Continuities in Cultural Evolution* (771).

Seguí experimentando con distintos niveles y clases de escritos hasta 1935 cuando compuse *Sexo y temperamento en las sociedades primitivas* (79), obra que me pareció un acierto porque combinaba, para un público culto, las exigencias estéticas con la presentación de una materia etnográfica difícil y deconocida. Entonces dejé de escribir poesía. Reconozco que me esmero más en el oficio de escribir un ensayo destinado a lectores exigentes, como los de *The American Scholar* (470) o *Daedalus* (543), pero por lo general no me persiguen esos remordimientos que padecen los que han aprendido a escribir en un género distinto al de sus sueños. De este modo me libré de las frustraciones de tantos científicos que escriben con gusto pero siempre con la esperanza de que algún día les saldrá la gran novela. Una vez que me hube convencido de que las culturas humanas eran infinitamente más complejas e interesantes que cualquiera invención mía, y que en mis tentativas de escribir obras de ficción había estado todo el tiempo tratando de comprender situaciones reales con las cuales me había enfrentado en mi niñez, no me asaltaron deseos de contribuir a la literatura novelesca.

Me sigue interesando la forma, y me resulta provocadora y emocionante cada petición fuera de lo normal – por ejemplo la de narrar una película (*29, 29*), la de escribir el guión para acompañar unas fotografías (832), la de grabar la cinta para un audiógrafo (en la sala de las gentes del Pacífico del Museo Americano de Historia Natural) (1146, 1151), la de escribir para un público extranjero, o la de dar una conferencia empleando una mezcla del inglés correcto y *Pidgin English* (inglés chapurreado) para un público de la Nueva Guinea de diversas aptitudes en este idioma.

Al cabo de cinco años de escribir profesionalmente, se podía distinguir un maracado contraste entre el estilo empleado en la composición de mis libros y largos estudios monográficos y aquel empleado en escribir artículos, reseñas y libros que se encontraban en la periferia de mi interés central, especialmente obras de las cuales yo era co-autora o co-redactora. Así que para todas las publicaciones principales que hice sobre mi propio trabajo de campo – *Adolescencia, sexo y cultura en Samoa* (6), *Social Organization of Manu'a* (25), *Growing Up in New Guinea* (22), *Kinship in the Admiralty Islands* (66), *Sexo y temperamento en las sociedades primitivas* (79), *The Mountain Arapesh* (94, 107, 269, 313), *El hombre y la mujer* (312), *New Lives for Old* (467), *Continuities in Cultural Evolution* (711), y *Cultura y compromiso* (1063) – fui yo quien decidí lo que quería escribir: la contribución de editores e impresores fue relativamente pequeña. Mi primer impresor, William Morrow, me sugirió que agregara los dos últimos capítulos a *Adolescencia, sexo y cultura en Samoa*, en los que relaciono mis descubrimientos acerca de Samoa con la cultura norteamericana – tema que ha había emprendido en algunas conferencias y clases. El señor Morrow también se quejaba de la excesiva dificultad del capítulo central sobre los Mundugumor en *Sexo y temperamento en las sociedades primitivas*. Por lo tanto lo destruí y volví a escribirlo. Thayer Hobson, mi editor en la casa de William Morrow, propuso el título de *New Lives for Old*. En el título de *Growing Up in New Guinea* se repetía de algún modo y desafortunadamente el de *Adolescencia, sexo y cultura en Samoa*, y las palabras *New Guinea* – bastante precisas para el territoria dentro del cual se situaban los Manus – se emplearon porque mi impresor lamentó que nadie supiera donde estaba situado. Me habían destinado al personal del Museo de Bernice P. Bishop de socio honorífico, y mi estudio monográfico, *Social Organization of Manu'a* se adecuaba a su serie de redacciones sobre Polinesia. *Kinship in the Admiralty Islands* fue escrito como respuesta a un juicio crítico de Malinowski; él alegaba que yo no sabía nada de sistemas de parentesco. Con el objeto de preparar mi respuesta para la colección del Museo Americano de Historia Natural, postergué cuatro meses un viaje de campo que tenía proyectado. Les estudios extensos sobre los Arapesh montañeses que se incluirían en la colección del Museo fueron concebidos primero como una obra de colaboración entre Reo Fortune y yo, y luego hubo que revisarlos debido al aumento de los gastos de reproducción que nos obligaba a excluir una sección entera para la cual ya se había hecho todo el trabajo gráfico preliminar.

A partir de mi viaje a Samoa, todo mi trabajo de campo se ha llevado a cabo en colaboración con otros; esa modalidad ha tenido como resultado varias publicaciones entre las cuales se encuentran *Balinese Character*, con Gregory Bateson (140); "The Cult as a Condensed Social Process" (607), y un estudio sobre "Micro- and Macro Cultural Models for Cultural Evolution" (644), con Theodore Schwartz. En cada caso las ediciones han sido dispuestas después de trazar e indicar lo que escribiría yo y lo que escribiría mi colega, el orden que seguirían los estudios, y la medida en que nuestros textos por separado contaran con el trabajo de campo del otro.

En la segunda categoría se encuentran libros que han surgido de proyectos ideados por otro individuo u otra institución. *The Changing Culture of an Indian Tribe* (53) fue redacción de un proyecto que yo emprendí a instancias de Clark Wissler, jefe del departamento donde yo trabajaba en el Museo Americano de Historia Natural, para cumplir con una obligación que él habia asumido al aceptar una donación de $ 750 de la Señora Leonard Elmhirst, destinada al estudio de la vida familiar de los indios norteamericanos. No fue elección mía ni el asunto ni la tribu (los Omaha, a quienes les puse el seudónomi de "los astas"), aunque diseñé el libro y encontré un editor para él. Cuarenta y cuatro años más tarde, cuando se gestionaba la reimpresión de algunas obras en la imprenta universitaria de la Universidad de Columbia, redacté una nueva introducción sobre "The Consequences of Racial Guilt" para un libro de bolsillo publicado por Capricorn Books, Putnam (866).

Cooperation and Competition Among Primitive Peoples (89) se derivó de un proyecto iniciado por la Subcomisión Sobre los Usos Competitivos y Cooperativos de la Comisión Sobre la Personalidad y la Cultura del Consejo de Investigaciones de Ciencias Sociales de los Estados Unidos. Había asumido la responsabilidad de preparar la sección que tenía que ver con el posible aporte de material etnológico en la planificación e investigación de sociedades competidoras y cooperativas. También había desarrollado un nuevo método que consistía en utilizar investigadores de campo como fuentes vivas y primarias que responderían a preguntas que no habían surgido antes en el curso de su propia investigación de terreno. Esto se hacía dentro del contexto académico de un seminario en que se les daba la tarea de reexaminar sus datos extraídos del trabajo de campo; tenían acceso a la vez a trabajos inéditos efectuados por otros colegas. Esta experiencia se transformó en un libro que yo dispuse y actualicé en 1961 para un libro de bolsillo de la Beacon Press. El impresor fue elegido a base de una conexión que tenían los iniciadores del proyecto con la casa McGraw Hill.

Balinese Character: A Photographic Study (140) provino de un examen atento que efectuamos Gregory Bateson y yo sobre la fase que nos parecía la más innovadora en cuanto a metodología de nuestro viaje de campo a Bali (99) durante los años 1936–1939. En el mismo momento de convenir en un estudio conjunto de las 25000 y pico de fotografías que teníamos, habíamos superado los límites anteriores en los usos de la fotografía. Al planear el libro agrupamos en una página algunas actividades que se diferenciaban inmensamente entre si para mostrar puntos de semejanzas sin destruir la integridad de cada acontecimiento. Esta disposición en sí significaba una innovación en métodos de presentación, que repetimos hasta cierto punto nueve años más tarde en *Growth and Culture: A Photographic Study of Balinese Childhood* (363), que emprendí como respuesta al interés de Frances MacGregor en perfeccionar su experiencia fotográfica respecto a las ciencias sociales.

And Keep Your Powder Dry (142), escrito durante la Segunda Guerra Mundial, fue consecuencia de una decisión mutua a que llegamos Gregory Bateson y yo en el sentido de que no sería mala la idea de hacer una edicion "Penguin" de los artículos y conferencias de los primeros dos años de la guerra. Cuando empecé a reunir los materiales, juzgué mejor escribir un nuevo libro utilizando, sin embargo, las ideas de los estudios anteriores. Esto que llegó a ser más tarde un "Penguin", apareció primero como libro de bolsillo en Inglaterra en 1944, bajo el titulo de *The American Character* (142).

Cultural Patterns and Technical Change (399) fue otra vez una respuesta a un proyecto que pasó por una serie de etapas y en cuyo resultado desempeñé un papel en la primera y última etapa. Como Secretaria Ejecutiva de la Comisión Sobre Costumbres Alimenticias durante la Segunda Guerra Mundial (1941-1945) – presidida en sus últimos jornadas por Lawrence K. Frank, yo había dirigido unas sesiones sobre hábitos cotidianos. Estas discusiones fueron elaboradas en una nota preparada por Lawrence K. Frank en los E.E.U.U., autorizada por la Asociación Nacional para la Salud Mental y recomendada a la Federación Mundial para la Salud Mental. Esta llamó en seguida la atención de la División de Ciencias Sociales de UNESCO sobre el plan. UNESCO le ofreció a la Federación Mundial para la Salud Mental un contrato con ciertas restricciones bastantes severas sobre la selección de un redactor. En medio de muchas otras responsabilidades, tuve que afrontar la amenaza de la pérdida de una donación de la UNESCO por la FMSM, donación imprescindible para fusionarla con otra igual, a no ser que yo aceptara ser redactora. Este trabajo llegó a ser *Cultural Patterns and Technical Change*, de nuevo escrito con esmero en un inglés corriente porque se dirigía a especialistas de varios tipos: peritos en nutrición, trabajadores en salud pública, agrónomos, etc. Después de una ambiciosa publicación inicial por UNESCO (Tensions and Technology Series), Mentor Book (399) lo publicó como libro de bolsillo en 1955 y se convirtió en constante éxito.

A menudo la preparación de un libro de este índole tenía que ver simultáneamente con otros proyectos. *Cultural Patterns and Technical Change*, por ejemplo, fue escrito para orientar la asistencia técnica multilateral y vincularla al mismo tiempo con un tomo redactado por Arensberg y Niehoff (1971) sobre el Programa de Asistencia Bilateral de los EE.UU. y con un volumen de Spicer. Asimismo participé en el esbozo de una serie de tomos sobre personalidad y cultura: *Readings in Social Psychology*, redactado por T.M. Newcomb y E.L. Hartley (1958); *Personal Character and Cultural Milieu*, redactado por D.S. Haring (1956); y *Personality in Nature, Society and Culture*, redactado por C. Kluckhohn y H.A. Murray (1962). En estos yo fui consejera de redacción y colaboradora.

Otra categoría de escritos exigía la preparación de algunos capítulos sintéticos basados en nuevas investigaciones para libros especializados: dos capítulos sobre los niños primitivos para manuales de psicología infantil (39, 109, 243); un capítulo sobre "Cultural Determinants of Sexual Behavior" (624) y sobre la adolescencia (75); artículos para varias enciclopedias, entre las cuales se incluían *The Encyclopedia of Psychology* (241), *The Encyclopedia of the Social Sciences* (32, 33), la *International Encyclopedia of the Social Sciences* (953), *The Encyclopedia of Mental Health* (719, 725), y *The Encyclopedia of Photography* (713), en varias de las cuales yo desempeñé un papel de consejera de redacción.

An Anthropologist at Work: Writings of Ruth Benedict (537) fue compilado a petición del editor de Ruth Benedict, Paul Brooks de Houghton Mifflin, que quería hacer una colección póstuma de sus escritos. Aunque ella escribía con poca frecuencia, cada una de sus obras más importantes ya había sido reeditada. Por eso, en conversaciones con Paul Brooks, concebí la idea de un libro que comprendiera una especie de conversación cuádruple entre Ruth Benedict, Franz Boas, Edward Sapir y yo misma. Mientras trabajaba en el libro, me empezó a interesar un estil antropológico de biografía que presentara materiales en grandes trozos coherentes. Las memorias de Ruth Benedict, desde 1923 a 1926, sus poesías inéditas, las cartas de Sapir a Benedict, fueron dispuestas como materiales cuya integridad interna no sufrió la fragmentación del estilo biográfico habitual en que se recurre a pequeños trozos de citas. El segundo libro sobre Ruth Benedict (1291) contenía una nueva selección de sus trabajos más breves, y fue escrito especialmente para los estudiantes. Formó parte de una serie de la Universidad de Columbia acerca de antropólogos, bajo la dirección de Charles Wagley.

El estímulo de *People and Places* (557) se me presentó cuando Velma Varner, talentosa e imaginativa redactora de libros para niños, me pidió que escribiera un libro sobre antropología para niños. Me dí cuenta de que, como se esperaba una obra de ese tipo y profusamente ilustrada sin ser muy cara, podría conseguir que el libro cumpliera dos fines a la vez: el de texto para niños y el de historia evolutiva de los métodos de registro y de presentación de otras culturas – desde las interpretaciones caprichosas de un ilustrador artístico, a los dibujos minuciosos de los artefactos del Museo, las pinturas primitivas, la fotografía, e incluso la fotografía en colores.

Family (832), con fotografías por Ken Heyman, fue trazado después que los dos hicimos varias expediciones fotográficas, para satisfacer su deseo de componer los dos un libro sobre el tema de la familia. Una vez establecido el tema de los papeles de parentesco — madres, padres, hermanos — Ken recorrió el mundo y sus archivos en busca de fotografías, y yo escribí la narración que iba a acompañarlas. Se ha seguido el mismo procedimiento en nuestra obra colaborativa, *World Enough: Rethinking the Future* (1976).

Tres libros surgieron de grandes proyectos de otras personas: *The Study of Culture at a Distance*, con Rhoda Metraux (412); *Childhood in Contemporary Cultures*, con Martha Wolfenstein (440); y *Soviet Attitudes Toward Authority* (359), este último escrito con la ayuda de todos los miembros de personal del proyecto entitulado Estudios de la Cultura Soviética del Museo Americano de Historia Natural. Esas obras basaron en los estudios extensos de culturas contemporáneas comenzados por Ruth Benedict, que murió antes de verlos terminados.

La antología, *Primitive Heritage* (411), que preparé con Nicolas Calas, tuvo su origen en una sugerencia que Leo Rosten le formuló a Bennet Cerf de Random House. Fue proyectado como colaboración entre un crítico surrealista y un antropólogo, pero se malogró a cause de la nota biográfica de la portada que identificó a Calas también como antropólogo.

The Small Conference (971) fue el resultado de una larga colaboración con Paul Byers. A raíz de la muerte del colega con quien él había esperado escribir la descripción de un solo congreso, Wilton Dillon sugirió que Byers y yo rescatáramos algunos de los materiales originales para componer un libro general sobre congresos.

De vez en cuando me pedían escritos que habían de aparecer en otro idioma o en algun compendio extranjero: un capítulo sobre "Ethnology and Psychiatry" para una enciclopedia alemana (635); un capítulo para *The Policy Sciences* redactado por Lasswell y Lerner (360), de primera edición francesa (razón por la cual tuve que ajustar las referencias conforma a lo que había en la biblioteca del Musée de L'Homme); un capítulo sobre "Cross-Cultural Approach to the Study of Personality" (466), diseñado para una traducción al castellano (que nunca tuvo lugar), con las notas y las ilustraciones más indicadas para un público español; y un capítulo que escribí con Walter Fairservis en 1975 para un libro alemán sobre el medio ambiente.

Cuando me avisaban previamente que mi libro iba dirigido a un público extranjero, solía asesorarme con los hablantes de esa lengua que además conocían al alcance cultural y teórico de lo que yo quería decir. Por otro lado, hay versiones extranjeras de mis libros que han sido hechas sin consulta previa, hasta en el caso de las dos traducciones casi simultáneas de *And Keep Your Powder Dry* (142), la una en Alemania en 1946 y la otra en Austria en 1947.

propósito inicial de publicar en conjunto los tres libros anteriores a la Segunda Guerra Mundial sobre los mares del sur, — *Adolescencia, sexo y cultura en Samoa* (6), *Growing Up in New Guinea* (22), y *Sexo y temperamento en las sociedades primitivas* (79) tuvo que ser abandonado porque el editor francés no aprobaba *Growing Up in New Guinea*. Para colmo de males, luego se publicaron el primero y el tercero de aquellos, pero sin quitar antes las ilutraciones seleccionadas para acompañar *Growing Up in New Guinea*; aparecieron además varias fotos de otras gentes de Melanesia, fotos incluídas por los especialistas en antropología, sin preguntarme. La publicación de *El hombre y la mujer* (312) se demoró porque el editor francés quería suprimir el capítulo de "Cada familia en una casa propia" porque se ocupaba de un fenómeno americano y por lo tanto nada tenía que ver con Francia. No obstante, por fin se publicó en francés bajo el título de *L'Un et L'Autre Sexe* en 1966. A menudo, cuando algo se dirigía específicamente a un público francés, me pedían la alteración de alguna frase o incluso de la idea en sí porque era imposible de traducir al francés. Hubo graves dificultades, por ejemplo, con palabras tales come patrones de cultura (cultural patterns), donde la dificultad estribaba no en la palabra patrón (pattern), que tenía con varios equivalentes franceses, sino en la terminación plural, ya que era inconcebible pensar en más de un patrón de cultura — el francés, de encopetado linaje clásico.

Las traducciones al italiano dieron lugar a otros problemas. Las ediciones se caracterizan por su hermosura y por su espíritu apasionado, pero prescinden de un detalle importante como el de emparejar las fotografías con el texto. Por ejemplo, en la traducción italiana de *Childhood and Contemporary Cultures* (453), en 1963, las ilustraciones fotográficas de un *shtetl* de Europa del Este se encuentran desparramadas por las otras secciones del libro.

Hay otra clase de problemas con las ediciones inglesas. Tuve que cambiar ciertas palabras para *Growing Up in New Guinea* (22): "pantalones de trabajo" (*overalls*), por ejemplo, fue sustituida por "pantalones vaquero" (*jeans*), y había que aludir a libros ingleses en vez de americanos. Cuando *And Keep Your Powder Dry* (142) se publicó en Inglaterra (1967), le puse una introducción en inglés británico. En otras ocasiones modifiqué la ortografía de una edición americana conforme a la ortografía inglesa. (Aunque los americanos podían leer la ortografía inglesa sin fijarse en la diferencia, los ingleses se habrían quejado de la ortografía americana. Desde luego, esto no ocurriría hoy). Después de la Segunda Guerra Mundial ya me parecía importante escribir como americana con la ortografía de mi país. Aun así cuando publiqué *New Lives for Old* (467), donde reproducía algunas partes de la edición de *Growing Up in New Guinea* de hacía veintisiete años, se creó toda clase de confusiones al redactarlo, prepararlo para la imprenta y corregir las pruebas.

Por lo común, las publicaciones de los científicos están escritas de acuerdo a las sociedades científicas a las cuales asisten y donde presentan ponencias. El diseño de estas ponencias a menudo depende de los requisitos de las revistas en que luego se publican. Este procedimiento puede ser sumamente caprichoso. No fueron publicados hasta 1970 (1054) los extractos de las contribuciones al Séptimo Congreso Internacional de las Ciencias Antropológicas y Etnológicas, que tuvo lugar en Moscú en 1964. Por otra parte, una de mis contribuciones al Noveno Congreso, celebrado en Chicago en 1973, ya ha sido publicada por Mouton (1975 (1352)), mientras que otra todavía no ha entrado en prensa "A Re-examination of Major Themes of the Sepik Area, Papua, New Guinea".

No obstante, puesto que una parte tan extensa de mis publicaciones ha brotado de otros estímulos, no he tenido que depender tanto de las publicaciones profesionales como muchos científicos. En cambio, otros tipos de congresos y coloquios internacionales dan lugar a distinta clase de publicación en la cual contribuciones individuales son sencillamente parte de las actas: los informes de las diez reuniones del Coloquio Delos, que se publicaron en *Ekistics* (1963-1972), las actas de los varios grupos de estudios de la Federación Mundial para la Salud Mental (853, 935); y publicaciones del Consejo Mundial de Iglesias (867). También cabe en esa categoría el tipo de conferencia que se ha desarrollado bajo la dirección de la Fundación Josiah Macy, hijo (1955) que publica una mezcla de discusiones y presentaciones: *Cybernetics*, redactado por H. von Foerster (1951-1955), *Problems of Consciousness*, redactado por H.A. Abramson (1951-1955), *Group Processes*, redactado por B. Schaffner (1955-1960) y *Discussions on Child Development*, redactado por J.M. Tanner y B. Inhelder (1957-1960).

Otro incentivo para preparar materiales han sido las peticiones de dar conferencias a grupos tan inverosímiles como la Asociación Nacional de Decanas (118), el Servicio de Personal del Oeste (220), o la Asociación de los Estados Centrales de Universidades y Colegios (105). Aunque en esas conferencias solía presentar a menudo nuevas ideas, el hecho de que fueran publicadas después en alguna revista que mis colegas nunca verían, determinaba la segura probabilidad de que el artículo se perdería del todo. Yo hice el esfuerzo de compensar esta posible pérdida republicando los artículos en tomos de reimpresiones tales como *Anthropology: A Human Science* (1964); *A Way of Seeing*, que redactamos Rhoda Metraux y yo (1970); y *Twentieth Century Faith*, redactado por Ruth N. Anshen (1972).

Desde 1943 hasta principios de los años 1960, el Instituto de Estudios Interculturales repartió reimpresiones seleccionadas pertinentes al campo de cultura y personalidad y pertinentes también a la aplicación de métodos antropológicos para la comprensión de problemas contemporáneos. Esto permitió cierta distribución sistemática de artículos publicados en sitios poco ortodoxos. Pero el cambio de direcciones era tan frecuente que esta distribución se hizo poco factible. Ahora distribuyo periódicamente una lista de mis publicaciones a unos 450 colegas, rogándoles que me pidan cualquier reimpresión que deseen, ya que se ha hecho tan agobiante recibir reimpresiones que yo misma suelo leer sólo los ejemplares que he pedido o los que me mandan acompañados de una carta personal.

La evolución de nuevos medios electrónicos también ha influído mucho en la clase de solicitudes para publicación que una recibe. Comenzando con la estenografía, la audiografía y luego la cinta magnética, las organizaciones o reuniones han podido transcribir las palabras de un conferenciante de manera bastante mutilada y luego pedirle que redacte la transcripción para publicarle. Estas solicitudes adoptan varias formas: un compromiso anticipado que se lleva en condiciones extremamente difíciles – cintas que se pierden, transcripciones incoherentes, etc.: transcripciones de conferencias o charlas para las cuales no hubo previo acuerdo de publicación y que implicaban cierta urgencia, incluso la posibilidad de reproducirlas sin permiso, lo que ocurrió con el trabajo que presenté ante la Reunión Sobre la Píldora (919); y las súplicas por parte de causas beneméritas, el acopio de fondos, los informes anuales, etc. Estas prácticas dan por resultado un número enorme de publicaciones, cuyo contenido repite el de otras y cuya calidad varía según los plazos fijados y la asequibilidad. Todo esto parace inevitable en el mundo contemporáneo, con su plétora de publicaciones; cada organización e institución trata de individualizar sus actividades y tiende a exaltar a unas cuantas personas una y otra vez, sin dar paso a nuevas personas que pueden ocupar luego el lugar de ese grupo privilegiado.

Disponemos de escasos medios oportunos para incorporar a los jóvenes en los coloquios, los congresos y otras reuniones públicas, siendo ellos los que podrían llegar a ser los verdaderos continuadores y enriquecedores del proceso, si se les diera la oportunidad. Me ha valido de todos los métodos a mi disposición – el de negarme a participar en un congreso o en un debate a menos que participaran los jóvenes, el de facilitar por medio de referencias el contacto entre los organizadores de los congresos y los jóvenes – pero con poco éxito. También he usado otras estratagemas. Después del Congreso de la Casa Blanca sobre los niños en 1950 (en los Estados Unidos), propuse que nadie que hubiese figurado como personaje principal en aquella ocasión se le permitiera tener un papel en el Congreso próximo de 1960, sino que se invitara en cambio, a un grupo de participantes de edad menor. Peso a mis esfuerzos, se volvió a recurrir al mismo grupo anterior, con resultados nada satisfactorios. Por fin fue necesario que yo les redactara un artículo que se agregó de suplemento a los papeles originales de la serie. A continuación del congreso convocado por el ahora fallecido C.H. Waddington en Chichén Itzá,

México (1216), donde me quejé de la ausencia de los jóvenes, pasó parecido; se perdió mucho tiempo en procurar la participación retrospectiva de los jóvenes en la publicación subsiguiente, pero luego prescindieron de ella.

Más tarde, en parte como capítulo final al congreso de Waddington, se convocó en Suecia un congreso de jóvenes nombrados por científicos y eruditos ilustres antes del Coloquio Nobel 14 (1067). Para que las conocieran a los estudiantes que asistieron se les entregaron las ponencias de los distinguidos participantes; su reacción fue la de recortarlas y volverlas a juntar, pegando con goma los párrafos en sentido disparatado — reacción propia del estado de ánimo durante los años sesenta pero de valor limitado como aporte a lo que se discutió en esa.

Con mucho pesar he llegado a la conclusión de que el único medio practicable de reclutar la participación de los jóvenes consiste en despertar el interés de los hijos de los investigadores que han alcanzado fama en la misma disciplina. Se puede señalar dos ventajas: hay más posibilidad de que se acepte su participación a cause de su apellido, y puesto que han conocido de cerca a sus distinguidos padres, no son tímidos, ni tienen necesidad de mostrar resentimientos para disimular el peso excesivo de lo que se les exige. Por lo tanto, aunque juzgo importante el papel de descubrir y animar a los colegas más jóvenes y menos conocidos, es tarea difícil de ejecutar.

Intento recibir las peticiones personalmente para poder examinar las posibilidades de que acepten a otra persona; leo las invitaciones a congresos aun cuando sé por la fecha que no puedo asistir, para luego reflexionar y proponer a sustitutos merecedores. Suelo alentar a otros a que pidan la participación de personas tan ocupadas que lógicamente se habrán de negar pero que sentirán la obligación de sugerir algunos nombres. Uno de los atolladeros del mundo actual es la calidad cumulativa del renombre: cuanto más se publica, con mayor insistencia se es solicitado.

Otro problema que se plantea hoy es el efecto amplificador del sinnúmero de medio baratos de fácil reproducción, junto con el carácter insaciable de esta sociedad de consumo y de despilfarro. Proliferan las colecciones; vuélvense a escribir artículos bajo títulos diferentes o se aprovechan algunos trozos para la exhibición de un museo, para un catálogo, para un libro de citas oportunas, en narraciones para adormecer a los niños, y en calendarios. A su vez otros coleccionistas y explotadores recogen una cita de la prensa y me escriben con toda sinceridad para averiguar el nombre de la publicación que corresponde. Libros que se publicaron hace años, a los cuales contribuí con un capítulo, de repente vuelven a aparecer, como es el caso de la obra recientemente revisada, *While You Were Gone* (251) libro publicado en 1946 y agotado durante años.

Este efecto amplificador se agrega a la tendencia actual de editar un sinfín de tomos sobre temas especiales para el uso en las aulas; constan de reimpresiones preparadas con miras al programa de un profesor determinado. La casa que imprime la colección por medio de un procedimiento barato luego intenta valerse de la coyuntura para conseguir los derechos permanentes a las reimpresiones. Cada uno de estos trámites de escribir cartas, comprobar datos, dar o negar permiso, le va enrodando a una hasta tel punto que, según un crítico, "Te pueden citar fuero de contexto sobre cualquier asunto para comprobar lo que quiera, y a menudo están equivocados".

Este efecto penetrante y difundido de la publicación reiterativa se aumenta aun más a causa de la radio. Los discursos que se hicieron con algún "motivo pedagógico", archivados desde hace años, de pronto vuelvan a escucharse, con anacronismos que el auditor no llega a descifrar. Por ejemplo, el tono de voz q que yo habría empleado al aludir al "presidente" en otro tiempo sería completamente distinto si yo hablara del "presidente" en el momento de la reemisión del programa. Por más que yo intente evitar la confusión, exigiendo que digan la fecha y el lugar del discurso cada vez que ponen la cinta, es imposible obligarlo por fuerza. La existencia de las cintas grabadas de emisiones de radio permite comprobar lo que se ha dicho pero por lo general la radio sigue siendo un medio insidioso, y es a través de ella que se es blanco de recriminaciones injustas y citas equivocadas. Nadie puede asegurarse de lo que se dijo, ni de quién habló, y las malas lenguas parecen sobrevivir.

Se ven además otros resultados de los avances en la tecnología. En la reproducción de las fotografías, por ejemplo, es posible mejorar el tono de las que se han ido destiñendo con el paso del tiempo, como en el caso de las que incluí en mi autobiografía *Blackberry Winter* (1178). Y ya no hay que agrupar todas las fotos en una sección del libro como se hizo en *New Lives for Old* (467), sino que se las puede distribuir entre las páginas apropiadas. Pero en otros sentidos hemos sufrido. No hay comparación entre la belleza de la primera edición de 1942 de *Balinese Character* (140), donde se produjeron 2,000 ejemplares por un procedimiento de fotogelatine, y la reimpresión en 1962, hecha con los mismos grabados de la colección de Gregory Bateson. Estos grabados aparecieron asimismo en el libro que preparé con Frances MacGregor, *Growth and Culture* (363). Los métodos modernos de reproducción dan mucho más libertad, pero siguen siendo sumamente caros para cualquier clase de obra científica. Yo posterqué la publicación de la última parte de mi etnografia sobre los Arapesh, "The Bark Paintings of the Mountain Arapesh of New Guinea" (715) hasta disponer de la reproducción en colores, para luego descubrir que me permitían sólo una.

En este tomo sólo ha registrado las cintas que se han hecho específicamente para la venta, que llevan un número de catálogo, y para las cuales se señala un local donde comprarlas. Representan una mínima parte de las cintas que existen en los archivos de las universidades, en las emisoras de las mismas, y en otras instituciones.

Son muchas las consecuencias curiosas al haber sostenido una larga vida como autora de muchas publicaciones. Los libros que una escribe quedan como testimonio permanente de investigaciones que no se volverán a acometer; mientras tanto la teoría, sobre la cual una basó su último trabajo de otros en la disciplina, esta cambiando constantemente. Cuando un antropólogo muere es posible reproducir su obra ya publicada en ediciones continuas por muchos años; generalmente se la agrega un nuevo prefacio o una introducción nueva que la sitúa en un contexto histórico y contemporáneo. Tuve la oportunidad de escribir tal prólogo y de preparar un nuevo apéndice fotográfico al *Expression of the Emotions in Man and Animals* (456) de Darwin, en que se dejaba ver la influencia de los últimos descubrimientos en el estudio de la cinética del Congreso sobre la Cultura y Comunicación de la Universidad da Lousiville, en 1954. Los editores querían que yo incluyera fotografías nuevas en el texto, lo cual habría significado una profanación de la integridad del libro.

He tenido que rechazar sugerencias de críticos en el sentido de que vuelva a escribir *Coming of Age in Samoa*, porque ya no refleja las costumbres actuales de esa comunidad. Los críticos que me lo han sugerido no comprenden que yo no podría "volver a escribirlo" sin más; habría que hacer con mucho cuidado un nuevo estudio, posiblemente intercalando selecciones del primer libro en el segundo, tal como lo hice en *New Lives for Old*, trabajo llevado a cabo veinticinco años después de *Growing Up in New Guinea*. Los cambios constantes de ediciones, los libros de bolsillo, las ediciones de vida corta, los libros de lujo, las ediciones para el extranjero, etc., me dan la oportunidad de escribir nuevos prólogos o introducciones. Lo he hecho para *Adolescencia, sexo y cultura en Samoa* (6) que tiene seis ediciones y para el cual he redactado tres prólogos nuevos. *Growing Up in New Guinea* (22) se ha publicado en cuatro ediciones, con dos prólogos nuevos; *Sexo y temperamento en las sociedades primitivas* (79), en tres ediciones, con dos prólogos nuevos; y *El hombre y la mujer* (312), en cuatro ediciones, con cuatro prólogos y un apéndice nuevos.

De este manera puedo introducir nuevas ideas, colocar un libro en perspectiva, corregir aquellos casos en que en el pasado puse demasiado o poco énfasis en algún tema y en alguna manera introducir mediante cambios en la terminología, un sentido del clima cambiante de opinión en el mundo. Estas oportunidades de volver sobre un tema antiguo me han sido importantes, especialmente en el caso de un libro como *Adolescencia, sexo y cultura en Samoa*. Cuando lo escribí me cuidé de encubrir bien las identidades de los informantes pero sin tomar en cuenta la posibilidad de que los jóvenes de Samoa con el tiempo irían a la universidad, donde sus compañeros se informarían a través de la lectura de las actividades pasadas de sus abuelas.

Estos apuros en parte se deben a que los títulos tenían que ser más generales en esa época cuando los lectores de habla inglesa no conocían bastante bien la geografía para que se pudiera escribir de la mayoría de edad en Manu'a, o del crecimiento en Manus. Hoy día, expresando los mismos reparos que los jóvenes de otras partes de Samoa, los jóvenes de algunos de los más de seiscientos distintos grupos lingüísticos de Papua Nueva Guinea se quejan y oponen de que su versión especial de "Nueva Guinea" – que creen es la única representativa – es diferente de aquella versión dada por mí en la que describo a los Manus en los años 1920. Desde su posición como gente moderna hoy, citan, airados, una frase de *Growing Up in New Guinea*, diciendo que los he falsificado. Durante el verano de 1975 hablé con el Colegio Lorengau en la Isla de Manus, donde enseñaba el joven poeta Kumalau Tawali (1970). Se puso de pie un estudiante y dijo: "En su libro *Growing Up in New Guinea*, usted dijo que a los niños de Manus les faltaba imaginación creativa. ¿En qué criterio basa usted esa declaración?" Pude contestarle: "En una colección de 35,000 de dibujos de niños," (56) y agregué, "Pero ahora ustedes tienen de profesor a un poeta de Manus y por lo tanto tienen una oportunidad de ir desarrollando su creatividad."

Ha habido otras dificultades que han tenido que ver con el paso del tiempo. Cuando empecé a escribir, la palabra *salvaje* se usaba indistintamente con *primitivo*, ambos términos se referían a las gentes sin lengua escrita. Yo no me oponía a los títulos periodísticos como *Savage Masters of the Sea* (40), aunque siempre prefería emplear *primitivo*. Hoy día, muchas naciones emergentes se oponen a la palabre *primitivo* y se ha creado toda clase de eufemismos para quitarles a algunas palabras la supuesta afrenta: *nativo* se ha convertido en *local* o *indígena*; "*Pidgin English*" (el inglés chapurreado) fue redesignado *Neo-melanesio* después de la Segunda Guerra Mundial (véase *New Lives for Old*), pero ahora ha vuelto a emplearse el término "*Pidgin English*". En los EE.UU., *Negro*, con obligatoria mayúscula "N" señalando situación social minoritaria, fue reemplazado por "*black*", y a veces *Afro-Americano*. Cuando escribo una nueva introducción o prólogo u otro capítulo para una nueva edición, empleo los eufemismos actuales: *los seres humanos* ("*humankind*") en lugar de *los hombres* ("*mankind*"), o "*chairperson*" en vez de "*chairman*" (jefe o presidente), perfectamente aceptable con tal de estar precedido de *Señor* o *Señora*. Pero me asombra la falta de sentido histórico que lleva a los antropólogos más jóvenes a poner reparos al uso de términos anticuados en las obras escritas hace años. Por ejemplo, las memorias de Malinowski (1967) fueron calumniadas por el uso en 1914 de una palabra polaca que en inglés fue traducida a *nigger*; refiriéndose a los habitantes de las Islas Trobriand a quienes su obra ha inmortalizado.

Ni siquiera se resuelve mucho el problema con añadir una introducción que subraya las fechas cuidadosamente. En 1939, cuando el extenso tomo *From the South Seas* (96), que contenía mis primeros tres libros fue publicado, escribí una nueva introducción en que hablaba de lo que no sabíamos en 1925, cuando llevé a cabo mi primer trabajo de campo. Los estudiantes reaccionaron expresándose en tono peyorativo, "La Señorita Mead misma concede..." y a continuación sugerían que yo debía haber empleado métodos todavía no concebidos cuando hice aquel trabajo de campo. Así es como el publicar y republicar a través de tanto tiempo, aunque dada la oprtunidad de contribuir a fijar perspectiva histórica, al misma tiempo introduce nuevos desconciertos e incertidumbres en el trabajo de los antropólogos cuyas primeras obras tienden a ser el blanco de muchas críticas.

Pienso que sólo se puede actuar con plena integridad en el presente cuando se acepta la crónica entera del pasado. Mis trabajos archivados sobre épocas anteriores de las culturas de la Nueva Guinea, ilustran la distancia asombrosa transcurrida en una generación, que ha efectuado el progreso más rápido que jamás se ha visto en el mundo — desde el aislamiento propio de la Edad de Piedra hasta la participación en la Edad del Poder Atómico. Su historia puede enorgullecer a la gente de Nueva Guinea si se encaran con ella; pero si se inventan un pasado ficticio, llegarán a ser cautivos de sus fabricaciones. Hoy día la gente de Manus puede leer las relaciones más técnicas de lo que he escrito acerca de ellos (22, 66, 467), así como las publicaciones de otros antropólogos come Reo Fortune (1935) y Theodore Schwartz (1962) que han escrito durante los últimos cuarenta y siete años — le major historia de su pasado que tiene cualquier pueblo como ellos.

Este necesidad de encararse con el pasado es una cuestión que preocupa de manera constante a los antropólogos. Fue precisamente por la buena voluntad de James Baldwin de afirmar su propio pasado como americano que no tenía vínculos de parentesco directos con Africa, que me complació escribir con él *A Rap On Race* (1144). Una reseña en *The New York Times* critic con aspereza el diseño del libro, diciendo que una conversación grabada en cinta era demasiado fácil y que envilecía el arte de escribir. Pero la grabadora hace posible una clase de intercambio que raras veces se da en las discusiones sobre cuestiones raciales, y una vez impresa la discusión, el lector no puede menos de ver los dos lados del asunto.

Con respecto a los libros que he reseñado: al principio, es claro, aceptaba cualquier libro que me mandaran — un surtido bien raro. Más tarde, preparé muchas reseñas para los *Annals of the American Academy of Political and Social Science* (30, 48, 83, 659, 941, 990) porque admitían reseñas cortas, y asi yo podía cumplir la tarea revisando libros que realmente queria leer con cuidado. Con el paso del tiempo decidí que sólo iba a hacer juicios críticos sobre aquellos que estimara dignos de atención y que merecían leerse por completo, libros valiosos en sí. A veces escribía una reseña para una obra que me parecía peligrosamente extraviada, como *The Hopi Child* (134) de Wayne Dennis o *The Individual and His Society* (137) de Kardiner. Puedo señalar el valor de contadas reseñas mías, porque en ellas formulé algún problema teórico: la de *Himalayan Village* (101) de Geoffrey Gorer, la de *Methods in Structural Lingusitics* (395) de Z.S. Harris, la de *Riddle of the Sfinx* (84) de Roheim, y la de *The Individual in Cultural Adaptation* (1975) de Edgerton. El tamaño del libro influye cada vez más; eso de cargar con tomos descomunales como *Coming of Age* (1271) de Simone de Beauvoir mientras viajo por todas partes, ya me resulta excesivo.

Como uno de mis deberes personales con estudiantes, colegas o jóvenes cuyas carreras he seguido con interés, suelo aceptar las peticiones de escribir prólogos e introducciones relacionados con su trabajo. En el pasado escribí algunos prólogos para libros con los cuales no había tenido nada que ver previamente (568), pero el número de solicitaciones de ese tipo, sobre todo a instancias de editores o de empresarios, representa una cantidad excesiva e inaceptable. Y en los últimos diez años, si no tengo algún motivo personal, como el de haber leído y criticado el manuscrito durante su preparación, o el de haber sido profesora, colega o amiga del autor, acostumbro negarme a prologar libros. Aun así, no es escasa la suma de prólogos e introducciones que se han acumulado.

Persuadida por la iniciativa de otra persona, he escrito también comentarios, artículos, o libros de tipo autobiográfico. Tanto *An Anthropologist at Work: Writings of Ruth Benedict* (537) como *Ruth Benedict: A Biography* (1291) contienen muchos datos autobiográficos sobre mis años de estudiante graduada y sobre mi asociación más tarde con ella. "Apprenticeship under Boas" (538) es otro ejemplo de esta clase. Y *Blackberry Winter: My Earlier Years* (1178) es una autobiografía personal que subraya mi ediucación bajo la tutela de padres dedicados a las ciencias sociales, y mi preparación para el casamiento con colegas antropólogos. El capítulo del tomo redactado por Gardiner Lindzey (1287) habla de la contribución de mis estudios de psicología a mi trabajo de campo. Varias redacciones más cortas – mis cartas en *Women in the Field* (1069) de Peggy Golde, "A Bread and Butter Letter from a Lecturer" (193), "Out of the Things I Read" (378), "Weaver of the Border" (601), "Field Work in High Cultures" (1186), "Retrospects and Prospects" (681), la introducción a *From the South Seas* (96), y los prólogos a diferentes tomos de *The Mountain Arapesh* (986, 1113, 1164a) – han combinado discusiones de método con comentarios. Pienso publicar un tomo de cartas que dirigí, a manera de boletines, a familiares, amigos y colegas, junto con otra correspondencia personal. Ha habido también narraciones más metódicas sobre determinados trabajos: las introducciones a *The Study of Culture at a Distance* (412), *Soviet Attitudes toward Authority* (359) y *Childhood in Contemporary Cultures* (453); "The Committee on Food Habits" (166); "The Anthropology of Human Conflict" (834); "The Vicissitudes of the Study of the Total Communication Process" (783); y tres películas (*35, 37, 41*).

Puesto que comencé en fecha temprana mi obra científica — creo que fui la primera antropóloga americana cuya carrera empezó con los estudios universitarios — he tenido la suerte de trabajar con personas mayores que me sirvieron de poderosa inspiración, y con colegas ya fallecidos: Lawrence K. Frank (1008, 1351), Ruth Benedict (319, 320), Robert Lamb (429), y Margaret Lowenfeld (1342). He ayudado a terminar la obra de Jane Belo (1112), Colin McPhee (1966), Edith Cobb (en prensa) y Margaret Lowenfeld (en prensa).

El balance final de mi trabajo de campo cubre tres categorías: (1) las publicaciones de mis seis viajes cuatro de las cuales he acabado — sola en Samoa, y con Reo Fortune entre los indios Omaha, los Manus, los Arapesh, los Mundugumor, y los Tchambuli. De entre estos estudios etnográficas tempranos, sólo queda por escribir la publicación sobre los Mudugumor (dejamos Reo Fortune y yo nuestro trabajo sobre esta cultura porque estaba tan fragmentada). Volví allá en 1973 para asegurarme de que ya no se podía hacer investigaciones eficaces sobre su cultura antigua: por eso estoy preparando un estudio monográfico que mostrará las primeras etapas de un trabajo de campo incompleto. (2) Los dos viajes con Gregory Bateson a Bali y a los Iatmul de Nueva Guinea, durante los cuales se emplearon por primera vez la fotografía y la película, produjeron cantidades de datos suficientes para un número ilimitado de estudios. Las publicaciones subsecuentes han sido forzosamente parciales, tanto las mías (91, 99, 100, 103, 104, 105, 110, 118, 145, 149, 170, 260, 363, 440, 539, 624, *28, 29*), como las de Gregory Bateson (1937, 1941, 1942, 1946, 1949, 1975), y las que hicimos juntos (140). (3) Las sucesivas vueltas al tema, elaboradas desde la Segunda Guerra Mundial, en colaboración con colegas más jóvenes — con Theodore Schwartz (433, 607, 644, *33*), con Lenora Schwartz (*33*), con Lola Romanucci-Ross (1335), con Jane Belo (1112), con Ken Heyman (832, 1395), con Barbara Heath, con Rhoda Metraux, y con Hildred Geertz. Se puede decir que a estos estudios yo nunca pondré punto final y que me ocuparán durante el resto de mi vida.

He realizado siete expediciones a Manus, a lo largo de cuarenta y siete años y cuatro generaciones. He vuelto a visitar los Iatmul dos veces mientras estaba Rhoda Metraux en el campo. He vuelto a visitar la aldea Arapesh de

Alitoa, trasladada a nuevo sitio en Hoskins Bay en la isla de New Britain; y he vuelto a visitar Samoa en 1971. El hecho de que empecé mi trabajo con niños cuando yo era todavía muy joven, durante una época en que el mundo vio las transformaciones más radicales de toda la historia, ha tenido felices concecuencias para mí porque ha hecho posibles esos estudios sucesivos de cambio y ha permitido el establecimiento de un sistema de sucesores entre los antropólogos más jóvenes.

Casi la mitad de mi tiempo la he dedicado a la aplicación práctica de la experiencia, los datos, y la teoría antropológicos a los problemas de la alimentación y las costumbres alimenticias (165, 773), a los cambios tecnológicos (399), a la salud mental, a la vida familiar y a la educación de los niños. Hoy se han ampliado estos intereses hasta incluir estudios de problemas planetarios (732, 824, 1063, 1131, 1194, 1247, 1286, 1395), ya que nuestra experiencia con pequeñas sociedades abarcables, aisladas y enteras puede ser útil en el estudio del desarrollo de una sociedad mundial.

The Bibliography

1925

1   "For a Proud Lady," *The Measure*, No. 52 (June, 1925), 16. (Poem for Louise Bogan.)

2   "Rose Tree of Assisi," *The Measure*, No. 57 (November, 1925), 15. (Poem.)

1926

3   "The Methodology of Racial Testing: Its Significance for Sociology," *American Journal of Sociology*, 31, No. 5 (March, 1926), 657-667.

1927

4   "Group Intelligence Tests and Linguistic Disability among Italian Children," *School and Society*, 25, No. 642 (April 16, 1927), 465-468.

5   "The Need for Teaching Anthropology in Normal Schools and Teachers' Colleges," *School and Society*, 26, No. 667 (October 8, 1927), 466-469.

1928

6   *Coming of Age in Samoa: A Psychological Study of Primitive Youth for Western Civilization*. New York: Morrow, 1928. Reprinted in paperback 1932, Blue Ribbon Books. New York: Doubleday; 1943, Editions for the Armed Services No. 826. Council on Books in Wartime; 1949, Mentor. New York: New American Library; 1953, Modern Library Books. New York: Random House; 1961 (with new preface), Apollo Editions. New York: Morrow; 1968, Laurel Editions. New York: Dell.
——

English edition: *Coming of Age in Samoa*. London: Cape, 1929; Harmondsworth: Penguin, 1943, 1969.
Argentinian edition: *Adolescencia y Cultura en Samoa*. Buenos Aires: Editorial Abril, 1946.
Dutch edition: *De groei naar volwassenheid*. Utrecht: Aula-Boeken, 1965.

German edition: *Jugend und Sexualität in Primitiven Gesellschaften*. Munich: Deutscher Taschenbuch Verlag, 1970.
Hungarian edition: *Férfi és nő*. Budapest: Gondolat, 1970.
Italian edition: *L'adolescente in una Società Primitiva*.
Firenze: Editrice Universitaria, 1954.
Spanish edition: *Adolescencia sexo y cultura en Samoa*.
Barcelona: Editorial Laia, 1972.

7   *An Inquiry into the Question of Cultural Stability in Polynesia*.
("Columbia University Contributions to Anthropology," Vol.
9.) New York: Columbia University Press, 1928.
Reprinted in paperback 1969, New York: AMS Press.

8   "A Lapse of Animism among a Primitive People," *Psyche*, 9,
No. 1 (July, 1928), 72-77.

9   *The Maoris and Their Arts*. ("The American Museum of Natural
History Guide Leaflet Series," No. 71.) New York:
The American Museum of Natural History, May, 1928.

10   "The Rôle of the Individual in Samoan Culture," *Journal of
the Royal Anthropological Institute*, 58 (July-December, 1928),
481-495.

11   "Samoan Children at Work and Play," *Natural History*, 28, No. 6
(November-December, 1928), 26-36.

12   Review of *History and Traditions of Niue*, by Edwin M. Loeb,
American Anthropologist, 30, No. 1 (January-March, 1928),
151-155.

1929

13   "Americanization in Samoa," *American Mercury*, 16, No. 63
(March, 1929), 264-270.

14   "And Your Young Men Shall See Visions." In *The City Day*, by
Edna Lou Walton. New York: Ronald Press, 1929, 95. (Poem.)

15   "Broken Homes," *Nation*, 128, No. 3321 (February 27, 1929),
253-255.

16   "South Sea Hints on Bringing Up Children," *Parents' Magazine*,
4, No. 9 (September, 1929), 20-22, 49-52.

17   Review of *The History of Tattooing and Its Significance*, by
W. D. Hambly, *American Anthropologist*, 31, No. 1 (January-
March, 1929), 176-177.

18   Review of *Orokaiva Magic*, by F. E. Williams, *American
Anthropologist*, 31, No. 3 (July-September, 1929), 528-531.

1930

19   "Adolescence in Primitive and Modern Society." In *The New Generation: The Intimate Problems of Modern Parents and Children*, V. F. Calverton and S. D. Schmalhausen, eds. New York: Macaulay, 1930, 169-188.

20   "Are We Mature? " *The Thinker*, 2, No. 7 (December, 1930), 25-32.

21   "An Ethnologist's Footnote to *Totem and Taboo*," *Psychoanalytic Review*, 17, No. 3 (July, 1930), 297-304.

22   *Growing Up in New Guinea: A Comparative Study of Primitive Education*. New York: Morrow, 1930.
       Reprinted in paperback 1933, Blue Ribbon Books. New York: Doubleday; 1953, Mentor. New York: New American Library; 1962 (with new preface), Apollo Editions. New York: Morrow; 1968, Laurel Editions. New York: Dell.
       ————
       English edition: *Growing Up in New Guinea*. London: Routledge, 1931; Harmondsworth: Penguin, 1942, 1970.
       Dutch edition: *Natuurvolk en westerse beschaving*. Utrecht: Aula-Boeken, 1964.
       French edition: *Une Education en Nouvelle-Guinée*. Paris: Payot, 1973.
       Hebrew edition: Tel Aviv: Meass-dah, 1953.

23   "Melanesian Middlemen," *Natural History*, 30, No. 2 (March-April, 1930), 115-130.

24   "Misericordia," *Poetry*, 35, No. 5 (February, 1930), 253. (Poem.)

25   "Social Organization of Manu'a," *Bernice P. Bishop Museum Bulletin*, 76. Honolulu, Hawaii, 1930. Reissued 1969.

26   "Water Babies of the South Seas," *Parents' Magazine*, 5, No. 9 (September, 1930), 20-21, 61.

27   Review of *Rossel Island: An Ethnological Study*, by W. E. Armstrong, *American Anthropologist*, 32, No. 1 (January-March, 1930), 176-178.

28   Review of *Amazon and Andes*, by Kenneth G. Grubb, *New Freeman*, 2, No. 14 (December 17, 1930), 331-332.

29   Review of *The Evolution of Modern Marriage*, by F. Muller-Lyer, *Birth Control Review*, 14, No. 12 (December, 1930), 355.

30   Review of *Human History*, by G. Elliot Smith, *Annals of the American Academy of Political and Social Science*, 152 (November, 1930), 422.

1931

31   "Civil Government for Samoa," *Nation*, 132, No. 3425
(February 25, 1931), 226-228.

32   "Education, Primitive." In *Encyclopedia of the Social Sciences*,
5, Edwin R. A. Seligman and Alvin Johnson, eds. New York:
Macmillan, 1931, 399-403.

33   "Family, Primitive." In *Encyclopedia of the Social Sciences*, 6,
Edwin R. A. Seligman and Alvin Johnson, eds.
New York: Macmillan, 1931, 65-67.

34   "Jealousy: Primitive and Civilized." In *Woman's Coming of
Age: A Symposium*, Samuel Schmalhausen and V. F. Calverton,
eds. New York: Liveright, 1931, 35-48.

35   "Life as a Samoan Girl." In *All True! The Record of Actual
Adventures That Have Happened to Ten Women of Today*.
New York: Brewer, Warren and Putnam, 1931, 94-118.

36   "Living with the Natives of Melanesia," *Natural History*, 31,
No. 1 (January-February, 1931), 62-74.

37   "The Meaning of Freedom in Education," *Progressive Education*,
8, No. 2 (February, 1931), 107-111.

38   "New Fields for the Curious Minded," *Publishers' Weekly*, 119,
No. 11 (March 14, 1931), 1355-1357.

39   "The Primitive Child." In *A Handbook of Child Psychology*, ed.
Carl Murchison. Worcester, Massachusetts: Clark University
Press, 1931, 669-686.

40   "Savage Masters of the Sea," *Safety Education*, 10, No. 9,
Sec. 1 (May, 1931), 228-230.

41   "Standardized America vs. Romantic South Seas," *Scribner's
Magazine*, 40, No. 5 (November, 1931), 486-491.

42   "Stevenson's Samoa Today," *World Today*, 58 (September,
1931), 343-350.

43   "Talk-Boy," *Asia*, 31, No. 3 (March, 1931), 144-151.

44   "Two South Sea Educational Experiments and Their American
Implications,"in "Eighteenth Annual Schoolmen's Week
Proceedings, March 18-21, 1931," *University of Pennsylvania
School of Education Bulletin*, 31, No. 36 (June 20, 1931),
493-497.

45   Review of *The Half-Way Sun*, by R. F. Barton, *New Freeman*,
2, No. 23 (February 18, 1931), 547.

46   Review of *Through Oriental Gates*, by James Saxon Childers
and Review of *The Romantic East*, by Sydney Greenbie,

New Freeman, 3, No. 3 (April 1, 1931), 69-70.

47 Review of *Eskimo: An Epic of the North*, by Peter Freuchen and Review of *Turi's Book of Lappland*, by Johan Turi, *Nation*, 133, No. 3444 (July 8, 1931), 43-44.

48 Review of *Californian Indian Nights Entertainments*, compiled by E. W. Gifford and B. G. Harris and Review of *Missions and Pueblos of the Old Southwest*, by Earle R. Forrest, *Annals of the American Academy of Political and Social Science*, 154 (March, 1931), 199.

49 Review of *Source Book in Anthropology*, by A. L. Kroeber and T. T. Waterman and Review of *Culture and Progress*, by W. D. Wallis, *Annals of the American Academy of Political and Social Science*, 155, Part I (May, 1931), 257-258.

50 Review of *Samoa under the Sailing Gods*, by N. A. Rowe, *Nation*, 133, No. 3448 (August 5, 1931), 138-139.

1932

51 "Absolute Benison," *New Republic*, 72, No. 933 (October 19, 1932), 255. (Poem.)

52 "Are Your Children Shockproof? " *Delineator*, 120, No. 1 (January, 1932), 15.

53 *The Changing Culture of an Indian Tribe*. New York: Columbia University Press, 1932.
Reprinted in paperback 1966, Cap Giant. New York: Capricorn Books (Putnam); 1969, New York: AMS Press.

54 "Contrasts and Comparisons from Primitive Society," *Annals of the American Academy of Political and Social Science*, 160, No. 2409 (March, 1932), 23-28.

55 "Growing Up in the South Seas," *Forum*, 87 (May, 1932), 285-288.

56 "An Investigation of the Thought of Primitive Children, with Special Reference to Animism," *Journal of the Royal Anthropological Institute*, 62 (January-June, 1932), 173-190.

57 "Note from New Guinea," *American Anthropologist*, 34, No. 4 (1932), 740.

58 "Parents and Children in Samoa," *Child Study*, 9, No. 8 (April, 1932), 231-232.

59 "South Sea Tips on Character Training," *Parents' Magazine*, No. 3 (March, 1932), 13, 66-68.

60   Review of *Samoan Material Culture*, by Te Rangi Hiroa
            (Peter H. Buck), *American Anthropologist*, 34, No. 2 (April-
            June, 1932), 347-348.

                              1933

61   "The Marsalai Cult among the Arapesh, with Special Reference
            to the Rainbow Serpent Beliefs of the Australian Aboriginals,"
            Oceania, 4, No. 1 (September, 1933), 37-53.
62   "More Comprehensive Field Methods," *American Anthropologist*,
            35, No. 1 (January-March, 1933), 1-15.
63   "Where Magic Rules and Men Are Gods," *The New York Times
            Magazine*, June 25, 1933, 8-9, 18.

                              1934

64   "Arapesh—New Guinea," in "Marrying Around the World,"
            Cosmopolitan, 97, No. 1 (July, 1934), 63-64.
65   "How the Papuan Plans His Dinner," *Natural History*, 34,
            No. 4 (July-August, 1934), 377-388.
66   "Kinship in the Admiralty Islands," *Anthropological Papers
            of The American Museum of Natural History*, 34, No. 2.
            New York, 1934, 183-358.
67   "The Sex Life of the Unmarried Adult in Primitive Society."
            In *The Sex Life of the Unmarried Adult*, ed. Ira S. Wile.
            New York: Vanguard Press, 1934, 53-74.
68   "Suggestions for Working Out the Backgrounds for the Case
            Studies on Adolescents." Adolescent Study, 1934-1935.
            (Mimeographed.)
69   "Tabu." In *Encyclopedia of the Social Sciences*, 14, Edwin
            R. A. Seligman and Alvin Johnson, eds. New York: Macmillan,
            1934, 502-505.
70   "Tamberans and Tumbuans in New Guinea," *Natural History*,
            34, No. 3 (May-June, 1934), 234-246.
71   "The Use of Primitive Material in the Study of Personality,"
            Character and Personality, 3, No. 1 (September, 1934), 3-16.
72   "Where Sorcerers Call the Tune," *Asia*, 34, No. 4 (April, 1934),
            232-235.
73   Review of *Patterns of Culture*, by Ruth Benedict, *Nation*, 139,

No. 3623 (December 12, 1934), 686.

74   Review of *Rebel Destiny*, by Melville J. Herskovits and Frances
S. Herskovits, *Natural History*, 34, No. 5 (September, 1934),
503.

1935

75   "Beginning with the Adolescent in Social Studies," *Social
Studies*, 26, No. 5 (May, 1935), 321-329.

76   "Position of Women of Native Races," *International Women's
News*, 29, No. 10 (July, 1935), 96-97.

77   Report to the Committee on the Social Studies of the
Commission on the Secondary School Curriculum. October 26,
1935. (Mimeographed.)

78   "Sex and Achievement," *Forum*, 94, No. 5 (November, 1935),
301-303.

79   *Sex and Temperament in Three Primitive Societies.* New York:
Morrow, 1935.
Reprinted in paperback 1950, Mentor. New York: New American
Library; 1963 (with new preface), Apollo Editions. New York:
Morrow; 1968, Laurel Editions. New York: Dell.

—

English edition: *Sex and Temperament in Three Primitive
Societies.* London: Routledge, 1935.
Argentinian edition: *Sexo y Temperamento.* Buenos Aires:
Abrile, 1947.
Danish edition: *Kvinde og Mande.* Copenhagen: Schultz, 1957.
Dutch edition: *Seksualiteit en temperament.* Utrecht: Aula-Boeken,
1962.
Finnish edition: *Sukupuoli ja luonne.* Helsinki:
Kustannvososakeyhtio otava, 1963.
French edition: *Moeurs et Sexualité en Océanie.* Paris: Plon, 1963.
German edition: *Geschlecht und Temperament in Primitiven
Gesellschaften.* Hamburg: Rowahlt, 1959.
Hebrew edition: Tel Aviv: Massada, 1970.
Italian edition: *Sesso E Temperamento in tre Societa Primitive.*
Milan: Il Saggiatore, 1967.
Spanish edition: *Sexo y Temperamento en Las Sociedades
primitivas.* Barcelona: Editorial Laia, 1947.
Swedish edition: *Kvinnlight Manlight Mänsklight.*

Stockholm: Tidens, 1948; Stockholm: Bonniers, 1957. Yugoslavian edition: *Spol i Temperament U Tri Primitivna Drustva.* Zagreb: Naprijed, 1968.

80   "Studies in Cooperative and Competitive Habits in Selected Primitive Cultures." Part of a report to the Psychological Subcommittee of the Committee on Personality and Culture of the Social Science Research Council, 1935. (Mimeographed.)

81   "Woman: Position in Society: Primitive." In *Encyclopedia of the Social Sciences*, 15, Edwin R. A. Seligman and Alvin Johnson, eds. New York: Macmillan, 1935, 439-442.

82   Review of *Law and Order in Polynesia*, by H. Ian Hogbin, *Saturday Review of Literature*, 12, No. 11 (July 13, 1935), 12.

83   Review of *The Pawnee Ghost Dance Hand Game*, by Alexander Lesser, *Annals of the American Academy of Political and Social Science*, 180 (July, 1935), 249.

84   Review of *The Riddle of the Sphinx*, by Géza Róheim, *Character and Personality*, 4, No. 1 (September, 1935), 85-90.

1936

85   "Anthropology." In *Encyclopaedia Sexualis*, ed. V. Robinson. New York: Crown, 1936, 16-27.

86   "Culture and Personality," *American Journal of Sociology*, 42, No. 1 (July, 1936), 84-87.

87   "On the Institutionalized Role of Women and Character Formation," *Zeitschrift für Sozialforschung*, 5, No. 1 (1936), 69-75.

88   Review of *Coral Gardens and Their Magic*, by Bronislaw Malinowski, *Zeitschrift für Sozialforschung*, No. 3 (1936), 469-470.

1937

89   Editor. *Cooperation and Competition among Primitive Peoples.* New York: McGraw-Hill, 1937.
Reprinted in paperback 1961 (enlarged edition), Boston: Beacon Press.

90   "Primitive Society." In *Planned Society, Yesterday, Today and Tomorrow: A Symposium*, ed. T. F. Mackenzie. New York: Prentice-Hall, 1937, 3-25.

91 "Public Opinion Mechanisms among Primitive Peoples,"
Public Opinion Quarterly, 1, No. 3 (July, 1937), 5-16.
92 "A Reply to a Review by R. C. Thurnwald of 'Sex and
Temperament in Three Primitive Societies,' " *American
Anthropologist*, 39, No. 3 (July-September, 1937), 558-561.
93 "A Twi Relationship System," *Journal of the Royal
Anthropological Institute*, 67 (July-December, 1937), 297-304.

1938

94 "The Mountain Arapesh. I. An Importing Culture,"
*Anthropological Papers of The American Museum of Natural
History*, 36, Part 3. New York, 1938, 139-349.
Reprinted in paperback 1970, as *The Mountain Arapesh II.
Arts and Supernaturalism*, American Museum Science Books
B 19b. Garden City, New York: Natural History Press.
95 "A Reply to the Review of 'Cooperation and Competition
among Primitive Peoples,' " *American Anthropologist*, 40, No. 3
(July-September, 1938), 530-531.

1939

96 *From the South Seas: Studies of Adolescence and Sex in
Primitive Societies*. New York: Morrow, 1939.

German edition: *Leben in der Südsee*. Munich: Szczesny, 1965.
97 "Men and Gods of a Bali Village," *The New York Times Magazine*,
July 16, 1939, 12-13, 23.
98 "Native Languages as Field-Work Tools," *American Anthropologist*, 41, No. 2 (April-June, 1939), 189-205.
99 "Researches in Bali, 1936-1939," *Transactions of The New York
Academy of Sciences*, Ser. 2, 2, No. 1 (November, 1939), 24-31.
(This paper consists of two parts: I. On the Concept of Plot in
Culture, 24-27, and II. Methods of Research in Bali and New
Guinea, 28-31.)
100 "The Strolling Players in the Mountains of Bali," *Natural
History*, 43, No. 1 (January, 1939), 17-26, 64.
101 Review of *Himalayan Village*, by Geoffrey Gorer, *Oceania*,
9, No. 3 (March, 1939), 344-353.

1940

102   (With Sidney Hook and Ruth Benedict.)
"Alexander Goldenweiser: Three Tributes," *Modern Quarterly*,
11, No. 6 (Summer, 1940), 31-34.

103   "The Arts in Bali," *Yale Review*, 30, No. 2 (December, 1940),
335-347.

104   "Character Formation in Two South Sea Societies." In *Trans-
actions of the American Neurological Association, Sixty-Sixth
Annual Meeting, June 6, 7, and 8, 1940.* Richmond, Virginia:
William Byrd Press, 1940, 99-103.

105   "Conflict of Cultures in America." In *Proceedings of the 54th
Annual Convention of the Middle States Association of Colleges
and Secondary Schools, November 22-23, 1940.*
Philadelphia: Middle States Association of Colleges and
Secondary Schools, 1940, 30-44.

106   "Material Conditions Affect Our Character Structure," in "The
Perils of Democracy, a Panel Discussion," *Journal of Adult
Education*, 12, No. 3 (June, 1940), 269-277.

107   "The Mountain Arapesh. II. Supernaturalism," *Anthropol-
ogical Papers of The American Museum of Natural History*,
37, Part 3. New York, 1940, 319-451.
Reprinted in paperback 1970, as *The Mountain Arapesh II.
Arts and Supernaturalism.* American Museum Science Books
B 19b. Garden City, New York: Natural History Press.

108   "On Behalf of the Sciences," in "Toward an Honorable World,
a Symposium," *Wilson College Bulletin*, 3, No. 4 (December,
1940), 19-29.

109   "Research on Primitive Children," *Oceania*, 10, No. 3 (March,
1940), 363.

110   "Social Change and Cultural Surrogates," *Journal of Educational Sociology*, 14, No. 2 (October, 1940), 92-109.

111   "Speech of Acceptance (National Achievement Award),"
Eleusis of Chi Omega, 42, No. 3 (September, 1940), 396-402.

112   "The Student of Race Problems Can Say...," *Frontiers of
Democracy*, 6, No. 53 (April, 1940), 200-202.

113   "Toward a New Role for Women," *Womans Press*, 34, No. 10
(November, 1940), 466-467.

114   "Warfare Is Only an Invention — Not a Biological Necessity,"
Asia, 40, No. 8 (August, 1940), 402-405.

115   (With Goodwin Watson and Sidonie Gruenberg.) "Discipline: The Challenge of Our Times," *Child Study*, 18, No. 2 (Winter, 1940-1941), 36-38, 64.

116   Review of *Experiments in Civilization*, by H. Ian Hogbin, *Oceania*, 11, No. 1 (September, 1940), 116-118.

1941

117   (With Gregory Bateson.) "Principles of Morale Building," *Journal of Educational Sociology*, 15, No. 4 (December, 1941), 206-220.

118   "Administrative Contributions to Democratic Character Formation at the Adolescent Level," *Journal of the National Association of Deans of Women*, 4, No. 2 (January, 1941), 51-57.

119   "Back of Adolescence Lies Early Childhood," *Childhood Education*, 18, No. 1 (January, 1941), 13-17.

120   "Democracy's Scapegoat: Youth," in "Defending the Younger Generation," by Margaret Mead and Irwin Ross, *Harper's Magazine*, 184, No. 1088 (January, 1941), 132-136.

121   "For Children from Different Backgrounds," *Progressive Education*, 18, No. 1 (Januari, 1941), 13-17.

122   "Museums in the Emergency," *Natural History*, 48, No. 2 (September, 1941), 67.

123   "New Inventions Needed," in "How Meet Today's Crisis (Symposium)," by Major George Fielding Eliot and others, *Independent Woman*, 20, No. 6 (June, 1941), 190.

124   "Not Head-hunters, nor Appeasers, but Men," *The New York Times Magazine*, November 30, 1941, 3, 29.

125   "On Methods of Implementing a National Morale Program," *Applied Anthropology*, 1, No. 1 (October-December, 1941), 20-24.

126   "Personality Development of Youth: A Bulwark in Sex Adjustment." In *Papers on Social Hygiene Read at the Regional Conference on Social Hygiene, February 5, 1941*. New York: New York Tuberculosis and Health Association, 1941, 106-107.

127   "Report on the Macy Family Study as a Research Study." (Mimeographed.)

128 "Shall Hitler Call Our Tune?" *Independent Woman*, 20, No. 1 (January, 1941), 5, 28-29.

129 "When Were You Born?" *Child Study*, 18, No. 3 (Spring, 1941), 71-72.

130 "Youth Would Be Valiant," *National Parent-Teacher*, 36, No. 2 (October, 1941), 14-16.

131 (With Gregory Bateson.) "Summary of Seminar of Department of Sociology: Interpretation in Anthropology." October 31, 1941. (Mimeographed.)

132 Review of *Within the Sound of These Waves*, by William H. Chickering, *Natural History*, 48, No. 4 (November, 1941), 249.

133 Review of *Deep South*, by Allison Davis, Burleigh Gardner and Mary Gardner, *New York Herald Tribune Books*, December 7, 1941, 38.

134 Review of *The Hopi Child*, by Wayne Dennis, *American Anthropologist*, 43, No. 1 (January-March, 1941), 95-97.

135 Review of *The Work of the Gods in Tikopia*, by Raymond Firth, *Review of Religion*, 5, No. 3 (March, 1941), 396.

136 Review of *Escape from Freedom*, by Erich Fromm, *New York Herald Tribune Books*, September 21, 1941, 18.

137 Review of *The Individual and His Society*, by Abram Kardiner, *American Journal of Orthopsychiatry*, 11, No. 3 (July, 1941), 603-605.

138 Review of *Married Life in an African Tribe*, by I. Schapera, *New York Herald Tribune Books*, November 23, 1941, 32.

139 Review of *Essays in Polynesian Ethnology*, by Robert W. Williamson, ed. Ralph Piddington, *American Historical Review*, 46, No. 4 (July, 1941), 846-847.

1942

140 (With Gregory Bateson.) *Balinese Character: A Photographic Analysis*. ("Special Publications of The New York Academy of Sciences," 2.) New York: New York Academy of Sciences, 1942. Reissued 1962.

141 "Against the Backdrop," *Mademoiselle*, December, 1942, 77, 130, 133-135.

142 *And Keep Your Powder Dry: An Anthropologist Looks at America*. New York: Morrow, 1942.
Reprinted in paperback 1965 (with new chapter), Apollo Editions.

New York: Morrow; 1971, Freeport, New York: Libraries Press.
—

English edition: *And Keep Your Powder Dry*. London: Whiting and Wheaton, 1967.

English edition: *The American Character*. Harmondsworth: Penguin, 1944.

Braille edition: *And Keep Your Powder Dry: An Anthropologist Looks at America*. Watertown, Massachusetts: School for the Blind, 1945.

Austrian edition: *Und Halte Dein Pulver Trocken*. Vienna: Phönix, 1947.

German edition: *Und Haltet Euer Pulver Trocken*. Munich: Desch, 1946.

Italian edition: *Carattere degli Americani*. Firenze: Edizioni U, 1946.

143 "Anthropological Data on the Problem of Instinct," in "Symposium–Second Colloquia on Psychodynamics and Experimental Medicine," *Psychosomatic Medicine*, 4, No. 4 (October, 1942), 396-397. (Abstract.)

144 "An Anthropologist Looks at the Teacher's Role," *Educational Method*, 21, No. 5 (February, 1942), 219-223.

145 "Community Drama, Bali and America," *American Scholar*, 11, No. 1 (Winter, 1941-1942), 79-88.

146 "The Comparative Study of Culture and the Purposive Cultivation of Democratic Values." In *Science, Philosophy and Religion, Second Symposium*, Lyman Bryson and Louis Finkelstein, eds. New York: Conference on Science, Philosophy and Religion in Their Relation to the Democratic Way of Life, 1942, 56-69.

147 "Cultural Patterns and Problems of Morale." In *Abstracts of the General Lectures Given at the Vassar Summer Institute for Family and Child-care Services in War Time, June 22- August 1, 1942*. Poughkeepsie, New York: Vassar College, September 1942, 107-108. (Mimeographed.)

148 "Customs and Mores," *American Journal of Sociology*, 47, No. 6 (May, 1942), 971-980.

149 "Educative Effects of Social Environment as Disclosed by Studies of Primitive Societies." In *Environment and Education*, ed. E. W. Burgess. ("Human Development Series, I. Supplementary Educational Monographs," 54.) Chicago: University of Chicago Press, 1942, 48-61.

150 "Has the 'Middle Class' a Future?" *Survey Graphic*, 31, No. 2

(February, 1942), 64-67, 95.

151   "Help Them Grow Up," *Parents' Magazine*, 17, No. 7 (July, 1942), 24-25, 44.

152   "The Problem of Training the Volunteer in Community War Work," *School and Society*, 56, No. 1457 (November 28, 1942), 520-522.

153   "Reaching the Last Woman down the Road," *Journal of Home Economics*, 34, No. 10 (December, 1942), 710-713.

154   "To Keep the Children Safe from Fear," *Guild Teacher*, 7, No.4 (February-March, 1942), 15-17.

155   "War Need Not Mar Our Children," *The New York Times Magazine*, February 15, 1942, 13, 34.

156   "When Do Americans Fight? " *Nation*, 155, No. 16 (October 17, 1942), 368-371.

157   Review of *A Field Study in Siam of the Behavior and Social Relations of the Gibbon (Hylobates Lar)*, by R. C. Carpenter, *American Anthropologist*, 44, No. 3 (July-September, 1942), 511-512.

158   Review of *Bali*, by Philip Hanson Hiss, *Natural History*, 49, No. 3 (March, 1942), 84.

159   Review of *Growing Up in the Black Belt*, by Charles S. Johnson, *American Journal of Sociology*, 48, No. 3 (November, 1942), 433-434.

1943

160   (Assistant with Gregory Bateson, Phyllis M. Kaberry, and Stephen W. Reed to Robert A. Hall, Jr. , primary author.) *Melanesian Pidgin English*. ("Special Publications of the Linguistic Society of America.") Baltimore: Waverly Press, 1943.

161   "Anthropological Approach to Dietary Problems," *Transactions of The New York Academy of Sciences*, Ser. 2, 5, No. 7 (May, 1943), 177-182.

162   "Anthropological Techniques in War Psychology," *Bulletin of the Menninger Clinic*, 7, No. 4 (July, 1943), 137-140.

163   "Art and Reality from the Standpoint of Cultural Anthropology," in "Art and Reality: A Symposium," by George Boas, C. L. Watkins and Margaret Mead, *College Art Journal*, 2, No. 4, Part 1 (May, 1943), 119-121.

164   "Can You Tell One American from Another? " *The Listener*, 30,

No. 777 (December 2, 1943), 640.

165 "Changing Food Habits." In *The Nutrition Front*. Report of the New York State Joint Legislative Committee on Nutrition. Legislative Document, No. 64, 1943, 37-43.

166 "The Committee on Food Habits," *Psychological Bulletin*, 40, No. 4 (April, 1943), 290-293.

167 "The Cultural Picture," in "Problems of a War-Time Society: II. The Modification of Pre-War Patterns," *American Journal of Orthopsychiatry*, 13, No. 4 (October, 1943), 596-599.

168 "Dietary Patterns and Food Habits," *Journal of the American Dietetic Association*, 19, No. 1 (January, 1943), 1-5.

169 "The Factor of Food Habits," *Annals of the American Academy of Political and Social Science*, 225 (January, 1943), 136-141.

170 "The Family in the Future." In *Beyond Victory*, ed. Ruth Nanda Anshen. New York: Harcourt, Brace, 1943, 66-87.

171 "Food and Feeding in Occupied Territory," *Public Opinion Quarterly*, 7, No. 4 (Winter, 1943), 618-628.

172 "Food Therapy and Wartime Food Problems," *Journal of the American Dietetic Association*, 19, No. 3 (March, 1943), 201-202.

173 "News of Developing Research Methods," *Applied Anthropology*, 2, No. 2 (January-March, 1943), 35-37.

174 "Our Educational Emphases in Primitive Perspective," *American Journal of Sociology*, 48, No. 6 (May, 1943), 633-639.

175 "The Problem of Changing Food Habits." In Report of the Committee on Food Habits, 1941-1943, "The Problem of Changing Food Habits," *National Research Council Bulletin*, 108, 1943, 20-31.

176 "The Problem of Changing Food Habits: With Suggestions for Psychoanalytic Contributions," *Bulletin of the Menninger Clinic*, 7, No. 2 (March, 1943), 57-61.

177 "The Problem of Training the Volunteer as Seen from the Standpoint of the Operating Agency." In *Handbook on Education and the War*. Based on Proceedings of the National Institute on Education and the War, Sponsored by the U. S. Office of Education Wartime Commission, at American University, Washington, D. C., August 28-31, 1942. Washington, D. C., 1943, 191-193.

178 "The Role of Small South Sea Cultures in the Post War World," *American Anthropologist*, 45, No. 2 (April-June, 1943), 193-196.

179 "Report on a Small Town Study, Conducted in June, 1943." (Mimeographed.)

180 "Shortage of Nurse Volunteers Linked to 'Synthetic Living,' " *New York Herald Tribune*, May 23, 1943, Sec. 5, 1, 13.

181 Speech on Post-War World, in New York Times Conference "On the World after the War," *The New York Times*, April 8, 1943, 16.

182 "What Makes Americans Tick?" *Vogue* (February 1, 1943), 53, 114-115.

183 "When Mother Joins Up," *Forecast for Home Economists*, 59, No. 6 (June, 1943), 54, 56.

184 "Why We Americans Talk Big," *The Listener*, 30, No. 772 (October 28, 1943), 494.

185 (With Karl Menninger and Mary Shattuck Fisher.) "The Roots of War in Human Nature: Aggression and Hate in Childhood and Family Life," *Child Study*, 20, No. 3 (Spring, 1943), 77, 91.

186 Introduction to *Is Germany Incurable?* by Richard M. Brickner. New York: Lippincott, 1943, 7-13.

187 Review of *Smoke from Their Fires: The Life of a Kwakiutl Chief*, by Clellan S. Ford, *Clinical Supplement to Journal of Abnormal and Social Psychology*, 38, No. 2 (April, 1943), 197-199.

188 Review of *The Making of Modern New Guinea*, by Stephen W. Reed, *Pacific Affairs*, 16, No. 1 (March, 1943), 121-122.

189 Review of *On Becoming a Kwoma*, by John M. Whiting, *American Journal of Sociology*, 48, No. 6 (May, 1943), 773-774.

190 "The Americans—Are They Human," London, BBC, October 10, 1943. (Manuscript.)

1944

191 (With A. Murray Dyer.) "It's Human Nature," *Education*, 65, No. 4 (December, 1944), 228-238.

192 *The American Troops and the British Community: An Examination of the Relationship between the American Troops and the British*. London: Hutchinson, 1944. (Pamphlet.)

193 *A Bread and Butter Letter from a Lecturer*. Los Angeles: Occidental College, 1944. (Pamphlet.)

194 "Can America Afford Families? " *Look*, 8, No. 25 (December 12, 1944), 90.

195 "Cultural Approach to Personality: Anthropological Comment on the Frame of Reference of Andras Angyal," *Transactions of*

The New York Academy of Sciences, Ser. 2, 6, No. 3 (January, 1944), 93-101.

196 "Decorators Hold the Cards," *House and Garden* (May, 1944), 29, 98.

197 "Ferment in British Education: Some Impressions of Educational Thinking in England," *Journal of the American Association of University Women*, 37, No. 3 (Spring, 1944), 131-133.

198 "Food as a Basis for International Cooperation," *Africa*, 14, No. 5 (January, 1944), 258-264.

199 "A GI View of Britain," *The New York Times Magazine*, March 19, 1944, 18-19, 34.

200 "The Home Changes with the World," in "The Home Changes with the World," by Dorothy Canfield Fisher, Margaret Mead and Eugene Meyer, *The New York Times Magazine*, April 9, 1944, 14, 40.

201 "One Mother Goes a Long Way," *Harriet Johnson Nursery School Souvenir Program*, 1944, 11.

202 "Preface from England." *The American Character*. Pelican A-138. Harmondsworth, Middlesex: Penguin, 1944, vii-xi.

203 "Preparing Children for a World Society," *Childhood Education*, 20, No. 8 (April, 1944), 345-348.

204 "Summary of a Communication, 5 October, 1943," *Man*, 44, No. 34 (March-April, 1944), 48-49.

205 "Training of Regional Specialists," in "Psychology—In the War and After (VII)," by Gregory Bateson, Margaret Mead and Walter Miles, *Junior College Journal*, 14, No. 7 (March, 1944), 311-312.

206 "Wellesley School of Community Affairs 1944: A Retrospective View," *Wellesley Magazine*, 29, No. 1 (October, 1944), 12-13.

207 "What Is a Date," *Transatlantic*, No. 10 (June, 1944), 54, 57-60.

208 "Why Not a Year of National Service? " *Parents' Magazine*, 19, No. 11 (November, 1944), 18.

209 "Will Women Be Able to Choose?" *Woman's Day* (May, 1944), 20-21, 69.

210 "Women Can Help Apply Science to Human Problems," *Science News Letter*, 45, No. 12 (March 18, 1944), 189-190.

211 "Women's Social Position," *Journal of Educational Sociology*, 17, No. 8 (April, 1944), 453-462.

1945

212   "The Choice Before Us," *Common Ground*, 6, No. 1 (Autumn, 1945), 103-104.

213   "The Dietitian as a Member of a Therapeutic Team," *Journal of the American Dietetic Association*, 21, No. 7 (July-August, 1945), 424-426.

214   "Group Living as a Part of Intergroup Educational Workshops," *Journal of Educational Sociology*, 18, No. 9 (May, 1945), 526-534.

215   "How Religion Has Fared in the Melting Pot." In *Religion in the Post-War World*, III: *Religion and Our Racial Tensions*, ed. Willard L. Sperry. Cambridge: Harvard University Press, 1945, 61-81.

216   "Human Differences and World Order." In *World Order: Its Intellectual and Cultural Foundations*, ed. F. Ernest Johnson. New York: Harper, 1945, 40-51.

217   "Intercultural Relations—A Priority in 1945," *The Bookshelf* (YWCA) (February, 1945), 1.

218   "Methods and Techniques," in "Translation of Scientific Findings into Living Habits." Washington, D. C. : Committee of Food Habits, National Research Council, 1945, 3-10; discussion 19-65. (Mimeographed.)

219   "Observations on Emotions and Thinking in the Living Room," in "A Social Evening at Mrs. Fairchild's—Prejudice and Emotion in the Living Room," *Journal of Social Issues*, 1, No. 2 (May, 1945), 43-46.

220   *Social Anthropology*. Pasadena, California: Western Personnel Service, 1945. (Pamphlet.)

221   "Wellesley School of Community Affairs," *Progressive Education*, 22, No. 4 (February, 1945), 4-8.

222   "What Is the Immediate Action Role of American Educators? Dr. Mead's Reply." In *Human Nature and Enduring Peace*, ed. Gardner Murphy. Boston: Houghton Mifflin, 1945, 285-288.

223   "What's the Matter with the Family? " *Harper's Magazine*, No. 1139 (April, 1945), 393-399.

224   "Youth in an Unchartered Landscape," *Junior Bazaar* (November, 1945), 91.

225   (With others.) "American Group Conflicts," *CCI Facts on Friction*, No. 7 (December 26, 1945), 1-9.

226   (With others.) "What Does It Mean to Us? An Unrehearsed

Discussion." In *Script: AAUW National Convention, 1945*. Washington, D. C. : American Association of University Women, 1945, 12-17.

227   Report of the Committee on Food Habits. "Manual for the Study of Food Habits," *National Research Council Bulletin*, No. 111. Washington, D. C. , 1945. Reissued 1962.

228   Review of *Studies in the Anthropology of Oceania and Asia*, by James M. Andrews and others, *Far Eastern Quarterly*, 4, No. 3 (May, 1945), 295-296.

229   Review of *The Psychology of Women: A Psychoanalytic Interrelation*, by Helene Deutsch, *Journal of Abnormal and Social Psychology*, 40, No. 2 (April, 1945), 277-278.

230   Review of *Native Peoples of the Pacific World*, by Felix M. Keesing, *Saturday Review of Literature*, 28, No. 34 (August 25, 1945), 11.

1946

231   "The American People." In *The World's Peoples and How They Live*. London: Odhams Press, 1946, 143-163.

232   "Are You Making Your Child a Snob? " *Two to Six*, 1, No. 3 (May, 1946), 11, 56.

233   "Can Homemaking Really Be a Career?" *Seventeen* (April, 1946), 116-117, 202.

234   "Changing Food Habits in the Post-War Period." In *Nutrition for Young and Old*. New York State Joint Legislative Committee on Nutrition, Legislative Document, No. 76, 1946, 60-64.

235   "Cuando Se Habla de Los Otros Grupos," *Alma Latina*, 16, No. 527 (January, 1946), 5, 36.

236   "Cultural Aspects of Women's Vocational Problems in Post World War II," *Journal of Consulting Psychology*, 10, No. 1 (January-February, 1946), 23-28.

237   "How Effective Are Your Education Methods? " *Program Information Bulletin*, 3, No. 3 (March, 1946), 3.

238   "Is It... Like Mother Like Daughter? " *House Beautiful*, 88, No. 10 (October, 1946), 124, 230-233.

239   "Learning a Food Pattern," *Practical Home Economics*, 24, No. 1 (January, 1946), 22, 58-60.

240   "Masks and Men," *Natural History*, 55, No. 6 (June, 1946), 280-285.

241   "Personality, the Cultural Approach to." In *The Encyclopedia of Psychology*, ed. Philip Lawrence Harriman. New York: Philosophical Library, 1946, 477-488.

242   "Professional Problems of Education in Dependent Countries," *Journal of Negro Education*, 40, No. 3 (Summer, 1946), 346-357.

243   "Research on Primitive Children." In *Manual of Child Psychology*, ed. Leonard Carmichael. New York: Wiley, 1946, 667-706.

244   "Shall Mankind Go On Living? " *Readers Scope*, 4, No. 6 (November, 1946), 101-104.

245   "Significant Aspects of Regional Food Patterns." In *Committee on Food Research Conference on Food Acceptance Research*. QMC 17-9. Washington, D. C. : War Department, Office of The Quartermaster General, 1946, 64-67.

246   "The Teacher's Place in American Society," *Journal of the American Association of University Women*, 40, No. 1 (Fall, 1946), 3-5.

247   "There's One Thing We Can Do About Atomic Energy," *Woman's Day* (April, 1946), 20, 54, 57.

248   "Trends in Personal Life," *New Republic*, 115, No. 12 (September 23, 1946), 346-348.

249   "What Women Want," *Fortune*, 34, No. 6 (December, 1946), 172-175, 218-224.

250   "Will Winners in War Be Losers in Peace? " *National Parent-Teacher*, 40, No. 8 (April, 1946), 15.

251   "The Women in the War." In *While You Were Gone*, ed. Jack Goodman. New York: Simon and Schuster, 1946, 274-289.

252   "Workshop for Democracy," *Better Times*, 27, No. 23 (March 1, 1946), 3, 12.

253   "Youth Needs New Models," *Clubwoman* (April, 1946), 13.

254   (With Harlow Shapley and Malcolm Sharp.) "Must Men Fight," *University of Chicago Round Table*, No. 444 (September 22, 1946).

255   Review of *Woman as Force in History*, by Mary R. Beard, *Chicago Sun Book Week*, March 24, 1946, 6.

256   Review of *Color Blind*, by Margaret Halsey, *The New York Times Book Review*, October 13, 1946, 3, 36.

257   Review of *Small Town*, by Granville Hicks, *The New York Times Book Review*, December 15, 1946, 4.

258   Review of *A House in Bali*, by Colin McPhee, *The New York Times Book Review*, September 29, 1946, 7.

259   Review of *America's Stake in Britain's Future*, by George Soule, *Survey Graphic*, 35, No. 5 (May, 1946), 176-178.

1947

260   "Age Patterning in Personality Development," *American Journal of Orthopsychiatry*, 17, No. 2 (April, 1947), 231-240.

261   "The Application of Anthropological Techniques to Cross-National Communication," *Transactions of The New York Academy of Sciences*, Ser. 2, 9, No. 4 (February, 1947), 133-152.

262   "Babies in Primitive Society," *Child Study*, 24, No. 3 (Spring, 1947), 71-72.

263   "The Concept of Culture and the Psychosomatic Approach," *Psychiatry*, 10, No. 1 (February, 1947), 57-76.

264   "Contributions from the Study of Primitive Cultures." In *Problems of Early Infancy, Transactions of the First Conference, March 3-4, 1947*, ed. Milton J. E. Senn. New York: Josiah Macy, Jr. Foundation, 1947, 36-39.

265   "The English as a Foreigner Sees Them," *The Listener*, 38, No. 973 (September 18, 1947), 475-476.

266   "Fundamental Education and Cultural Values." In *Fundamental Education: Common Ground for All Peoples: Report of a Special Committee to the Preparatory Commission of Unesco, Paris, 1946*. New York: Macmillan, 1947, 150-178.

267   "The Implications of Culture Change for Personality Development," *American Journal of Orthopsychiatry*, 17, No. 4 (October, 1947), 633-646.

268   "Maturity and Society," *American Journal of Psychoanalysis*, 7, No. 1 (1947), 79-81.

269   "The Mountain Arapesh. III. Socio-Economic Life, and IV. Diary of Events in Alitoa," *Anthropological Papers of The American Museum of Natural History*, 40, Part 3. New York, 1947, 163-419.
Reprinted in paperback 1971, as *The Mountain Arapesh III. Stream of Events in Alitoa*. American Museum Science Books B 19c. Garden City, New York: Natural History Press.

270   "Must Marriage Be for Life? " *'47: The Magazine of the Year*, 1, No. 9 (November, 1947), 28-31.

271   "On the Implications for Anthropology of the Gesell-Ilg Approach to Maturation," *American Anthropologist*, 49, No. 1 (January-March, 1947), 69-77.

272   "Reference List: 1926-1947," *Psychiatry*, 10, No. 1 (February, 1947), 118-120.

273   "Setting New Patterns for Women's Work," *Responsibility*, 5, No. 1 (Spring, 1947), 13-14.

274   "Some Relations between Cultural Anthropology and Sociometry," *Sociometry*, 10, No. 4 (November, 1947), 312-318.

275   "What Is Happening to the American Family? " *Journal of Social Casework*, 28, No. 9 (November, 1947), 323-330.

276   (With Alex Bavelas.) "The Dallas Convention and the Future of AAUW," *Journal of the American Association of University Women*, 41, No. 1 (Fall, 1947), 23-25.

277   Comment in "General Discussion," in "Physiological and Psychological Factors in Sex Behavior," by S. Bernard Wortis, Gregory Bateson and others, *Annals of the New York Academy of Sciences*, 47, Art. 5 (May, 1947), 631.

278   Comment in "I Remember a Teacher...," *Glamour* (January, 1947), 130.

279   Participant in "Problems in Clinical Research: Round Table, 1946," *American Journal of Orthopsychiatry*, 17, No. 2 (April, 1947), 227.

280   Foreword to *Counseling Girls in a Changing Society*, by Rosalind Cassidy and Hilda Clute Lozman. New York: McGraw-Hill, 1947, xv-xix.

281   Review of *Touchstone for Ethics*, by T. H. Huxley and Julian Huxley, *The New York Times Book Review*, November 16, 1947, 8.

282   Review of *Modern Women: The Lost Sex*, by Ferdinand Lundberg and Marynia F. Farnham, *The New York Times Book Review*, January 26, 1947, 18.

283   Review of *Sex in Our Changing World*, by John McPartland, *The New York Times Book Review*, July 20, 1947, 21.

284   Review of *Sex and the Social Order*, by Georgene H. Steward, *American Anthropologist*, 49, No. 2 (April-June, 1947), 309-311.

285   Review of *Richer by Asia*, by Edmond Taylor, *The New York Times Book Review*, July 13, 1947, 3.

1948

286   "An Anthropologist Looks at the Report." In *Proceedings of a Symposium on the First Published Report of a Series of Studies of Sex Phenomena by Professor Alfred C. Kinsey, Wardell B. Pomeroy and Clyde E. Martin.* New York: American Social Hygiene Association, 1948, 58-69.

287   "Are Children Savages?" *Mademoiselle* (July, 1948), 33, 110-111.
288   "A Case History in Cross-National Communications." In *The Communication of Ideas*, ed. Lyman Bryson. New York: Institute for Religious and Social Studies, 1948, 209-229.
289   "The Contemporary American Family as an Anthropologist Sees It," *American Journal of Sociology*, 53, No. 6 (May, 1948), 453-459.
290   "Cultural Contexts of Nutritional Patterns," *Science*, 108, No. 2813 (November 26, 1948), 598-599.
291   "Growing Older in Our Community." In *Age Will Be Served, a Digest of Papers Given at the Annual Meeting of the Brooklyn Council for Social Planning, May 12, 1948*. New York: Brooklyn Council for Social Planning, 1948, 26-28.
292   "Mémoire sur la recherche internationale à effectuer concernant les effets de la guerre sur les enfants. Mesures thérapeutiques à envisager." In *Rapport du Secrétaire Général sur le problème de la création des laboratoires de recherche des Nations Unies*. E/620. Paris: UNESCO, January 23, 1948, 429-441. (Mimeographed.)
293   "Mental Health: A New Profession," *The Listener*, 40, No. 1028 (October 7, 1948), 511-512.
294   "New Relationships between Ethnographic Studies of the American Indian Cultures and the Study of the Modern Cultures of the Americas." In *Actes du XXVIIIe Congrès International des Américanistes, Paris 1947*. Paris: Musée de l'Homme, 1948, 353-354. (Abstract.)
295   "Positive Motivation in Health Education." In *Motivation in Health Education: The 1947 Health Education Conference of the New York Academy of Medicine*. New York: Columbia University Press, 1948, 45-53.
296   "The Role of the Scientist in Society." In *Orthopsychiatry 1923-1948: Retrospect and Prospect*, Lawson G. Lowrey and Victoria Sloane, eds. New York: American Orthopsychiatric Association, 1948, 367-373.
297   "Some Cultural Approaches to Communication Problems." In *The Communication of Ideas*, ed. Lyman Bryson. New York: Institute for Religious and Social Studies, 1948, 9-26.
298   "World Culture." In *The World Community*, ed. Quincy Wright. Chicago: University of Chicago Press, 1948, 47-94.
299   (With Jean Rhys.) "Cultural Anthropology." In *College Reading and Religion*. New Haven: Yale University Press, 1948, 286-306.

300   Review of *Malay Fishermen: Their Peasant Economy*, by Raymond Firth, *American Anthropologist*, 50, No. 2 (April-June, 1948), 319.

301   Review of *The Americans*, by Geoffrey Gorer, *The Observer* (London), August 29, 1948.

1949

302   (With Lawrence K. Frank.) "The International Preparatory Commission." In *International Congress on Mental Health London 1948*. Vol. I. *History, Development and Organisation*, J. C. Flugel and others, eds. London: Lewis; New York: Columbia University Press, 1949, 74-89.

303   "An Anthropologist Looks at Our Marriage Laws," *Virginia Law Weekly Dicta*, 2, No. 3 (October 6, 1949), 1, 4.

304   "Character Formation and Diachronic Theory." In *Social Structure: Studies Presented to A. R. Radcliffe-Brown*, ed. Meyer Fortes. Oxford: Clarendon Press, 1949, 18-34.

305   "Collective Guilt." In *International Congress on Mental Health London 1948*. Vol. III. *Proceedings of the International Conference on Medical Psychotherapy, 11-14 August*, J. C. Flugel and others, eds. London: Lewis; New York: Columbia University Press, 1949, 56-66.

306   "Crossing Cultural Barriers: Sixth Address of the Edward Corbin Jenkins Lectureship, George Williams College, Chicago, November 1, 1948," *Religious Education*, 44 (March, 1949), 67-71.

307   "Cultural Patterning of Nutritionally Relevant Behavior," *Journal of the American Dietetic Association*, 25, No. 8 (August, 1949), 677-680.

308   *The Family's Food*. ("Bureau of Current Affairs Pamphlet," 85.) London: Bureau of Current Affairs, July 23, 1949. (Pamphlet.)

309   "The Higher Education Survey," *Journal of the American Association of University Women*, 43, No. 1 (Fall, 1949), 8-12.

310   "The Individual and Society." In *International Congress on Mental Health London 1948*. Vol. IV. *Proceedings of the International Conference on Mental Hygiene, 16-21 August*, J. C. Flugel and others, eds. London: Lewis; New York: Columbia University Press, 1949, 121-127.

311   "The International Preparatory Commission of the London Conference on Mental Hygiene," *Mental Hygiene*, 33, No. 1 (January, 1949), 9-16.

312   *Male and Female: A Study of the Sexes in a Changing World.*
New York: Morrow, 1949.
Reprinted in paperback 1955, Mentor. New York: New American
Library; 1967, Apollo Editions. New York: Morrow; 1968, Laurel
Editions. New York: Dell; 1975, Paperback Editions. New York:
Morrow.
—
English edition: *Male and Female.* London: Gollancz, 1949;
Harmondsworth: Penguin, 1962, 1975.
Argentinian edition: *El Hombre y la Mujer.* Buenos Aires:
Comparria General Fabril, 1961.
Danish edition: *Kon og Kultur.* Copenhagen: Schultz, 1962, 1969.
Dutch edition: *Man en Vrouw.* Utrecht: Bijleveld, 1953, 1962.
Finnish edition: *Mies ja Nannen.* Helsinki: Kustannvsosakeyhtio
okavan, 1957.
French edition: *L'un et l'autre sexe.* Paris: Gonthier, 1966.
German edition: *Mann und Weib.* Stuttgart: Diana, 1955.
Hebrew edition: Tel Aviv: Meass-dah, 1964.
Italian edition: *Mascho e Femma.* Milan: Il Saggiatore, 1962.
Japanese edition: Tokyo: Tuttle, 1961.
Portuguese edition: *O Homem e a Mulher.* Lisbon: Meridiano, 1971.
Venezuelan edition: *Macho y Hembra.* Caracas: Tiempo Nuevo,
1972.

313   "The Mountain Arapesh. V. The Record of Unabelin with
Rorschach Analyses," *Anthropological Papers of The American
Museum of Natural History*, 41, Part 3. New York, 1949, 285-390.
Reprinted in paperback 1968, as *The Mountain Arapesh I. The
Record of Unabelin with Rorschach Analyses.* American Museum
Science Books B 19a. Garden City, New York: Natural History
Press.

314   "Preface to Mentor edition," *Coming of Age in Samoa.* MP418.
New York: New American Library, 1949, ix-x.

315   "Primitive Cultures." In *Encyclopedia of Vocational Guidance*,
2 vols. , ed. Oscar J. Kaplan. New York: Philosophical Library,
1949, II, 1102-1106.

316   "Problems of the Atomic Age," *Survey*, 85, No. 7 (July, 1949),
385.

317   "Problems of Leadership and Mental Health," *Bulletin of the
World Federation for Mental Health*, 1, No. 6 (December, 1949),
7-12.

318   "Psychologic Weaning: Childhood and Adolescence." In *Psychosexual Development in Health and Disease*, ed. Paul Hoch. New York: Grune and Stratton, 1949, 124-135.

319   "Ruth Fulton Benedict." In *The Memorial Meeting at Viking Fund*. New York: Viking Fund, November 4, 1949, 25-27.

320   "Ruth Fulton Benedict, 1887-1948," *American Anthropologist*, 51, No. 3 (July-September, 1949), 457-468.

321   "Two Projects," *Human Organization*, 8, No. 1 (Winter, 1949), 28.

322   "Which Way? " *The Good Neighbor*, 1, No. 1 (February, 1949), 5-8.

323   (With Eliot D. Chapple and G. Gordon Brown.) "Report of the Committee on Ethics," *Human Organization*, 8, No. 2 (Spring, 1949), 20-21.

324   Discussion of "Child Rearing in Certain European Countries," by Ruth Benedict, *American Journal of Orthopsychiatry*, 19, No. 2 (April, 1949), 349-350.

325   Review of *The American People*, by Geoffrey Gorer, *American Journal of Psychiatry*, 106, No. 1 (August, 1949), 156-157.

326   Review of *Birth and Childhood among the Arabs*, by Hilma Granquist, *Middle East Journal*, 3, No. 2 (April, 1949), 217-218.

327   Review of *An Introduction to Samoan Custom*, by F. J. H. Grattan, *Pacific Affairs*, 22, No. 4 (December, 1949), 440-441.

328   Review of *The Political Community: A Study of Anomie*, by S. de Grazia, *UN World*, 3, No. 6 (June, 1949), 42.

329   Review of *Evolution and Ethics*, by Arthur Keith, *Journal of the History of Medicine*, 4, No. 3 (Summer, 1949), 345-346.

1950

330   "Change and Growth through Understanding," in "The Next Half Century in Science,"*Natural History*, 59, No. 4 (April, 1950), 150.

331   "The Comparative Study of Cultures and the Purposive Cultivation of Democratic Values, 1941-1949." In *Perspectives on a Troubled Decade: Science, Philosophy and Religion, 1939-1949*, Lyman Bryson, Louis Finkelstein and R. M. MacIver, eds. New York: Harper, 1950, 87-108.

332   "Cultural Contexts of Nutritional Patterns." In *Centennial: Collected Papers Presented at the Centennial Celebration, Washington, D. C. , September 13-17, 1948*. Washington, D. C. : American Association for the Advancement of Science, 1950, 103-111.

333   "Do Our Democratic Liberties Depend on Mental Health? " *The Northwestern University Reviewing Stand*, 14, No. 15 (April 23, 1950), 3-9.

334   "Grownups in the Making," *Child Study*, 27, No. 3 (Summer, 1950), 76, 91.

335   "It's about Time," *Flair*, 1 (March, 1950), 100-101.

336   Preface to 1950 edition, *Sex and Temperament in Three Primitive Societies*. New York: Morrow, 1950, unpaged.

337   "The Role of the Arts in a Culture." In *The Integrative Function of Art Education*. ("The Art Education Bulletin Yearbook," 1950.) Kutztown, Pennsylvania: Eastern Arts Association, 1950, 10-16.

338   "Some Anthropological Considerations Concerning Guilt." In *Feelings and Emotions: The Mooseheart Symposium*, ed. Martin L. Reymert. New York: McGraw-Hill, 1950, 362-373.

339   "Towards Mutual Responsibility," *Journal of Social Issues*, 6, No. 3 (1950), 45-56.

340   "Unique Possibilities of the Melting Pot." In *The Social Welfare Forum: Official Proceedings, 76th Annual Meeting, National Conference of Social Work, Cleveland, Ohio, June 12-17, 1949*. New York: Columbia University Press, 1950, 79-89.

341   "Unitarianism Too Intellectual: Must Satisfy 'Whole Man,' " *Christian Register*, 129, No. 7 (August, 1950), 34-36.

342   "What Psychoanalysis Does for You," *Look*, 14, No. 20 (September 26, 1950), 114, 116, 119-120, 122.

343   Discussion of "Anxiety Factors: Relation to Bodily Disease," by Leo W. Simmons; discussion of "Communication and Bodily Disease," by Jurgen Ruesch and Rodney Prestwood. In *Life Stress and Bodily Desease: Proceedings of the Association, December 2-3, 1949, New York, N. Y.* ("Research Publications, Association for Research in Nervous and Mental Diseases," 29.) Baltimore: Williams and Wilkins, 1950, 135-136, 226.

344   Preface to *The Samoan Dance of Life*, by John Copp. Boston: Beacon, 1950, ix-x.

345   (With T. F. Main and T. S. Simey.) *"Training in Community Relations*: A Critical Appreciation of a Book by Ronald Lippitt," *Human Relations*, 3, No. 2 (June 1950), 201-214.

346   Review of *The Coming of the Maori*, by Peter Buck (Te Rangi Hiroa), *Natural History*, 59, No. 7 (September, 1950), 293.

1951

347 "Anthropologist and Historian: Their Common Problems," *American Quarterly*, 3, No. 1 (Spring, 1951), 3-13.

348 "Changing Role of Physical Education in Our Culture," *Journal, American Association for Health, Physical Education, Recreation*, 22, No. 3 (March, 1951), 13.

349 "Contributions of Cultural Anthropology." In *The Selection of Military Manpower: A Symposium*, Leonard Carmichael and Leonard C. Mead, eds. Publication, 209. Washington, D. C. : National Academy of Sciences—National Research Council, 1951, 177-183.

350 "Cultural Contexts of Aging." In *No Time to Grow Old*. New York State Joint Legislative Committee on Problems of the Aging, Legislative Document, No. 12, 1951, 49-51.

351 "Experience in Learning Primitive Languages through the Use of Learning High Level Linguistic Abstractions." In *Cybernetics: Circular Causal and Feedback Mechanisms in Biological and Social Systems, Transactions of the Seventh Conference, March 23-24, 1950*, ed. Heinz von Foerster. New York: Josiah Macy, Jr. Foundation, 1951, 159-185.

352 "Group Psychotherapy in the Light of Anthropology," *International Journal of Group Psychotherapy*, 1, No. 3 (September, 1951), 193-199.

353 "The Impact of Culture on Personality Development in the United States Today." In *Midcentury White House Conference on Children and Youth, Proceedings of the Report of Conference Sessions, Washington, D. C., December 3-7, 1950*, ed. E. A. Richards. Raleigh, N. C.: Health Publications Institute, 1951, 84-86.

354 "Live and Learn," *Camp Fire Girl*, 30, No. 5 (January, 1951), 1.

355 "Mental Health Problems in a Changing World," *Tasmanian Education*, 6, No. 6 (December, 1951), 1-13.

356 "Race Majority—Race Minority." In *The People in Your Life: Psychiatry and Personal Relations by Ten Leading Authorities*, ed. Margaret Hughes. New York: Knopf, 1951, 120-157.

357 "Research in Contemporary Cultures." In *Groups, Leadership and Men*, ed. Harold Guetzkow. Pittsburgh: Carnegie Press, 1951, 106-117.

358 *The School in American Culture*. ("The Inglis Lecture," 1950.)

Cambridge: Harvard University Press, 1951. Reissued 1964.

359 *Soviet Attitudes toward Authority*. New York: McGraw-Hill, 1951.
Reprinted in paperback 1955, New York: Morrow; 1966, New York: Schocken.
Italian edition: *Società e Authorità nell'Unione Sovietica*. Firenze: Nuova Italia, 1956.

360 "The Study of National Character." In *The Policy Sciences: Recent Developments in Scope and Method*, Daniel Lerner and Harold D. Lasswell, eds. Stanford: Stanford University Press, 1951, 70-84.

361 "Teen-Agers in Time of Crisis," *Junior League Magazine*, 39, No. 3 (December, 1951), 2-3.

362 "What Makes the Soviet Character? " *Natural History*, 60, No. 7 (September, 1951), 296-303, 336.

363 (With Frances Cooke Macgregor and photographs by Gregory Bateson.) *Growth and Culture: A Photographic Study of Balinese Childhood*. New York: Putnam, 1951.

364 "A Rejoinder to Jules Henry's Review of *Male and Female*," *American Journal of Orthopsychiatry*, 20, No. 4 (April, 1951), 427-428.

365 Participant in *Problems of Consciousness, Transactions of the Second Conference, March 19-20, 1951*, ed. Harold A. Abramson. New York: Josiah Macy, Jr. Foundation, 1951.

366 Preface to *Song, Dance and Customs of Peasant Poland*, by Sula Benet. New York: Roy, 1951, 11-14.

367 Review of *Birth and Childhood among the Arabs: Studies in a Muhammadan Village in Palestine*, and Review of *Child Problems among the Arabs: Studies in a Muhammadan Village in Palestine*, by Hilma Granquist, *American Anthropologist*, 53, No. 2 (April-June, 1951), 254-255.

368 Review of *The Lonely Crowd*, by David Riesman, *American Journal of Sociology*, 56, No. 5 (1951), 495-497.

369 "Night after Night," review of *Movies: A Psychological Study*, by Martha Wolfenstein and Nathan Leites, *Trans/formation: Arts, Communication, Environment*, 1, No. 2 (1951), 94-96.

1952

370 Editor. (With Heinz von Foerster and Hans Lucas Teuber, eds.) *Cybernetics: Circular Causal and Feedback Mechanisms in*

Biological and Social Systems, Transactions of the Eighth Conference, March 15-16, 1951. New York: Josiah Macy, Jr. Foundation, 1952.

371   "The Anthropological Film: U. S. : Trance and Dance in Bali," *Cinema 16 (Bill of Fare)*, October, 1952.

372   "Child Rearing in Two Primitive Societies," *Journal, Brooklyn State Hospital Psychiatric Forum*, 5, No. 11 (December, 1952), 4-6.

373   "College Education: An American Dowry," *Barnard Alumnae Magazine*, 41, No. 7 (June, 1952), 5.

374   "Family Relationships," *Tasmanian Education*, 7, No. 1 (February, 1952), 28-38.

375   "The Myth That Threatens America." In *Readings in Democracy*, ed. M. David Hoffman. New York: Globe, 1952, 101-105.

376   "A New Control of Destiny." In *This I Believe: The Personal Philosophies of 100 Thoughtful Men and Women in All Walks of Life*. As written for Edward R. Murrow, ed. Edward P. Morgan. New York: Simon and Schuster, 1952, 115-116.

377   "One Aspect of Male and Female." In *Women, Society and Sex*, ed. Johnson E. Fairchild. New York: Sheridan House, 1952, 15-32.

378   "Out of the Things I Read." In *Moments of Personal Discovery*, ed. R. M. MacIver. New York: Harper, 1952, 37-45.

379   "Personality Adjustment in a Changing World," *Tasmanian Education*, 7, No. 1 (February, 1952), 39-49.

380   "Report on an Educational Journey," *New Horizons in Education*, New Ser. , No. 8 (Summer, 1952), 4-23.

381   "Sharing Child Development Insights around the Globe," *Understanding the Child*, 21, No. 4 (October, 1952), 98-103.

382   "Some Relationships between Social Anthropology and Psychiatry." In *Dynamic Psychiatry*, Franz Alexander and Helen Ross, eds. Chicago: University of Chicago Press, 1952, 401-448.

383   Statement, United States House of Representatives, Committee on the Judiciary. *Hearings before the President's Commission on Immigration and Naturalization, September and October, 1952*. 82nd Congress, 2nd Session, 1952, 70-75.

384   Editor. *Studies in Soviet Communication*, 2 vols. Cambridge: Center for International Studies, Massachusetts Institute of Technology, 1952, I. Part 1: "Introduction," 1-34; I. Part 3: "Oral Communication in the Soviet Union," 175-208. (Mimeographed.)

385   "Symposium Summary." In *Symposium on Human Freedoms:*

Proceedings of the Coe College Symposium, Cedar Rapids, Iowa,
March 28-29, 1952. Cedar Rapids: Coe College, 1952, 106-111.

386   "Teacher-Pupil Relationships," *Tasmanian Education*, 7, No. 1
        (February, 1952), 50-61.

387   "Technical Change and Child Development," *Understanding the*
        Child, 21, No. 4 (October, 1952), 109-112.

388   "The Training of the Cultural Anthropologist," *American*
        Anthropologist, 54, No. 3 (July-September, 1952), 343-346.

389   Participant in *Creating an Industrial Civilization: A Report on the*
        Corning Conference, ed. Eugene Staley. New York: Harper, 1952.

390   Participant in *Problems of Consciousness, Transactions of the*
        Third Conference, March 10-11, 1952, ed. Harold A. Abramson.
        New York: Josiah Macy, Jr. Foundation, 1952.

391   Foreword to *The Human Frame*, by Giovanna Lawford.
        New York: Duell, Little, 1952, 9-11.

392   Foreword to *Life Is with People: The Jewish Little-Town of*
        Eastern Europe, by Mark Zborowski and Elizabeth Herzog.
        New York: International Universities Press, 1952, 9-19.

393   Review of *Sex and Marriage*, by Havelock Ellis, *The New York*
        Times Book Review, September 28, 1952, 39.

394   Review of *Patterns of Sexual Behavior*, by Clellan S. Ford and
        Frank A. Beach, *American Anthropologist*, 54, No. 1
        (January-March, 1952), 75-76.

395   Review of *Methods in Structural Linguistics*, by Zellig S. Harris,
        International Journal of American Linguistics, 18, No. 4
        (October, 1952), 257-260.

1953

396   Editor. (With Heinz von Foerster and Hans Lucas Teuber, eds.)
        Cybernetics: Circular Causal and Feedback Mechanisms in
        Biological and Social Systems, Transactions of the Ninth
        Conference, March 20-21, 1952. New York: Josiah Macy, Jr.
        Foundation, 1953.

397   "America and the Intellectuals." In *America and the Intellec-*
        tuals: A Symposium. (PR Series, 4.) New York: Partisan Review,
        1953, 70-75. (Pamphlet.)

398   "Cultural Bases for Understanding Literature," *PMLA*, 68, No. 2

98

(April, 1953), 13-23.

399   Editor. *Cultural Patterns and Technical Change: A Manual Prepared by the World Federation for Mental Health*. Tensions and Technology Series. Paris: UNESCO, 1953.
Reprinted in paperback 1955 (with new preface), Mentor. New York: New American Library.

400   "Enter the European: I—Into the South Pacific," *Beaver* (June, 1953), 4-9.

401   "Expedition to the Admiralty Islands," *Natural History*, 62, No. 7 (September, 1953), 334.

402   "The Impact of Cultural Changes on the Family." In *The Family in the Urban Community: 1953 Spring Lecture Series of the Merrill-Palmer School*, ed. Dorothy Tyler. Detroit: Merrill-Palmer School, 1953, 3-17.

403   "Manus Revisited." In *Papua and New Guinea Scientific Society, Annual Report and Proceedings, Port Moresby, 1953*. Port Moresby: Papua and New Guinea Scientific Society, 1953, 15-18.

404   "Modern Marriage: The Danger Point," *Nation*, 177, No. 18 (October 31, 1953), 348-350.

405   "Modern Youth in a Changing World," *St. Louis Post-Dispatch, 75th Anniversary Supplement* (December 13, 1953), 16.

406   "National Character." In *Anthropology Today: An Encyclopedic Inventory*, ed. A. L. Kroeber. Chicago: University of Chicago Press, 1953, 642-667.

407   Preface to *Coming of Age in Samoa*. Modern Library Books, 126. New York: Random House, 1953.

408   Preface to *Growing Up in New Guinea*. Mentor M91. New York: New American Library, 1953, v-vi.

409   "Sex and Censorship in Contemporary Society." In *New World Writing*. 3rd Mentor Selection, Ms85. New York: New American Library, 1953, 7-24.

410   "Spiritual Issues in the Problem of Birth Control," *Pastoral Psychology*, 4, No. 34 (May, 1953), 39-44.

411   Editor. (With Nicolas Calas, ed.) *Primitive Heritage: An Anthropological Anthology*. New York: Random House, 1953.

English edition: *Primitive Heritage: An Anthropological Anthology*. London: Gollancz, 1954.

412   Editor. (With Rhoda Metraux, ed.) *The Study of Culture at a Distance*. Chicago: University of Chicago Press, 1953.
Paperback edition 1953.

413   (With Arie Querido.) "Mental Health and the Floods in Holland,"
        World Mental Health Bulletin, 5, No. 1 (February, 1953), 34-38.
414   Comment on "Would You Approve Your Child's Marrying a
        Protestant? a Catholic? (Companion Poll)," by Morton
        Sontheimer, *Woman's Home Companion*, 18, No. 3 (March,
        1953), 30.
415   Participant in *An Appraisal of Anthropology Today*, Sol Tax
        and others, eds. Chicago: University of Chicago Press, 1953.
416   Introduction to *The Lost and the Found*, by Robert Collis.
        New York: Woman's Press, 1953, v-vii.
417   Introduction to *Women: The Variety and Meaning of Their Sexual
        Experience*, ed. A. M. Krich. Dell D3. New York: Dell, 1953, 9-24.
418   Review of *The Second Sex*, by Simone de Beauvoir, in a SR Panel
        Review by Six Experts, *Saturday Review*, 36, No. 8 (February 21,
        1953), 30-31.
419   Review of *Faces in the Crowd: Individual Studies in Character
        and Politics*, by David Riesman, *American Quarterly*, 5, No. 1
        (Spring, 1953), 82-84.
420   "Analyzing a Prodigy," review of *Ex-Prodigy: My Childhood and
        Youth*, by Norbert Wiener, *Virginia Quarterly Review*, 29, No. 3
        (Summer, 1953), 438-441.

1954

421   "Cultural Discontinuities and Personality Transformation,"
        Journal of Social Issues, Supplement Series, No. 8 (1954), 3-16.
422   "Family Life Is Changing." In *Encyclopedia of Child Care and
        Guidance*, ed. Sidonie Matsner Gruenberg. New York: Doubleday,
        1954, 675-682.
423   "The Gifted Child in the American Culture of Today," *Journal
        of Teacher Education*, 5, No. 3 (September, 1954), 211-214.
424   "How Fares the American Family? " In *Proceedings, Annual
        Convention, Atlantic City, New Jersey, May 24-26, 1954*.
        ("National Congress of Parents and Teachers, Official Reports
        and Records," 58.) Chicago: National Congress of Parents and
        Teachers, 1954, 58-62.
425   "Manus Restudied: An Interim Report," *Transactions of The
        New York Academy of Sciences*, Ser. 2, 16, No. 8 (June, 1954),
        426-432.
426   "Melanesia 'Black Islands' of the Pacific 'Milky Way,' " *UNESCO*

100

Courier, 7, Nos. 8-9 (1954), 25-31.

427   "The Nicest Way to Live," *McCall's*, 81, No. 11 (August, 1954), 27.

428   "Orchestrating the Cultures of the World," *Delta Kappa Gamma Bulletin*, 21, No. 1 (Fall, 1954), 7.

429   "Robert K. Lamb: 1904-1952," *Human Organization*, 12, No. 4 (May, 1954), 33-37.

430   "Some Theoretical Considerations on the Problem of Mother-Child Separation," *American Journal of Orthopsychiatry*, 24, No. 3 (July, 1954), 471-483.

431   "The Swaddling Hypothesis: Its Reception," *American Anthropologist*, 56, No. 3 (June, 1954), 395-409.

432   "Twenty-fifth Reunion at Manus," *Natural History*, 63, No.2 (February, 1954), 66-68.

433   (With Theodore Schwartz.) "A Brief Description of the Admiralty Islands Expedition," *Clearinghouse Bulletin of Research in Human Organization*, 2, No. 4 (1954), 10.

434   (With Rhoda Metraux.) *Themes in French Culture: A Preface to a Study of French Community*. ("Hoover Institute Studies," Ser. D, Communities No. 1.) Stanford: Stanford University Press, 1954.

435   Introduction to *Men*, ed. A. M. Krich. Dell D15. New York: Dell, 1954, 9-25.

436   Review of *Don't Be Afraid of Your Child*, by Hilde Bruch, *American Journal of Orthopsychiatry*, 24, No. 2 (April, 1954), 426-429.

437   Review of *The African Mind in Health and Disease: A Study in Ethnopsychiatry*, by J. C. Carothers, *Psychiatry*, 17, No. 3 (August, 1954), 303-306.

438   Review of *The Story of Man*, by Carleton S. Coon, *New York Herald Tribune*, December 12, 1954.

439   Review of Film, "The Royal Tour of Elizabeth and Philip," *Natural History*, 63, No. 7 (September, 1954), 333.

1955

440   "Children and Ritual in Bali." In *Childhood in Contemporary Cultures*, Margaret Mead and Martha Wolfenstein, eds. Chicago: University of Chicago Press, 1955, 40-51.

441   "Christian Faith and Technical Assistance," *Christianity and*

Crisis, 14, No. 23 (January 10, 1955), 179-182.

442   "Different Cultural Patterns and Technological Change." In
Mental Health and Infant Development: Proceedings of the Inter-
national Seminar held by the World Federation for Mental
Health at Chichester, England, 2 vols. , ed. Kenneth Soddy.
London: Routledge and Kegan Paul, 1955; New York: Basic
Books, 1956, I, 161-185.

443   "Effects of Anthropological Field Work Models on Inter-
disciplinary Communication in the Study of National Character,"
Journal of Social Issues, 11, No. 2 (May, 1955), 3-11.

444   "Energy Changes under Conditions of Cultural Change,"
Sociometry and the Science of Man, 18, No. 4 (December, 1955),
201-211.

445   "I Can Come Home," *Perfect Home* (November, 1955), 3.

446   "Introduction to the Study of the Case Histories." In *Mental*
Health and Infant Development: Proceedings of the International
Seminar held by the World Federation for Mental Health at
Chichester, England, 2 vols. , ed. Kenneth Soddy. London:
Routledge and Kegan Paul, 1955; New York: Basic Books, 1956,
II, 8-13.

447   "The New Isolationism," *American Scholar*, 24, No. 3 (Summer,
1955), 378-382.

448   Preface to the Mentor edition, *Male and Female*. Mentor, MD150.
New York: New American Library, 1955, v-vii.

449   "Summary." In *Education and Anthropology*, ed. George D.
Spindler. Stanford: Stanford University Press, 1955, 271-280.

450   "What Is Human Nature? " *Look*, 19, No. 8 (April 19, 1955),
56-62.

451   "Why Large Families Are Fashionable Today," *pb*, *The Pocket*
Book Magazine No. 2. New York: Pocket Books, 1955, 31-43.

452   (With Norman Holmes Pearson and Lyman Bryson.) "William
Dean Howells, *The Rise of Silas Lapham*." In *The Invitation to*
Learning Reader: An American Portrait, ed. Ralph Backlund.
New York: Herbert Muschel, 1955, 300-308.

453   Editor. (With Martha Wolfenstein, ed.) *Childhood in Contempo-*
rary Cultures. Chicago: University of Chicago Press, 1955.
Reprinted in paperback 1963, Phoenix Books. Chicago:
University of Chicago Press.
—
Italian edition: *Il mondo del bambino*. Milano: Comunità,
1963.

454   Participant in *Group Processes: Transactions of the First Conference, September 26-30, 1954, Ithaca, New York*, ed. Bertram Schaffner. New York: Josiah Macy, Jr. Foundation, 1955.

455   Participant in *Problems of Consciousness: Transactions of the Fifth Conference, March 22-24, 1954*, ed. Harold A. Abramson. New York: Josiah Macy, Jr. Foundation, 1955.

456   Preface to *The Expression of the Emotions in Man and Animals*, by Charles Darwin. New York: Philosophical Library, 1955, v-vi.

457   Foreword to *Education, the Lost Dimension*, by W. R. Niblett. New York: Morrow, 1955, vii-x.

458   Review of *A Study of Abortion in Primitive Societies*, by George Devereux, *Guide to Psychiatric and Psychological Literature*, 2, No. 2 (October, 1955), 10.

459   Review of *The Lowenfeld Mosaic Test*, by Margaret Lowenfeld, *American Anthropologist*, 57, No. 6 (December, 1955), 1346-1347.

460   Review of *Russian Assignment*, by Leslie C. Steven, *American Anthropologist*, 57, No. 2 (April, 1955), 400-401.

461   (Interviewed by Jane Dennis.) "Desegregation and Growing Up," *Views* (University of Louisville), 111, No. 11 (1955), 11-13.

1956

462   "Applied Anthropology, 1955." In *Some Uses of Anthropology: Theoretical and Applied*, Joseph B. Casagrande and Thomas Gladwin, eds. Washington, D. C. : The Anthropological Society of Washington, 1956, 94-108.

463   "Are You Still in Love," *Family Circle* (April, 1956), 17, 85-87.

464   "Commitment to Field Work." In *Gladys A. Reichard, 1893-1955*. New York: Barnard College, 1956, 22-27.

465   "The Concept of Mental Health and Its International Implications." In *Ninth Annual Report with Proceedings: Mental Health in Home and School, Papers Presented in Berlin, August 1956*. London: World Federation for Mental Health, 1956, 10-13.

466   "The Cross-Cultural Approach to the Study of Personality." In *Psychology of Personality: Six Modern Approaches*, ed. J. L. McCary. New York: Logos Press, 1956, 201-252.

467   *New Lives for Old: Cultural Transformation—Manus, 1928-1953*. New York: Morrow, 1956.

Reprinted in paperback 1961, Mentor. New York: New American
Library: 1966 (with new preface), Apollo Editions. New York:
Morrow; 1968, Laurel Edition. New York: Dell.

English edition: *New Lives for Old*. London: Gollancz, 1956.
Italian edition: *Crescita di una Comunità Primitiva*. Milan:
Bompiani, 1962.
Braille edition: *New Lives for Old*. New York: Recording for the
Blind, 1956.

468   "Nursing–Primitive and Civilized," *American Journal of Nursing*,
       56, No. 8 (August, 1956), 1001-1004.
469   "One Vote for This Age of Anxiety," *The New York Times
       Magazine*, May 20, 1956, 13.
470   "Our Documentary Culture," *American Scholar*, 25, No. 4
       (Autumn, 1956), 401-409.
471   "She Has Strength Based on a Pioneer Past," in special issue,
       "The American Woman: Her Achievements and Troubles,"
       Life, 41, No. 26 (December 24, 1956), 26-27.
472   "Some Uses of Still Photography in Culture and Personality
       Studies." In *Personal Character and Cultural Milieu*, ed. Douglas
       G. Haring, 3rd rev. ed. Syracuse: Syracuse University Press, 1956,
       79-105.
473   "Summing Up Address." In *Ninth Annual Report with Proceedings:
       Mental Health in Home and School, Papers Presented in Berlin,
       August 1956*. London: World Federation for Mental Health, 1956,
       294-298.
474   "Understanding Cultural Patterns," *Nursing Outlook*, 4, No. 5
       (May, 1956), 260-262.
475   "Rejoinder to Omer C. Stewart," *American Anthropologist*, 58,
       No. 3 (June, 1956), 560.
476   Comment "To Help Your Husband Enjoy His Family," in "How
       to Enrich Your Husband's Life," by Mort Weisinger, *Family
       Circle* (January, 1956), 51.
477   Participant in *Discussions on Child Development: A Consideration
       of the Biological, Psychological, and Cultural Approaches to the
       Understanding of Human Development and Behaviour: Proceed-
       ings of the First Meeting of the World Health Organization
       Study Group on the Psychobiological Development of the Child,
       Geneva, 1953*. Vol. 1. J. M. Tanner and Bärbel Inhelder, eds.
       London: Tavistock, 1956; New York: International Universities
       Press, 1957.

478   Participant in *Discussions on Child Development: A Considera-tion of the Biological, Psychological, and Cultural Approaches to the Understanding of Human Development and Behaviour Proceedings of the Second Meeting of the World Health Organ-ization Study Group on the Psychobiological Development of the Child, London, 1954*. Vol. 2. J. M. Tanner and Bärbel Inhelder, eds. London: Tavistock, 1956; New York: International Universities Press, 1957.

479   Participant in *Group Processes: Transactions of the Second Con-ference, October 9-12, 1955, Princeton, N. J.* , ed. Bertram Schaffner. New York: Josiah Macy, Jr. Foundation, 1956.

480   Participant in "The New Frontier: A Review of the Scientific Achievements of 1956." In *At Year's End 1956, CBS Television*. New York: CBS Television, 1956.

481   Foreword to *Mental Health Planning for Social Action*, by George S. Stevenson. New York: McGraw-Hill, 1956, v-vi.

482   Review of *Nine Soviet Portraits*, by Raymond A. Bauer, *American Slavic and East European Review*, 15, No. 2 (April, 1956), 276-277.

483   Review of *The English People on the Eve of Colonization: 1607-1630*, by Wallace Notestein, *American Quarterly*, 8, No. 1 (Spring, 1956), 82-83.

484   Review of *Without the Chrysanthemum and the Sword*, by Jean Stoetzel, *Guide to Psychiatric and Psychological Literature*, 2, Nos. 4-5 (December, 1955-January, 1956), 9.

1957

485   "Adults Can Change Their Habits," *Vogue*, 129, No. 9 (May, 1957), 134-135.

486   "American Man in a Woman's World," *The New York Times Magazine*, February 10, 1957, 11, 20-23.

487   "Breaking the Barriers of Prejudice." In *New Frontiers of Knowledge: A Symposium by Distinguished Writers, Notable Scholars and Public Figures*. Washington: Public Affairs Press, 1957, 30-32.

488   "Changing Patterns of Parent-Child Relations in an Urban Culture," *International Journal of Psycho-Analysis*, 38, Part 6 (1957), 369-378.

489   "Children in American Culture," *National Elementary Principal*,

36, No. 6 (April, 1957), 16-19.

490   "The Development of Responsibility," *Education Summary* (March 5, 1957), 4-5.

491   "The Family: Its Unique Role in Meeting Today's Stress and Strain," *Family Service Highlights*, 18, No. 2 (February, 1957), 17-22.

492   "How Fast Can Men Change? " In *The Empire Club of Canada, Addresses 1956-1957*. Toronto: Empire Club of Canada, 1957, 336-351.

493   "Illness as a Psychological Defense." In *Personal Problems and Psychological Frontiers*, ed. Johnson E. Fairchild. New York: Sheridan House, 1957, 60-78.

494   "The Immortality of Man," *Pastoral Psychology*, 8, No. 75 (June, 1957), 17-22.

495   "The Impact of Automation on Ethics and Culture." In *The Impact of Automation...* Columbus, Ohio: Religion and Labor Foundation, 1957, 20-32. (Pamphlet.)

496   "Mental Health, a Moving Target." In *Steps for Today toward Better Mental Health*, Josephine Nelson and Elizabeth M. Dach, eds. New York: National Health Council, 1957, 12-14.

497   "One Who Is Greater than His Works." In *Why Teach?* ed. D. Louise Sharp. New York: Holt, 1957, 141-143.

498   "The Pattern of Leisure in Contemporary American Culture," *Annals of the American Academy of Political and Social Science*, 313 (September, 1957), 11-15.

499   "Raising Children Who'll Reach for the Moon," *Parents' Magazine*, 32, No. 10 (October, 1957), 44, 182-184.

500   "The Study of Social Evolution," *Proceedings of the Royal Institution of Great Britain*, 36, No. 164 (1957), 1-3, 7.

501   "Towards More Vivid Utopias," *Science*, 126, No. 3280 (November 8, 1957), 957-961.

502   "Values for Urban Living," *Annals of the American Academy of Political and Social Science*, 314 (November, 1957), 10-14.

503   "The Worm of Self-Consciousness in American Culture," *Advertising Age*, 28, No. 10 (March 11, 1957), 71-72, 74.

504   (With Rhoda Metraux.) "Image of the Scientist among High-School Students: A Pilot Study," *Science*, 126, No. 3270 (August 30, 1957), 384-390.

505   Participant in *Group Processes: Transactions of the Third Conference, October 7-10, 1956, Princeton, N. J. *, ed. Bertram Schaffner. New York: Josiah Macy, Jr. Foundation, 1957.

506   Foreword to *Annual Report of the World Federation for Mental Health, 1957*. London: World Federation for Mental Health, 1957, 8-9.

507   Preface to *The Twice-Born: A Study of a Community of High-Caste Hindus*, by G. Morris Carstairs. London: Hogarth, 1957, 5.

508   Review of *The American Woman*, by Eric John Dingwall, *New York Herald Tribune Book Review*, May 26, 1957, 10.

509   Review of *Sexual Behavior in American Society: An Appraisal of the First Two Kinsey Reports*, J. Himelhoch and S. F. Fava, eds. , *American Anthropologist*, 59, No. 2 (April, 1957), 383-384.

510   Review of *The American Teenager*, by H. H. Remmers and D. A. Radler, *New York Herald Tribune Book Review*, June 30, 1957, 5.

511   Review of *The Curve of the Snowflake*, by W. Gray Walter, *American Scholar*, 26, No. 2 (Spring, 1957), 261.

1958

512   "The Anthropologist Looks at Architecture," *AIA, Journal of the American Institute of Architects*, 30, No. 2 (August, 1958), 73-79.

513   "Anthropology." In *It Happened in 1957: The 1958 Compton Yearbook*. Chicago: Compton, 1958, 183.

514   "Changing Teacher in a Changing World." In *The Education of Teachers: New Perspectives, Official Report, Second Bowling Green Conference, June 24-28, 1958*. Washington: National Education Association of the United States, 1958, 121-134.

515   "Comment on 'Germany's New Flagellants,' " *American Scholar*, 27, No. 2 (Spring, 1958), 178-181.

516   "Cultural Determinants of Behavior." In *Behavior and Evolution*, Ann Roe and George Gaylord Simpson, eds. New Haven: Yale University Press, 1958, 480-503.

517   "The Dangerous Godless Brain," *Look*, 22, No. 2 (January 21, 1958), 20-27.

518   "Do Women Like Other Women? " *Chatelaine*, 31, No. 8 (August, 1958), 13, 56-58.

519   "The False Position of the Working Wife," *Chatelaine*, 31, No. 6 (June, 1958), 62-63.

520   "The Group as the Unit of Social Evolution," *Man*, 58, Art. 233 (November, 1958), 178.

521   "Growing Up in Different Cultures." In *Growing Up in a Changing*

World: Papers Presented at the Tenth Annual Meeting of the World Federation for Mental Health, Copenhagen, Denmark, August 1957. London: World Federation for Mental Health, 1958, 7-14.

522 "His Family Looks at the Businessman," *Alumni Newsletter* (Graduate School of Business of Columbia University) (January, 1958) .

523 *Israel and Problems of Identity.* ("Herzl Institute Pamphlets," 3.) New York: Theodor Herzl Foundation, 1958. (Pamphlet.)

524 "A Meta Conference: Eastbourne, 1956," *ETC.* , 15, No. 2 (March, 1958), 148-151.

525 "A New Look at Your Food Habits," *Parade* (February 23, 1958), 6.

526 "A Social Scientist Looks at Advertising Research." In *Advertising Research: Is It Time for an Agonizing Reappraisal?* New York: American Association of Advertising Agencies, 1958, 13-19. (Offset.)

527 "Why Is Education Obsolete," *Harvard Business Review*, 36, No. 6 (November-December, 1958), 23-36, 164-170.

528 (With Donald N. Michael, Harold D. Lasswell, and Lawrence K. Frank.) "Man in Space: A Tool and Program for the Study of Social Change," *Annals of The New York Academy of Sciences*, 72, Art. 4 (April 10, 1958), 165-214.

529 "Comments in Brief." In *American Education*, ed. Bower Aly. ("The Thirty-second Discussion and Debate Manual, I, 1958-1959.") Columbia, Missouri: Lucas Brothers, 1958, 94.

530 Participant in *Discussions on Child Development: A Consideration of the Biological, Psychological, and Cultural Approaches to the Understanding of Human Development and Behaviour: Proceedings of the Third Meeting of the World Health Organization Study Group on the Psychological Development of the Child, Geneva, 1955,*Vol. 3. J. M. Tanner and Bärbel Inhelder, eds. London: Tavistock; New York: International Universities Press, 1958.

531 Response to George F. J. LaMountain, in "The Reader Replies," *American Scholar*, 27, No. 3 (Summer, 1958), 400.

532 Review of *Free Society and Moral Crisis*, by Robert C. Angell, *The New York Times Book Review*, November 23, 1958, 44.

533 Review of *Elite Communication in Samoa: A Study of Leadership*, by Felix M. Keesing and Marie M. Keesing, *American Anthropologist*, 60, No. 6 (December, 1958), 1233-1234.

534   Review of *Algeria: The Realities*, by Germaine Tillion, *Science*, 128, No. 3328 (October 10, 1958), 835.

535   (Interviewed by Henry Brandon.) "A New Form of Escapism—Escape into Private Life," *New Republic*, 138, No. 25 (June 23, 1958), 14-17.

1959

536   "The American Family." In *The Search for America*, ed. Huston Smith. Englewood Cliffs, N. J. : Prentice-Hall, 1959, 116-122.

537   *An Anthropologist at Work: Writings of Ruth Benedict.* Boston: Houghton Mifflin, 1959.
       Reprinted in paperback 1966, Atheling Book. New York: Atherton Press; 1973, Equinox Books. New York: Avon.

538   "Apprenticeship under Boas." In *The Anthropology of Franz Boas*, ed. Walter Goldschmidt. ("Memoirs of the American Anthropological Association," 89.) *American Anthropologist*, 61, No. 5, Part 2 (October, 1959), 29-45.

539   "Bali in the Market Place of the World," *Proceedings of the American Academy of Arts and Letters and the National Institute of Arts and Letters*, Ser. 2, No. 9 (1959), 286-293.

540   "Bringing Up Children in the Space Age," *Space Digest*, 2, No. 2, in *Air Force and Space Digest*, 42, No. 2 (February, 1959), 71-73.

541   "Changing Culture: Some Observations in Primitive Societies." In *The Human Meaning of the Social Sciences*, ed. Daniel Lerner. Meridian M64. New York: Meridian, 1959, 285-307.

542   "The Climate of Opinion Necessary for Science." In *The Scientific Revolution: Challenge and Promise*, Gerald W. Elbers and Paul Duncan, eds. Washington: Public Affairs Press, 1959, 139-147.

543   "Closing the Gap between the Scientists and the Others," *Daedalus* (Winter, 1959), 139-146.

544   "Creativity in Cross-Cultural Perspective." In *Creativity and Its Cultivation*, ed. Harold H. Anderson. New York and Evanston: Harper and Row, 1959, 222-235.

545   "Culture Change and the Student." In *The Student and Mental Health, an International View: Proceedings of the First International Conference on Student Mental Health, Princeton, N. J. ,*

September 5-15, 1956, ed. Daniel H. Funkenstein. Cambridge: Riverside Press, 1959, 143-154; discussion, 154-163.

546 "Cultural Contexts of Puberty and Adolescence," *Bulletin of the Philadelphia Association for Psychoanalysis*, 9, No. 3 (September, 1959), 59-79.

547 "Cultural Factors in Community-Education Programs." In *Community Education: Principles and Practices from World-Wide Experience*, ed. Nelson B. Henry. ("Fifty-eighth Yearbook of the National Society for the Study of Education," Part 1.) Chicago: University of Chicago Press, 1959, 66-96.

548 "Discussion of the Symposium Papers," in "Urbanization and Standard Language: A Symposium Presented at the 1958 Meetings of the American Anthropological Association," *Anthropological Linguistics*, 1, No. 3 (March, 1959), 32-33.

549 "Feral Children and Autistic Children," *American Journal of Sociology*, 65, No. 1 (July, 1959), 75. (Letter to the editor.)

550 "God's Help." In *A New Treasury of Words to Live By*, ed. William Nichols. New York: Simon and Schuster, 1959, 174-175.

551 "Independent Religious Movements," *Comparative Studies in Society and History*, 1, No. 4 (June, 1959), 324-329.

552 "Is Our Picture of the Scientist Fair? " *Current Science and Aviation*, 44, No. 23 (March 9-13, 1959), 179-181.

553 "Job of the Children's Mother's Husband," *The New York Times Magazine*, May 10, 1959, 7, 66-67.

554 "A Letter from Margaret Mead," *Menninger Quarterly*, 13, No. 2 (Summer, 1959), 12-17.

555 "Mental Health in World Perspective." In *Culture and Mental Health*, ed. Marvin K. Opler. New York: Macmillan, 1959, 501-516.

556 "A New Kind of Discipline," *Parents' Magazine*, 34, No. 9 (September, 1959), 50-51, 86-87.

557 *People and Places*. Cleveland and New York: World Publishing, 1959. Reprinted in paperback 1963, Bantam Pathfinder. New York: Bantam.

—

Canadian edition: *People and Places*. Canada: Nelson, Foster, and Scott, 1959.
Dutch edition: *Verre Volken van Nabij*. Utrecht: Prisma-Boeken, 1965.
Hebrew edition: Tel Aviv: 3N, 1959.
Lebanese edition: Beirut: USIS, 1964.

558 "Possible Approaches to the Project on Men and Women in South and Southeast Asia." Part II of *A Background Paper on Men and Women in South and Southeast Asia, Based on Studies of Family Life in Various Asian Countries*, prepared by Margaret Mead through The Institute for Intercultural Studies on behalf of the World Federation for Mental Health for the Department of Social Sciences of the United Nations Educational Scientific and Cultural Organization, February, 1959. (Mimeographed.)

559 "A Redefinition of Education," *NEA Journal*, 48, No. 7 (October, 1959), 15-17.

560 "Research: Cult or Cure?" in "Approaches to Research in Mental Retardation," *American Journal of Mental Deficiency*, 64, No. 2 (September, 1959), 253-263; discussion, 263-264.

561 "The Significance of the Individual," *What's New*, No. 215 (Christmas, 1959), 2-7.

562 "Violence and Your Child," *T. V. Guide*, 7, No. 12 (March 21, 1959), 17-19.

563 "Who Are the World's Best Fathers? " *New York Herald Tribune This Week Magazine*, June 21, 1959, 12, 15, 18.

564 "Reply to Kardiner," *Science*, 130, No. 3391 (December 25, 1959), 1728-1732.

565 "Ruth Benedict," *Science*, 129, No. 3362 (June 5, 1959), 1514.

566 Participant in *Group Processes: Transactions of the Fourth Conference, October 13-16, 1957, Princeton, N. J. *, ed. Bertram Schaffner. New York: Josiah Macy, Jr. Foundation, 1959.

567 Foreword to *Race: Science and Politics*, by Ruth Benedict. Compass Books, C42. New York: Viking, 1959, vii-xi.

568 Introduction to *Premarital Dating Behavior*, by Winston Ehrmann. New York: Holt, 1959, xii-xiii.

569 Review of *The Patient Speaks*, by Harold A. Abramson, *Psychoanalysis and the Psychoanalytic Review*, 46, No. 2 (Summer, 1959), 126-127.

570 Review of *Social Change in the South Pacific: Raratonga and Aitutaki*, by Ernest Beaglehole, *Pacific Affairs*, 32, No. 2 (June, 1959), 229-230.

571 Review of *The Silent Language*, by Edward T. Hall, *New York Herald Tribune Book Review*, May 10, 1959, 13.

572 Review of *Children of the Kibbutz*, by Melford E. Spiro, *American Anthropologist*, 61, No. 4 (August, 1959), 697-699.

573 Review of *Race: Individual and Collective Behavior*, Edgar T. Thompson and Everett C. Hughes, eds. *American Journal of Sociology*, 65, No. 1 (July, 1959), 110-112.

1960

574   (With Lyman Bryson, Rudolf Arnheim, and Milton Nahm.)
       "The Conditions for Creativity." In *The Creative Mind and Method*,
       Jack D. Summerfield and Lorlyn Thatcher, eds. Austin: Univer-
       sity of Texas Press, 1960, 105-111.

575   "America's Many Faces," in "America, His Hope, His Future...,"
       Special Supplement Prepared by the National Urban League,
       The New York Times, Sec. 10, January 17, 1960, 2.

576   "Anthropology as Part of a Liberal Education." Background
       paper prepared for the Wenner-Gren Education Conference,
       "Teaching of Anthropology," August 9-16, 1960, Burg
       Wartenstein, Austria. (Mimeographed.)

577   "Are We Squeezing Out Adolescence? " *National Parent Teacher*,
       55, No. 1 (September, 1960), 4-6.

578   "The Changing American Food Pattern," *Living for Young Home-
       makers* (October, 1960), 140-141, 161-165.

579   "Cherishing the Life of the World," *Pastoral Psychology*, 11, No.
       104 (May, 1960), 10-11.

580   "The Contemporary Challenge to Education," *Fundamental and
       Adult Education* (UNESCO), 12, No. 3 (1960), 105-112.

581   "The Contribution of Cultural Anthropology to Nutrition."
       Background paper prepared for the Conference on Malnutrition
       and Food Habits, Cuernavaca, Mexico, 9-14 September, 1960.
       (Manuscript.)

582   "Cultural Contexts of Nursing Problems." In *Social Science in
       Nursing*, ed. Frances Cooke Macgregor. New York: Russell Sage
       Foundation, 1960, 74-88.

583   "Cultural Patterns and the American Diet," *School Lunch Journal*,
       14, No. 8 (October, 1960), 20-22.

584   "The Cultural Perspective." In *Communication or Conflict:
       Conferences: Their Nature, Dynamics and Planning*, ed. Mary
       Capes. London: Tavistock, 1960, 9-18.

585   "Epilogue." In *Reality and Vision: Report of the First Asian
       Seminar on Mental Health and Family Life, Baguio, Philippines,
       6-20 December 1958*, by Tsung-Yi Lin; Margarethe Stepan,
       Tsung-Yi Lin, and the Seminar Staff, eds. Manila: Bureau of
       Printing, 1960, 77-79.

586   "Growing Pains," *Every Week*, 26, No. 21 (February 29-March 4,
       1960), 163; *Current Events*, 59, No. 21 (February 29-March 4,
       1960), 163.

587   "High School of the Future," *California Journal of Secondary Education*, 35 (October, 1960), 360-369.

588   "I'm Sick of Being Shocked," *New York Herald Tribune This Week Magazine*, November 20, 1960, 8-9.

589   "Is College Compatible with Marriage? " Syndicated article written for Editorial Projects for Education, Inc. , and published in various Alumni magazines across the United States in 1960.

590   "John R. Rees," *International Mental Health Research Newsletter*, Nos. 1 and 2 (June, 1960), 1, 2.

591   "Mealtime: A Tradition of Family Sharing," *Family Circle*, 56, No. 1 (January, 1960), 19, 66-69.

592   "The Modern Study of Mankind." In *An Outline of Man's Knowledge of the Modern World*, ed. Lyman Bryson. New York: McGraw-Hill, 1960, 322-341.

593   "A New Framework for Studies of Folklore and Survivals." In *Men and Cultures: Selected Papers of the Fifth International Congress of Anthropological and Ethnological Sciences, Philadelphia, September 1-9, 1956*, ed. Anthony F. C. Wallace. Philadelphia: University of Pennsylvania Press, 1960, 168-174.

594   "New Thoughts on Old People," *Council Woman*, 22, No. 4 (October, 1960), 4-5.

595   "The Newest Battle of the Sexes," *Space Digest*, 3, No. 7, in *Air Force and Space Digest*, 43, No. 7 (July, 1960), 77-86.

596   "Problems of Cultural Acommodation in Israel." In *Assignment in Israel*, ed. Bernard Mandelbaum. New York: Harper, 1960, 99-114.

597   "Problems of the Late Adolescent and Young Adult." In *Children and Youth in the 1960's: Survey Papers Prepared for the 1960 White House Conference on Children and Youth*. Washington, D. C. : Golden Anniversary White House Conference on Children and Youth, 1960, 3-12.

598   "The Secret of Completeness," in "Symposium: The Gift of Self," *Good Housekeeping Magazine*, 150, No. 5 (May, 1960), 72, 157-162.

599   Statement of Margaret Mead, Ph.D. , Anthropologist. *The U. S. Government and the Future of International Medical Research. Hearings before the Subcommittee on Reorganization and International Organizations of the Committee on Government Operations, United States Senate, July 9 and 16, 1959*. 86th Congress, First Session. Washington, D. C. : Government Printing Office, 1960, 68-81.

600   *The Study of Cultures*. Washington, D. C. : Industrial College of
        the Armed Forces, Publication No. L60-65, 1960, 1-25.
        (Mimeographed pamphlet.)
601   "Weaver of the Border." In *In the Company of Man*, ed. Joseph
        B. Casagrande. New York: Harper, 1960, 175-210.
602   "What Makes Women Unhappy? " *Chatelaine*, 33, No. 3 (March,
        1960), 25, 44, 46, 47-48.
603   "Where Do We Live in Time? " *Grade Teacher*, 78, No. 1
        (September, 1960), 12, 92.
604   "Woman in Society," *Way Forum* (Brussels), No. 38 (December,
        1960), 5-9.
605   "Work, Leisure and Creativity," in special issue, "The Visual
        Arts Today," *Daedalus* (Winter, 1960), 13-23.
606   Editor. (With Ruth L. Bunzel, ed.) *The Golden Age of American
        Anthropology*. New York: Braziller, 1960.
607   (With Theodore Schwartz.) "The Cult as a Condensed Social
        Process." In *Group Processes: Transcations of the Fifth Confer-
        ence, October 12-15, 1958*, ed. Bertram Schaffner. New York:
        Josiah Macy, Jr. Foundation, 1960, 85-187.
608   (With Edward Berkowitz.) "Maturity, Mind, & Money: An
        Exchange," *Columbia University Forum*, 3, No. 4 (Fall, 1960),
        52-53.
609   Comment on "If You Had Several Billion Dollars...." In *1960
        Encyclopedia Yearbook: The Story of Our Time*. New York:
        Grolier, 1960, 315, 318.
610   Participant in *Discussions on Child Development: A Considera-
        tion of the Biological, Psychological, and Cultural Approaches
        to the Understanding of Human Development and Behaviour:
        Proceedings of the Fourth Meeting of the World Health Organi-
        zation Study Group on the Psychobiological Development of
        the Child, Geneva, 1956*, Vol. 4, J. M. Tanner and Bärbel
        Inhelder, eds. London: Tavistock; New York: International
        Universities Press, 1960.
611   Moderator of panel on "The Place of Mental Health in the
        Planning of Immigration Programmes." In *Uprooting and
        Resettlement: Eleventh Annual Meeting of the World Fed-
        eration for Mental Health, Vienna, Austria, August, 1958*.
        London: World Federation for Mental Health, 1960, 77-96.
612   Participant in panel discussion, "The Social Environment." In
        Man's Contracting World in an Expanding Universe, ed. Ben H.
        Bagdikian. Providence, Rhode Island: Brown University, 1960,
        90-101.

613   Participant in "Science and Human Welfare," *Science*, 132, No. 3419 (July, 1960), 68-73.

614   Preface to *Trance in Bali*, by Jane Belo. New York: Columbia University Press, 1960, v-vi.

615   Foreword to *A Punjabi Village in Pakistan*, by Zekiye Eglar. New York: Columbia University Press, 1960, ix-x.

616   Introduction to *The Golden Age of American Anthropology*, Margaret Mead and Ruth L. Bunzel, eds. New York: Braziller, 1960, 1-12.

617   "Anthropology and Archeology," in "Outstanding Selected Paperbacks," *Paperback Review* (October, 1960), 9.

618   (Interviewed by Lester and Irene David.) "American Husbands Are Too Domestic! " *Family Weekly* (August 14, 1960), 1.

1961

619   "Anthropology among the Sciences," *American Anthropologist*, 63, No. 3 (June, 1961), 475-482.

620   "Are Shelters the Answer? " *The New York Times Magazine*, November 26, 1961, 29, 124-126.

621   "Are We Neglecting the Social Sciences? " *Science Digest*, 50, No. 6 (December, 1961), 97, 80.

622   "Continuing Our Present System Isn't Enough." In *Today and Tomorrow: Three Essays on Adult Education in the Future*. Chicago: Center for the Study of Liberal Education for Adults, 1961, 34-38.

623   "Cultural Determinants," *American Journal of Public Health*, 51, No. 10 (October, 1961), 1552-1554.

624   "Cultural Determinants of Sexual Behavior." In *Sex and Internal Secretions*, 2 vols. , 3rd ed. , ed. William C. Young. Baltimore: Williams and Wilkins, 1961, 2, 1433-1479.

625   "Gender in the Honors Program," *(ICSS) Superior Student*, 4, No. 4 (May, 1961), 2-6.

626   "How You Can Help Your Child Develop a Sense of Responsibility," *Parents' Magazine*, 36, No. 5 (May, 1961), 35, 99-101.

627   "The Human Study of Human Beings," *Science*, 133, No. 3447 (January 20, 1961), 163.

628   "The Menninger Foundation: A Center of Innovation," *Menninger Quarterly*, 15, No. 1 (1961), 1-5.

629   "National Character and the Science of Anthropology." In
       *Culture and Social Character: The Work of David Riesman
       Reviewed*, Seymour M. Lipset and Leo Lowenthal, eds. New York:
       Free Press of Glencoe, 1961, 15-26.
630   "New Inventions for Survival," *NEA Journal (Journal of the
       National Education Association)*, 50, No. 8 (November, 1961),
       11-13.
631   "Old Traditions Can Help Young Moderns," *Parents' Magazine*,
       36, No. 9 (September, 1961), 50-51, 131, 133.
632   "Perspective on Technology, 2: Learning's Long, Long Road,"
       Technology and the Teacher, 7, No. 4 (December, 1961), 3.
633   "Preface 1961 edition." *Coming of Age in Samoa*. Apollo
       Editions, A-30. New York: Morrow, 1961, unpaged.
634   "Preface to the Beacon Press edition." *Cooperation and Compe-
       tition among Primitive Peoples*, ed. Margaret Mead. BP 123.
       Boston: Beacon, 1961.
635   "Psychiatry and Ethnology." In *Psychiatrie der Gegenwart:
       Forschung und Praxis*, III: *Soziale und Angewandte Psychiatrie*,
       H. W. Gruhle and others, eds. Berlin, Göttingen, Heidelberg:
       Springer, 1961, 452-470.
636   "Questions That Need Asking," *Teachers College Record*
       (Columbia University), 63, No. 2 (November, 1961), 89-93.
637   Report on the Preparation of Play Materials for International
       Use. The World Federation for Mental Health, United Nations,
       Bureau of Social Affairs, United Nations Children's Fund.
       December 20, 1961. (Mimeographed.)
638   "The Social Sciences in the College of Liberal Arts and Sciences."
       In *The College of Liberal Arts and Sciences–Its Role in the 1960's*.
       Minneapolis, Minnesota: Lutheran Brotherhood Insurance Society,
       1961, 11-15. (Pamphlet.)
639   "Some Anthropological Considerations Concerning Natural Law,"
       Natural Law Forum, 6 (1961), 51-64.
640   "They Learn from Living Things," *Parents' Magazine*, 36, No. 2
       (February, 1961), 48, 82-84.
641   "We're Robbing Our Children," *AP Newsfeature*, May 21, 1961.
642   *Women's Role in Today's World*. New York: National Council,
       1961, 3-12. (Pamphlet.)
643   "Youth Is a Time," *Boys' Life* (September, 1961), 17, 52.
644   (With Theodore Schwartz.) "Micro- and Macro-cultural Models
       for Cultural Evolution," *Anthropological Linguistics*, 3, No. 1
       (January, 1961), 1-7.

645   (With Margaret Truman.) "Margaret Truman and Margaret Mead Talk about Their Childhood, Their Children, Early Marriages, Working Mothers–and the Problem of Having Famous Parents," *Redbook Magazine*, 116, No. 3 (January, 1961), 30-33, 77-81.

646   "Are We Overworking the Holiday Spirit," *Redbook Magazine*, 118, No. 2 (December, 1961), 29, 99.

647   Comment on "How Do You Feel about Man's Attempt to Conquer Outer Space?" In *1961 Encyclopedia Yearbook: The Story of Our Time*. New York: Grolier, 1961, 43-44.

648   Comment, "I would choose *Childhood and Society*...," in "Outstanding Books, 1931-1961," *American Scholar*, 30, No. 4 (Autumn, 1961), 614-615.

649   "The Institute for Intercultural Studies and Japanese Studies," *American Anthropologist*, 63, No. 1 (January, 1961), 136-137. (Letter to the editor.)

650   " 'Thorny Issue,' " *European Herald Tribune*, August 29, 1961, 6. (Letter to the editor.)

651   Participant in *Identity; Mental Health and Value Systems*, ed. Kenneth Soddy. ("Cross-Cultural Studies in Mental Health.") London: Tavistock, 1961.

652   Participant in *Mental Health in International Perspective: A Review Made in 1961 by an International and Interprofessional Study Group*. London: World Federation for Mental Health, 1961.

653   Participant in "Science and Human Survival," *Science*, 134, No. 3496 (December 29, 1961), 2080-2083.

654   "A New Preface." *Patterns of Culture*, by Ruth Benedict. Sentry, SE 8. Boston: Houghton Mifflin, 1961, vii-x.

655   Preface to *Family Life Plays*, by Nora Stirling. New York: Association Press, 1961, vii-viii.

656   Review of *Symposium on Evolution*, by Frederick C. Bawden, Gottfried O. Lang, Andrew G. van Melsen and Cyril Vollert; and review of *Evolution and Christian Thought Today*, ed. Russell L. Mixter, *American Anthropologist*, 63, No. 2 (April, 1961), 395-396.

657   Review of *Becoming More Civilized*, by Leonard W. Doob, *Science*, 133, No. 3463 (May 12, 1961), 1471-1472.

658   Review of *Bali: Studies in Life, Thought and Ritual*, by H. J. Franken and others, *American Anthropologist*, 63, No. 5 (October, 1961), 117-118.

659   Review of *Amerika Samoa*, by John A. C. Gray, *Annals of the American Academy of Political and Social Science*, 334 (March,

1961), 173.

660 Review of *The Child Buyer*, by John Hersey, *Science*, 133, No. 3452 (February 24, 1961), 573.

661 Review of *Ta'u: Stability and Change in a Samoan Village*, by Lowell D. Holmes, *American Anthropologist*, 63, No. 2 (April, 1961), 428-430.

662 Review of *New Men of Papua*, by Robert F. Maher, *American Journal of Sociology*, 67, No. 2 (September, 1961), 233-235.

663 Review of *Summerhill: A Radical Approach to Child Rearing*, by A. S. Neill, *American Sociological Review*, 26, No. 3 (June, 1961), 504.

664 Review of *And the Poor Get Children: Sex, Contraception, and Family Planning in the Working Class*, by Lee Rainwater and Karol Weinstein, *American Anthropologist*, 63, No. 2 (April, 1961), 458-459.

665 (Interviewed by William Mitchell.) In *Wisdom for Our Time*, ed. James Nelson. New York: Norton, 1961, 65-75.

1962

666 "Brushes of Comets' Hair," *Menninger Quarterly*, 16, No. 2 (Summer, 1962), 1-5.

667 "Building Communities for the Builders of Tomorrow." In *Research and the Community*. Albany: State of New York, Department of Commerce, 1962, 47-54.

668 "The Challenge of Man." In "The Challenge of Tomorrow, Fifth International Food Congress," *Encore* (Autumn, 1962), 16-23.

669 "A Chill of Recognition," in "The Books I Can't Ever Forget," *Seventeen* (April, 1962), 151.

670 *A Creative Life for Your Children*. ("Children's Bureau Headliner Series," No. 1.) Washington, D. C. : U. S. Department of Health, Education, and Welfare, 1962.

671 "A Cultural Anthropologist's Approach to Maternal Deprivation." In *Deprivation of Maternal Care: A Reassessment of its Effects*. ("Public Health Papers," 14.) Geneva: World Health Organization, 1962, 45-62.

672 "A Force that Can Change the Nature of Society," *T V Guide*, 10, No. 10, Issue 467 (March 10, 1962), 8-11.

673 "Introduction to the Pelican edition: Fifteen Years Later."

Male and Female. A575. Harmondsworth, Middlesex: Penguin, 1962, 11-24.

674   "Mental Health and the Wider World," *American Journal of Orthopsychiatry*, 32, No. 1 (January, 1962), 1-4.

675   "More than a Manhattan Project," *Peace Opportunities*, 1, No. 3 (May, 1962), 2.

676   "Must Capitalism Crawl? " *Harvard Business Review*, 40, No. 6 (November-December, 1962), 6-19, 171-172.

677   "Outdoor Recreation in the Context of Emerging American Cultural Values." In *Trends in American Living and Outdoor Recreation*. ("Reports to the Outdoor Recreation Resources Review Commission," No. 22.) Washington, D. C. : U. S. Government Printing Office, 1962, 2-25.

678   "Patriotism Redefined," *Parents' Magazine*, 37, No. 9 (September, 1962), 52-53, 112-116.

679   "Preface to the Apollo edition." *Growing Up in New Guinea*. Apollo Editions. A58. New York: Morrow, 1962, iii-viii.

680   "Reply to Rajkumari Amrit Kaur." In *Proceedings of the Sixth International Congress on Mental Health, August 30-September 5, 1961, Paris, France*. ("International Congress Series," No. 45.) Amsterdam: Exerpta Medica Foundation, 1962, 42-43. (Abstract.)

681   "Retrospects and Prospects." In *Anthropology and Human Behavior*, Thomas Gladwin and William C. Sturtevant, eds. Washington, D. C. : The Anthropological Society of Washington, 1962, 115-149.

682   "The Social Responsibility of the Anthropologist," *Journal of Higher Education*, 33, No. 1 (January, 1962), 1-12.

683   "The Underdeveloped and the Overdeveloped," *Foreign Affairs*, 41, No. 1 (October, 1962), 78-89.

684   "What Makes College Kids Cut Up? " *Family Weekly* (April 22, 1962), 2.

685   "What Shall We Tell Our Children about Race? " In *Called Confronted Compelled*. ("Program Book, September 1962-August 1963, Woman's Societies of Christian Service, Wesleyan Service Guilds.") Cincinnati: Woman's Division of Christian Service Board of Missions, The Methodist Church, 1962, 133-140.

686   "Where Education Fits In," *Think*, 28, No. 10 (November-December, 1962), 16-22.

687   "Your Accident of Birth," in "The Human Comedy," *Cosmopolitan*, 153, No. 4 (October, 1962), 45-50.

688   "Is College Wasted on Women? " *Redbook Magazine*, 118, No. 3 (January, 1962), 6.

689 "A New Kind of First Lady," *Redbook Magazine*, 118, No. 4 (February, 1962), 8, 10.

690 "Must Our Children Fear the Future? " *Redbook Magazine*, 118, No. 5 (March, 1962), 6.

691 "What's the Matter with Children's Books? " *Redbook Magazine*, 118, No. 6 (April, 1962), 30, 33.

692 "What Does the American Man Expect of a Wife? " *Redbook Magazine*, 119, No. 1 (May, 1962), 28, 30.

693 "Why Not Pay Students to Go to College? " *Redbook Magazine*, 119, No. 2 (June, 1962), 26, 28.

694 "The Price We Pay for Democracy," *Redbook Magazine*, 119, No. 4 (August, 1962), 6, 8.

695 "Whatever Happened to the People Next Door? " *Redbook Magazine*, 119, No. 5 (September, 1962), 26, 28.

696 "Sex on the Campus: The Real Issue," *Redbook Magazine*, 119, No. 6 (October, 1962), 6, 8.

697 "Wanted: Perfect Babies Only," *Redbook Magazine*, 120, No. 1 (November, 1962), 56, 58.

698 "Peacekeeping: What Every Woman Knows," *Redbook Magazine*, 120, No. 2 (December, 1962), 30, 32.

699 Comment in "Christmas in Crisis," *Look*, 26, No. 27 (December 31, 1962), 16.

700 "For Moment of Silence," *The New York Times*, July 5, 1962, 24. (Letter to the editor.)

701 "Inaugurate Was Meant," *The New York Times*, November 1, 1962. (Letter to the editor.)

702 In "More on (Paul) Goodman." *Commentary*, 34, No. 5 (November, 1962), 446-447. (Letter to the editor.)

703 "No Victory in Nuclear War," *The New York Times*, October 30, 1962, 34. (Letter to the editor.)

704 "Reply to Comment by Suggs and Carr," *Fellow Newsletter: American Anthropological Association*, 3, No. 7 (September, 1962), 4.

705 Participant in *Malnutrition and Food Habits: Report of an International and Interprofessional Conference*, Anne Burgess and R. F. A. Dean, eds. London: Tavistock, 1962.

706 Introduction to *American Women: The Changing Image*, ed. Beverly B. Cassara. Boston: Beacon, 1962, ix-xv.

707 Introduction to *Specials for Women*, by George Lefferts. New York: Avon, 1962, ix-xvii.

708 Review of *Maori Youth*, by David P. Ausubel, *Mental Hygiene*,

46, No. 4 (October, 1962), 656.

709   Review of *National Character and National Stereotypes: A Trend Report Prepared for the International Union of Scientific Philosophy*, by H. C. J. Duijker and N. H. Frijda, *American Anthropologist*, 64, No. 3 (June, 1962), 688-690.

710   Review of *Psychological Anthropology: Approaches to Culture and Personality*, ed. Francis L. K. Hsu, *American Anthropologist*, 64, No. 3 (June, 1962), 627-630.

711   "For Fifteen Dollars: A Shelf of Archaeology and Anthropology," *New York Herald Tribune Book Review, Paperback Section*, January 14, 1962, 24.

1963

712   "Aging Differently in the Space Age." In *Proceedings of the Second Annual Governor's Conference on Aging*. Albany: New York State Office for the Aging, 1963, 3-13. (Offset.)

713   "Anthropology and the Camera." In *The Encyclopedia of Photography*, ed. Willard D. Morgan. New York: Greystone, 1963, I, 166-184.

714   "Anthropology and an Education for the Future." In *The Teaching of Anthropology*, 2 vols., David G. Mandelbaum, Gabriel W. Lasker and Ethel M. Albert, eds. Berkeley and Los Angeles: University of California Press, 1963, I, 595-607.

715   "The Bark Paintings of the Mountain Arapesh of New Guinea." In *Technique and Personality in Primitive Art*. ("Museum of Primitive Art Lecture Series," 3.) New York: The Museum of Primitive Art, 1963, 8-43.

716   "Beyond the Nuclear Family." In *The Future of the American Family: Dream and Reality*. New York: Better Homes & Gardens for Child Study Association of America, 1963, 13-17. (Pamphlet; mimeographed.)

717   "Continuities in Communication." In *VIe Congrès International des Sciences Anthropologiques et Ethnologiques, Paris, 30 juillet-6 août 1960*, Tome II: *Ethnologie*, André Leroi-Gourhan and others, eds. Paris: Musée de L'Homme, 1963, I, 197. (Abstract.)

718   "A Cruise on the *s.s. Delos*, Summer 1962," *Review of the Society for Hellenic Travel*, 3 (December, 1963), 8-9.

719   "Culture and Personality." In *The Encyclopedia of Mental Health*, 6 vols. , Albert Deutsch and Helen Fishman, eds. New York: Watts,

1963, II, 415-426.

720   "The Early Adolescent in Today's American Culture and Implications for Education," *Junior High School Newsletter*, 1, No. 2 (February, 1963), 1-6.

721   "The Factor of Culture." In *The Selection of Personnel for International Service*, ed. Mottram Torre. Geneva and New York: World Federation for Mental Health, 1963, 3-22.

722   "Families and Maternity Care around the World," *Bulletin of the American College of Nurse-Midwifery*, 8, No. 1 (Spring, 1963), 2-7.

723   "Geneva: Helping the Less Developed Nations—Lessons from the UN Conference," *International Science and Technology*, No. 16, (April, 1963), 86-87.

724   "Human Capacities." In *Man, Science, Learning and Education: The Semicentennial Lectures at Rice University*, ed. S. W. Higginbotham. ("Rice University Studies," Vol. 49, Supplement 2.) Houston, Texas: William Marsh Rice University, 1963, 241-254.

725   "Introduction, Optimum Mental Health." In *The Encyclopedia of Mental Health*, 6 vols., Albert Deutsch and Helen Fishman, eds. New York: Watts, 1963, I, 1-8.

726   "Male and Female." In *The Measure of Mankind*, by Joseph Bram, Colin M. Turnbull, Marvin Harris, Margaret Mead and Saul K. Padover. Dobbs Ferry, N. Y. : Oceana Publications, 1963, 55-72.

727   "An Open Letter," *Read*, 12, No. 18 (May 15, 1963), 28-29.

728   "Opening Address of the Conference." In *National Conference for Scientific Information, New York City, February 16, 17, 1963*, Ralph McCallister and Diana Brown, eds. New York: SIPI (Scientists' Institute for Public Information), 1963, 5-8.

729   "Our Growing Nation: Foreword," *Current Events*, 63, No. 3 (September 23-27, 1963), 19; and *Every Week*, 30, No. 3 (September, 1963), 19.

730   "Patterns of Worldwide Cultural Change in the 1960's." In *Social Problems of Development and Urbanization*, Vol. VII. *Science, Technology, and Development: United States Papers Prepared for the United Nations Conference on the Application of Science and Technology for the Benefit of the Less Developed Areas*. Washington, D. C. : Government Printing Office [1963], 1-15.

731   "Preface to the 1963 edition." *Sex and Temperament in Three Primitive Societies*. Apollo Editions, A-67. New York: Morrow,

122

1963, unpaged.

732 "The Psychology of Warless Man." In *A Warless World*, ed.
Arthur Larson. New York: McGraw-Hill, 1963, 131-142.

733 "Recurrent Crises—Democracy's Way of Life," *Lincoln University
Bulletin*, 66, No. 3 (Summer, 1963), 8-12.

734 "The Roots of Prejudice," *The Sunday Herald Tribune* (Special
School Edition), November 10, 1963.

735 "Scientist Reviewers Beware," *Science*, 141, No. 3578 (July 26,
1963), 312-313. (Letter to the editor.)

736 "Socialization and Enculturation," in "Papers in Honor of
Melville J. Herskovits," *Current Anthropology*, 4, No. 2
(April, 1963), 184-188.

737 "Some General Considerations." In *Expression of the Emotions
in Man*, ed. Peter H. Knapp. New York: International Universities
Press, 1963, 318-327.

738 "The Tele-Lecture," *Understanding* (Winter, 1962-1963), 1, 4.

739 "To the Students of Jamaica High School," *Nucleus* (March, 1963),
3.

740 "*Totem and Taboo* Reconsidered with Respect," *Bulletin of the
Menninger Clinic*, 27, No. 4 (July, 1963), 185-199.

741 "Violence in the Perspective of Culture History." In *Violence and
War*, ed. Jules Masserman. New York: Grune and Stratton, 1963,
93-106.

742 "What Makes a Man a Man," *Chatelaine*, 36, No. 7 (July, 1963),
17, 78-80.

743 "Where Americans Are Gods: The Strange Story of the Cargo
Cults," *Family Weekly* (March 24, 1963), 4-5.

744 (With Rhoda Metraux.) "The Human Sciences: Their Contribution."
In *A Guide to Science Reading*, ed. Hilary J. Deason. Signet
Science Library, P2283. New York: New American Library, 1963,
38-49.

745 "Mrs. Roosevelt," *Redbook Magazine*, 120, No. 3 (January, 1963),
6.

746 "Margaret Mead Answers: Questions about School Prayers,
Happiness, Telepathy, etc.," *Redbook Magazine*, 120, No. 4
(February, 1963), 21-22.

747 "Margaret Mead Answers: Questions about Drug Addiction,
Primitive Humor, Male and Female Creativity, etc.," *Redbook
Magazine*, 120, No. 5 (March, 1963), 28, 30, 32.

748 "What Is a Lady? " *Redbook Magazine*, 120, No. 6 (April,
1963), 22, 24.

749 "Margaret Mead Takes Issue with a Controversial Book, American Attitudes Toward Divorce—and Admiral Rickover," *Redbook Magazine*, 121, No. 1 (May, 1963), 10, 12.

750 "September to June: An Informal Report," *Redbook Magazine*, 121, No. 2 (June, 1963), 32, 34, 36.

751 "Margaret Mead Answers: Questions about the Kennedys—too much Publicity? Toy Soldiers—Should Children Play with them? Our Astronauts—Are They Really Heroes? etc. ," *Redbook Magazine*, 121, No. 3 (July, 1963), 24, 29.

752 "Why Americans Must Limit Their Families," *Redbook Magazine*, 121, No. 4 (August, 1963), 30, 32.

753 "Margaret Mead Answers: Questions about Children and Funerals, Our Race to the Moon, Some Curious American Attitudes toward the Private Lives of Political Candidates, etc. ," *Redbook Magazine*, 121, No. 5 (September, 1963), 24, 26.

754 "Apprenticeship for Marriage: A Startling Proposal," *Redbook Magazine*, 121, No. 6 (October, 1963), 14, 16.

755 "Do We Undervalue Full-Time Wives? " *Redbook Magazine*, 122, No. 1 (November, 1963), 22, 24, 26.

756 "Margaret Mead Answers: Should a Boy be Named after his Father? Should Gambling be Legalized? Are Russian Women Better off than American Women? etc. ," *Redbook Magazine*, 122, No. 2 (December, 1963), 24, 26, 28-29.

757 Comment on "Issues of the Sixties." In *Orientation 1963*. Nashville, Tenn. : Division of Higher Education of the Methodist Church, 1963, 39.

758 Comment on "What We Wish We'd Learned in School," by Arthur Henley, *Pageant*, 19, No. 3 (September, 1963), 101.

759 Statement on Home Economics in *Look at Home Economics*. Washington, D. C. : American Home Economics Association, 1963. (Portfolio.)

760 Preface to *The Javanese of Surinam*, by Annemarie de Waal Malefijt. The Netherlands: Royal VanGorcum, 1963, ix-x.

761 Introduction to *Sixty Years of Advertising from Redbook Magazine: 1903-1963*. ("Souvenir Book on the Occasion of Redbook's Sixtieth Anniversary.") New York: Redbook Magazine, 1963, 2 pp.

762 "Clocking the Timetable of Man," review of *The Origin of Races*, by Carleton S. Coon, *Saturday Review*, 46, No. 25 (June 22, 1963), 41.

763 "TV Effects: London View," review of *Television and the Child*,

by Hilde T. Himmelweit, A. N. Oppenheim and Pamela Vince, *Contemporary Psychology*, 8, No. 6 (June, 1963), 248-249.

764   (Interviewed by Staff.) "What's Happening to the American Family," *U. S. News and World Report*, 54, No. 20 (May 20, 1963), 48-50.

765   (Interviewed by Staff.) "We've got a Blending of Races Right Now," *U. S. News and World Report*, 55, No. 21 (November 18, 1963), 89-90.

1964

766   "Anthropology and American Civilization," *Thought*, 39, No. 155 (December, 1964), 485-509.

767   "Anthropological Contributions to the Development of Rational Dietary Practices." Paper presented at the VII. International Congress of Anthropological and Ethnological Sciences, Moscow, August 3-10, 1964. (Abstract.)

768   "Applied Anthropology." In *A Dictionary of the Social Sciences*, Julius Gould and William L. Kolb, eds. New York: Free Press of Glencoe, 1964, 32.

769   "Be Glad Your Child Is Different," *Parents' Magazine*, 39, No. 9 (September, 1964), 70-71, 146, 148.

770   "The Challenge of Cross-Cultural Research," *Journal of the American Dietetic Association*, 45, No. 5 (November, 1964), 413-414.

771   *Continuities in Cultural Evolution*. ("The Dwight Harrington Terry Foundation Lectures on Religion in the Light of Science and Philosophy.") New Haven: Yale University Press, 1964.
Reprinted in paperback 1966, New Haven: Yale University Press.

Italian edition: *Il Futuro Senza Volto*. Rome: Laterza Bari, 1972.

772   "Cultural Factors in the Cause and Prevention of Pathological Homicide," *Bulletin of the Menninger Clinic*, 28, No. 1 (January, 1964), 11-22.

773   *Food Habits Research: Problems of the 1960's.* Publication 1225. Washington D. C. : National Academy of Sciences—National Research Council, 1964.

774   "A Fresh Growing Plant," *Columbia University Forum*, 7, No. 4 (Fall, 1964), 35-36.

775 "Human Nature Will Flower, If--," in "The Fair, the City, the Future," *The New York Times Magazine*, April 19, 1964, 96-97, 99-101.

776 "The Idea of National Character." In *The Search for Identity: Essays on the American Character*, ed. Roger L. Shinn. ("Religion and Civilization Series.") New York: The Institute for Religious and Social Studies; Harper and Row, 1964, 15-27.

777 "The Liberal Church in an Urban Community," *Journal of the Liberal Ministry*, 4, No. 2 (Spring, 1964), 65-73.

778 "Memories of Walter Spies." In *Schönheit und Reichtum des Lebens: Walter Spies*, ed. Hans Rhodius. Den Haag: Boucher, 1964, 358-359.

779 "New Lives for Old: Discussion and Study Guide," *Horizons of Science*, 1, No. 6, 1964. Four-page pamphlet written to accompany film, see *33*.

780 "Nonliterate." In *A Dictionary of the Social Sciences*, Julius Gould and William L. Kolb, eds. New York: Free Press of Glencoe, 1964, 471-472.

781 "Problems of a One-Parent Family," *Rx Health*, 3, No. 2 (February, 1964), 22-23.

782 "Survival." In *A Dictionary of the Social Sciences*, Julius Gould and William L. Kolb, eds. New York: Free Press of Glencoe, 1964, 708-709.

783 "Vicissitudes of the Study of the Total Communication Process." In *Approaches to Semiotics*, Thomas A. Sebeok, Alfred S. Hayes and Mary Catherine Bateson, eds. The Hague: Mouton, 1964, 277-287.

784 (With Rhoda Metraux.) Comment on "Report on Regional Conferences," by Ruth L. Bunzel and Anne Parsons, *Current Anthropology*, 5, No. 5 (December, 1964), 440-442.

785 (With Elizabeth Steig.) "The City as the Portal of the Future," *Journal of Nursery Education*, 19, No. 3 (April, 1964), 146-153.

786 "More about Limiting Large Families," *Redbook Magazine*, 122, No. 3 (January, 1964), 14, 20.

787 "Margaret Mead Answers: Does the Bible Condemn Interracial Marriage? Can Disarmament Talks Work without Red China? Do Primitive Peoples Spank Their Children? etc. ," *Redbook Magazine*, 122, No. 4 (February, 1964), 12-14.

788 "Margaret Mead Answers: Questions about Young Conservatives, Fluoridation, the American Way of Death, etc. ," *Redbook*

Magazine, 122, No. 5 (March, 1964), 34, 36.

789 "What I Owe to Other Women," *Redbook Magazine*, 122, No. 6 (April, 1964), 18.

790 "Margaret Mead Answers: Why is there Less Crime among American Chinese than among American Negroes? Why are Americans so Fascinated with the British Royal Family? Are Standards for Teachers too Low? etc. ," *Redbook Magazine*, 123, No. 1 (May, 1964), 31, 33.

791 "A New Role for Jacqueline Kennedy? " *Redbook Magazine*, 123, No. 2 (June, 1964), 24, 26.

792 "Margaret Mead Answers: Questions about School Boycotts, Barry Goldwater's View on Poverty, her Preferences in Magazines, etc. ," *Redbook Magazine*, 123, No. 3 (July, 1964), 15, 17, 20.

793 "Time to Reflect, Time to Feel," *Redbook Magazine*, 123, No. 4 (August, 1964), 14-16, 20.

794 "Margaret Mead Answers: Should We Amend the Constitution to Allow School Prayers? Does All-digit Dialing Make Sense? Should Americans Be Permitted to Travel to Cuba? etc. ," *Redbook Magazine*, 123, No. 5 (September, 1964), 25-26, 28.

795 "Must Women Be Bored with Politics? " *Redbook Magazine*, 123, No. 6 (October, 1964), 20, 22.

796 "Margaret Mead Answers: Is Housework Easier than it Was 50 Years Ago? Was Shakespeare Really Shakespeare? What is the Fatal Fascination of Baseball? Is Juvenile Delinquency Really on the Rise? " *Redbook Magazine*, 124, No. 1 (November, 1964), 38, 40, 42.

797 "Margaret Mead Answers: Did You Bring Up Your Children to Believe in Santa Claus? Should American Presidents Be Permitted a Third Term in Office? How Would You Advise a Son or Daughter Who Wanted to Work for Civil Rights in Mississippi? Isn't Psychiatry Harmful as Often as it is Helpful? " *Redbook Magazine*, 124, No. 2 (December, 1964), 6-8.

798 (With AAAS Committee on Science in the Promotion of Human Welfare: Barry Commoner, Robert B. Brode, T. C. Byerly, Ansley J. Coale, John T. Edsall, Lawrence K. Frank,Walter Orr Roberts, Dael Wolfle.) Reply to "Science and the Race Problem," *Science*, 143, No. 3609 (February, 1964), 915. (Letter to the editor.)

799 Comment on "The Human Revolution," by Charles F. Hockett and Robert Ascher, *Current Anthropology*, 5, No. 3 (June, 1964), 160.

800 Comment on "Would You Vote for a Woman as President? "

Family Weekly (June 28, 1964), 14.

801   "Hazards Encountered in Publishing in Europe," *American Anthropologist*, 66, No. 3 (June, 1964), 638. (Letter to the editor.)

802   "Urban Violence Discussed," *The New York Times*, June 23, 1964, 32. (Letter to the editor.)

803   Preface to *You Can Raise Your Handicapped Child*, by Evelyn W. Ayrault. New York: Putnam, 1964, 13-15.

804   Preface to *Anthropology, a Human Science: Selected Papers 1939-1960*, by Margaret Mead. Insight Book, 22. Princeton: Van Nostrand, 1964, iii-v.

805   Foreword to *The Australian Aborigines*, 3rd ed. , by A. P. Elkin. Natural History Library, N37. Garden City, New York: Doubleday, 1964, vii-ix.

806   Introduction to *Christmas in a Technological Era*, ed. Hugh C. White, Jr. New York: Seabury Press, 1964, 11-23.

807   Review of *Man and Society in Disaster*, George W. Baker and Dwight W. Chapman, eds., *American Anthropologist*, 66, No. 3 (June, 1964), 718-719.

808   Review of *The Concept of Freedom in Anthropology*, ed. David Bidney, *American Anthropologist*, 66, No. 6 (December, 1964), 1402-1403.

809   "This Island Then," review of *This Island Now*, by G. M. Carstairs, *Crucible* (July, 1964), 107-111.

810   "A Savage Paradigm," film review of *Dead Birds*, by Robert Gardner, *Film Comment*, 2, No. 1 (Winter, 1964), 14-15.

811   Review of *The Universal Experience of Adolescence*, by Norman Kiell, *Teachers College Record*, 66, No. 1 (October, 1964), 86-87.

812   Review of *Six Cultures: Studies of Child Rearing*, ed. Beatrice B. Whiting, *American Anthropologist*, 66, No. 3 (June, 1964), 658-660.

813   Review of *The Widening World of Childhood: Paths toward Mastery*, by Lois Murphy and others, *American Anthropologist*, 66, No. 3 (June, 1964), 719.

814   (Interviewed by Staff.) "For Youth: A National Service," *U. S. News and World Report*, 56, No. 25 (June 22, 1964), 47-48.

1965

815   "Adult Roles." In *Transcultural Psychiatry: A Ciba Foundation*

Symposium, A. V. S. de Reuck and Ruth Porter, eds. London: Churchill, 1965, 236-257.

816   *Anthropologists and What They Do*. New York: Watts, 1965. Reprinted 1969, Eau Claire, Wisc. : Hale.

817   "Are Teen-Agers Taking Over," *Family Weekly* (October 3, 1965), 4-5.

818   "1. The City as a Point of Confrontation. 2. Megalopolis: Is It Inevitable? " *Transactions of the Bartlett Society*, 3 (1965), 9-22, 23-41.

819   "Do You Know as Much as Your Pupils Know About Today's World? " *Nature and Science*, 3, No. 6 (December, 1965), 1T, 4T.

820   "Early Adolescence in the United States," *Bulletin of the National Association of Secondary-School Principals*, 49, No. 300 (April, 1965), 5-10.

821   "From Black and White Magic to Modern Medicine," *Proceedings of the Rudolf Virchow Medical Society*, 22 (1965), 130-131. (Abstract.)

822   "The Future as the Basis for Establishing a Shared Culture," *Daedalus* (Winter, 1965), 135-155.

823   "Glauben die Amerikaner an den Fortschritt? " In *Amerika Deutet Sich Selbst*, ed. Peter Coulmas. Hamburg: Hoffmann and Campe, 1965, 103-124.

824   "The Information Explosion," *The New York Times*, Sect. 11, May 23, 1965, 18-20.

825   "Introduction," and "Epilogue." In *American Women*, Margaret Mead and Frances B. Kaplan, eds. New York: Scribner, 1965, 3-6, 181-204.

826   "Leisure is for Recollecting in Tranquility," *Nova*, 1, No. 3 (May, 1965), 62.

827   "Marriage Isn't for Every Woman," *Chatelaine*, 38, No. 6 (June, 1965), 25, 74-77.

828   "Preface—1965." *And Keep Your Powder Dry*. Apollo Editions A-105. New York: Morrow, 1965, xi-xv.

829   "Postscript 1928-1964," to *Growing Up in New Guinea*. Pelican A117. Harmondsworth: Penguin, 1965, 263-266.

830   "Social Aspects of Density: A Real Life Situation," *Ekistics*, 20, No. 119 (October, 1965), 214.

831   "Man and His World: A Special Message," *Read*, 15, No. 4 (October, 1965), 5.

832   (With Ken Heyman.) *Family*. New York: Macmillan, 1965.

833   Editor. (With Frances B. Kaplan, ed.) *American Women:*

The Report of the President's Commission on the Status of Women and Other Publications of the Commission. New York: Scribner, 1965.

834 (With Rhoda Metraux.) "The Anthropology of Human Conflict." In *The Nature of Human Conflict*, ed. Elton B. McNeil. Englewood Cliffs, N. J. : Prentice-Hall, 1965, 116-138.

835 (With Rhoda Metraux.) "Town and Gown: A General Statement." In *The Universities in Regional Affairs*, Vol. 2 of *Urban Research and Education in the New York Metropolitan Region: A Report to Regional Plan Association*, Harvey S. Perloff and Henry Cohen, eds. New York: Regional Plan Association, 1965, 1-42.

836 (With Niles Newton.) "Conception, Pregnancy, Labor and the Puerperium in Cultural Perspective." In *First International Congress of Psychosomatic Medicine and Childbirth.* Paris: Gauthier-Villars, 1965, 51-54.

837 (With others.) "The Integrity of Science: A Report by the AAAS Committee on Science in the Promotion of Human Welfare," *American Scientist*, 53 (June, 1965), 1-25.

838 (With H. S. Perloff.) "Social Aspects of Regional Development: Regional Development and Its Impact on Modernization, Migration and Human Settlement," *Ekistics*, 20, No. 119 (October, 1965), 220-222.

839 "Margaret Mead Answers: Questions about Horoscopes, Young Anthropologists, Outlandish English Hairdos, etc. ," *Redbook Magazine*, 124, No. 3 (January, 1965), 6, 8.

840 "New Guinea Revisited," *Redbook Magazine*, 124, No. 4 (February, 1965), 6, 8, 10, 12.

841 "Margaret Mead Answers: Questions about Jean-Paul Sartre, School Busing, Why People Like to Have their Hair Stand on End, etc. ," *Redbook Magazine*, 124, No. 5 (March, 1965), 36, 38, 40.

842 "Margaret Mead Re-examines Our Right to Privacy," *Redbook Magazine*, 124, No. 6 (April, 1965), 15-16.

843 "The Unwitting Partners to Youthful Violence," *Redbook Magazine*, 125, No. 1 (May, 1965), 24, 26.

844 "Margaret Mead Answers: Questions about the John Birch Society, Children with Too Much Home-work—and Boys with Too Much Hair," *Redbook Magazine*, 125, No. 2 (June, 1965), 10, 12, 14.

845 "Mrs. Lyndon B. Johnson: A New Kind of First Lady? " *Redbook Magazine*, 125, No. 3 (July, 1965), 12, 14, 20.

846 "What Can I Do for Peace? " *Redbook Magazine*, 125, No. 4 (August, 1965), 68-69, 123-127.

847   "Small Towns: A New Role for Old Communities? " *Redbook Magazine*, 125, No. 5 (September, 1965), 20, 22.

848   "Margaret Mead Answers: Do the More 'Civilized' Societies Produce a Greater Number of Neurotic Individuals? How Do Adults in Other Societies Control Teen-age Drinking? " *Redbook Magazine*, 125, No. 6 (October, 1965), 20, 22, 24.

849   "Margaret Mead Answers: Questions on Romantic Love, Psychological Testing of Children, and Whether 'Femininity' means Fulfillment," *Redbook Magazine*, 126, No. 1 (November, 1965), 22, 24.

850   "Christmas in Other Lands," *Redbook Magazine*, 126, No. 2 (December, 1965), 24, 26, 28.

851   Comment as Participant at Final Meeting of Delos 3, July 18, 1965. *ATI · ACE Newsletter*, 1, No. 3 (September, 1965), 7.

852   Comment on "The Los Angeles Riots: Handling the Topic in Class," *Scholastic Teacher*, 87, No. 4 (October, 1965), 17-18.

853   Participant in *Mental Health in a Changing World*. Vol. I of a *Report of an International and Interprofessional Study Group convened by the World Federation for Mental Health*, Kenneth Soddy and Robert H. Ahrenfeldt, eds. London: Tavistock, 1965.

854   Participant in "Ehe auf Amerikanisch," *Film und Frau 13*, No. 2 (June, 1965), 19-24.

855   Introduction to *Why Young Mothers Feel Trapped*, ed. Robert Stein. New York: Trident, 1965, v-viii.

856   Review of *Excess and Restraint*, by Ronald M. Berndt, *Journal of American Folklore*, 78, No. 308 (April-June, 1965), 174-175.

857   Review of *Culture Against Man*, by Jules Henry, *American Journal of Orthopsychiatry*, 35, No. 1 (January, 1965), 170-172.

858   Review of *The Next Generation*, by Donald N. Michael, *Science*, 149, No. 3680 (July, 1965), 174.

859   (Interviewed by Tanneguy de Quénétain.) "What Can Modern Man Learn from Primitive Societies? " *Réalités*, No. 180 (November, 1965), 68-71.

1966

860   (With Harvey Breit and Mason Gross.) Critic on *An American Tragedy*, by Theodore Dreiser. In *Invitation to Learning: English and American Novels*, ed. George D. Crothers. New York, London: Basic Books, 1966, 300-308.

861   "Anthropology and Ekistics," *Ekistics*, 21, No.123 (February, 1966), 88-89.

862   "Author's Précis," and "Reply," to Reviews of *Continuities in Cultural Evolution*, *Current Anthropology*, 7, No. 1 (February, 1966), 67-68, 78-82.

863   "Benedict, Ruth." In *Encyclopaedia Britannica*, 23 vols, ed. Warren E. Preece. Chicago: Encyclopaedia Britannica, 1966, 3, 465-466.

864   "The Challenge of Automation to Education for Human Values." In *Automation, Education, and Human Values*, William W. Brickman and Stanley Lehrer, eds. New York: School and Society Books, 1966, 67-70.

865   "Changing Patterns of Trust and Responsibility," *Journal of Higher Education*, 37, No. 6 (June, 1966), 307-311.

866   "Consequences of Racial Guilt: Introduction: 1965." *The Changing Culture of an Indian Tribe*. CAP Giant 266. New York: Capricorn Books, Putnam, 1966, ix-xxiii.

867   "Cultural Man." In *Man in Community*, ed. Egbert De Vries. London: SMC Press; New York: Association Press, 1966, 197-217.

868   "Equality Goals and Urban Progress." Prepared for the Goals for Metropolitan Areas Subcommittee, June 2, 1966, New York City. (Mimeographed.) Confidential.

869   "Forty Years from the Stone Age," *Think*, 32, No. 1 (January-February, 1966), 2-7.

870   "Letter from Peri Village, New Guinea," *ATI · ACE Newsletter*, 1, No. 9 (March, 1966), 6-7.

871   "Letter from Montserrat: Visiting in Somebody Else's Field." September 2, 1966. (Mimeographed.)

872   "A Letter from Margaret Mead," *Church Woman* (October, 1966), 20-24.

873   "Manus Revisited—Preface 1965." In *New Lives for Old*. Apollo 124. New York: Morrow, 1966, xi-xvi.

874   "Neighbourhoods and Human Needs," *Ekistics*, 21, No. 123 (February, 1966), 124-126.

875   "New Forms of Community in a Pluralistic Society," *Concern*, 8, No. 16 (September, 1966), 18, 22-23.

876   "Preface to the Paperback edition." *Soviet Attitudes Toward Authority*. SB 129. New York: Schocken, 1966, vii-ix.

877   "Problems of Population Balance," *Archives of Environmental Health*, 13 (December, 1966), 802-804.

878   "Rearing Children to Live in a Changing World," *Parents' Magazine*,

41, No. 1 (January, 1966), 33-35, 76-77.

879   "Ritual Expression of the Cosmic Sense," *Worship*, 40, No. 2 (February, 1966), 66-72.

880   "20th Century Faith Must Use Technology," *Methodist Woman*, 27, No. 4 (December, 1966), 9-11.

881   "The University and Institutional Change." In *Oakland Papers: Symposium on Change and Educational Continuity*, James B. Whipple and Gary A. Woditsch, eds. ("Notes and Essays on Education for Adults," 51.) Center for the Study of Liberal Education for Adults at Boston University, 1966, 52-62.

882   "The World Today," *Waverly Times*, 10, No. 686 (June 13, 1966), 1, 6. (Letter to the editor.)

883   (With Henry Brandon.) "Who Are the Americans? " In *Conversations with Henry Brandon*. London: Deutsch, 1966, 63-80.

884   (With Muriel Brown.) *The Wagon and the Star: A Study of American Community Initiative*. St. Paul, Minn.: Curriculum Resources; Chicago: Rand McNally, 1966.

—

Japanese edition: Tokyo: Tuttle, 1973.

885   (With Norman H. Pearson and Lyman Bryson.) Critic on *The Rise of Silas Lapham*, by William D. Howells. In *Invitation to Learning: English and American Novels*, ed. George D. Crothers. New York, London: Basic Books, 1966, 252-261.

886   "Trading Old Superstitions for New," *Redbook Magazine*, 126, No. 3 (January, 1966), 16, 24, 26.

887   "A Cruise into the Past—and a Glimpse of the Future," *Redbook Magazine*, 126, No. 4 (February, 1966), 30, 32, 34.

888   "Margaret Mead Answers: How Can Agnostic Parents Teach Their Children about Religion? What Do Dreams Mean to Primitive Peoples? Do Other Cultures Have Menstrual Taboos? " *Redbook Magazine*, 126, No. 5 (March, 1966), 32, 35, 37, 39-40.

889   "One World—But Which Language?" *Redbook Magazine*, 126, No. 6 (April, 1966), 34, 37, 39, 41.

890   "Letter from the Field," *Redbook Magazine*, 127, No. 1 (May, 1966), 30, 33, 34, 36.

891   "Margaret Mead Answers: What is the Modern Grandparent's Role? What Happens to Exceptional Children in Primitive Societies? Has the Medicine Man Anything in Common with the Psychoanalyst? " *Redbook Magazine*, 127, No. 2 (June, 1966), 28, 30.

892   "Marriage in Two Steps," *Redbook Magazine*, 127, No. 3 (July,

1966), 48-49, 84, 86.

893   "Different Lands, Different Friendship," *Redbook Magazine*,
127, No. 4 (August, 1966), 38, 40.

894   "The Case of Drafting All Boys—and Girls," *Redbook Magazine*,
127, No. 5 (September, 1966), 40, 42, 44.

895   "Margaret Mead Answers: Questions about Why the Laboratory
Study of Sex Repels Us, How an Anthropologist Keeps House in
the Field, Why Men are Wearing such Bright Clothes," *Redbook
Magazine*, 127, No. 6 (October, 1966), 36, 38, 40.

896   "Margaret Mead Reviews a Fascinating New Book that Asks:
What is the Purpose of Aggression? How is Agression Related
to Love? " *Redbook Magazine*, 128, No. 1 (November, 1966),
34, 36, 38, 40.

897   "The Gift of Personal Independence," *Redbook Magazine*,
128, No. 2 (December, 1966), 26, 28, 31.

898   Preface to *Huenun Namku*, by M. Inez Hilger. Norman:
University of Oklahoma Press, 1966, vii-viii.

899   Foreword to *Cultural Frontiers of the Peace Corps*, ed. Robert B.
Textor. Cambridge, Mass., and London: MIT Press, 1966, vii-x.

900   "Anthropologist in the Field," Review of *Stranger and Friend*,
by Hortense Powdermaker, *Holiday*, 39, No. 7 (July, 1966),
113-115.

901   Review of *Life Styles of Educated Women*, by Eli Ginzberg and
others, *Harvard Educational Review*, 36, No. 4 (Fall, 1966), 546-
550.

902   Review of *Growing Up in the Kibbutz*, by A. I. Rabin, *Midstream*
(October, 1966), 77-80.

1967

903   "Alternatives to War," in "War: The Anthropology of Armed
Conflict and Aggression," *Natural History*, 76, No. 10 (December,
1967), 65-69.

904   "Anthropologists, Scientists, and Laity," *The Sciences (The New
York Academy of Sciences)*, 7, Nos. 6-7 (November-December,
1967), 10-13.

905   "Background Papers." In *Women in National Service: A Report
on a Service Institute*, ed. Louise Saunders. New York: National
Council of Women of the United States, 1967, 48-51.

906   "Being Human in the Modern World," *Student World*, 60, No. 3

134

(1967), 216-225.

907   "Changing Cultural Patterns of Work and Leisure." In *Seminar on Manpower Policy and Program, February 16, 1966*. Washington, D. C. : U. S. Department of Labor, 1967, 3-16; discussion, 17-38.

908   "The Changing World of Living," in "Symposium on The Emotional Basis of Illness," *Diseases of the Nervous System*, Suppl. 28, No. 7 (July, 1967), 5-11.

909   "Ethnological Aspects of Aging," *Psychosomatics*, 8, Sect. 2 (July-August, 1967), 33-37.

910   "Homogeneity and Hypertrophy: A Polynesian-Based Hypothesis." In *Polynesian Culture History: Essays in Honor of Kenneth P. Emory*, Genevieve A. Highland and others, eds. Honolulu, Hawaii: Bishop Museum Press, 1967, 121-140.

911   "Introduction to the Apollo edition, 1967," *Male and Female*. Apollo Editions A-160. New York: Morrow, 1967, vii-xi.

912   Letter from Tambunam, June, 1967. Sepik River, New Guinea, 6 pp. (Mimeographed.)

913   "The Life Cycle and Its Variations: The Division of Roles," *Daedalus* (Summer, 1967), 871-875.

914   "A National Service System as a Solution to a Variety of National Problems." In *The Draft*, ed. Sol Tax. Chicago: University of Chicago Press, 1967, 99-109.

915   "New Forms of Community," *South African Outlook*, 97, No. 1149 (February, 1967), 21-23.

916   "Racial Differences and Cultural Attitudes," in "Race and Behavior: A Symposium," *Columbia University Forum*, 10, No. 3 (Fall, 1967), 35-36.

917   "Reciprocities Between Domestic and Overseas Health Service Inventions," *Journal of Medical Education*, 42, No. 9 (September, 1967), 822-825.

918   "The Rights of Primitive Peoples: Papua-New Guinea: A Crucial Instance," *Foreign Affairs*, 45, No. 2 (January, 1967), 304-318.

919   "Sexual Freedom and Culture Change," *Franciscan*, 1, No. 1 (Fall, 1967), 8-14.

920   "Universal National Service." *Round Table, Beloit College*, March 30, 1967, 5. (Letter to the editor.)

921   (With Niles Newton.) "Cultural Patterning of Perinatal Behavior." In *Childbearing—Its Social and Psychological Aspects*, Stephen A. Richardson and Alan F. Guttmacher, eds. Baltimore: Williams and Wilkins, 1967, 142-144.

922   "Margaret Mead Answers: Questions about How her Brothers and

Sisters Influenced Her, Our Chances of Achieving World Peace, Other Countries She Would Like to Live in, etc. ," *Redbook Magazine*, 128, No. 3 (January, 1967), 32, 34.

923   "And Children Shall Lead the Way," *Redbook Magazine*, 128, No. 4 (February, 1967), 46, 48, 50.

924   "Are the Natives Friendly," *Redbook Magazine*, 128, No. 5 (March, 1967), 31, 33, 34.

925   "The Right to Privacy vs. the Public Need to Be Informed," *Redbook Magazine*, 128, No. 6 (April, 1967), 30, 32, 34.

926   "Education for Tomorrow's World," *Redbook Magazine*, 129, No. 1 (May, 1967), 36, 38.

927   "Margaret Mead Answers: Do American Women Work Too Hard at Being Beautiful? How Do American Fathers Compare with those of Other Cultures? Do Members of Primitive Societies Ever Commit Suicide? Should College Professors Speak Out on Public Issues? " *Redbook Magazine*, 129, No. 2 (June, 1967), 36, 38, 40, 42.

928   "Is the Church Powerless in a Scientific World? " *Redbook Magazine*, 129, No. 3 (July, 1967), 44, 46, 47.

929   "Margaret Mead Answers: How Are Children Disciplined in Other Cultures? " *Redbook Magazine*, 129, No. 4 (August, 1967), 10.

930   "Margaret Mead Reviews: The Gypsies, by Jan Yoors," *Redbook Magazine*, 129, No. 5 (September, 1967), 52, 54-57.

931   "Margaret Mead Answers: The View from the Picture Window: Are the Suburbs Really Perfect? Has Extrasensory Perception Been Discredited? " *Redbook Magazine*, 129, No. 6 (October, 1967), 38, 40.

932   "Letter from the Field: Return to New Guinea," *Redbook Magazine*, 130, No. 1 (November, 1967), 20, 22, 24, 26, 27.

933   "Books for Christmas: An Anthropologist's Choice," *Redbook Magazine*, 130, No. 2 (December, 1967), 22, 24, 26.

934   Comment on "A Research Film Program in the Study of Changing Man," by E. Richard Sorenson, *Current Anthropology*, 8, No. 5 (December, 1967), 465.

935   Participant in *Mental Health and Contemporary Thought*. Vol. II of a *Report of an International and Interprofessional Study Group convened by the World Federation for Mental Health*, Kenneth Soddy and Robert H. Ahrenfeldt, eds. London: Tavistock; Philadelphia: Lippincott, 1967.

936   Participant in *Mental Health in the Service of the Community*.

136

Vol. III of a *Report of an International and Interprofessional Study Group convened by the World Federation for Mental Health*, Kenneth Soddy and Robert H. Ahrenfeldt, eds. London: Tavistock; Philadelphia: Lippincott, 1967.

937 Participant in *World Conference on Church and Society: Christians in the Technical and Social Revolutions of Our Time, Geneva, July 12-26, 1966*. Geneva: World Council of Churches, Official Report, 1967.

938 Introduction to "New Guinea People in Business and Industry: Papers from the First Waigani Seminar," *New Guinea Research Bulletin*, No. 20 (December, 1967), 3-9.

939 Introduction to *The Peaceful Revolution: Birth Control and the Changing Status of Women*. New York: Planned Parenthood-World Population, 1967, 3-8. (Pamphlet.)

940 Review of *Normality and Pathology in Childhood*, by Anna Freud; and *The Family and Individual Development*, by D. W. Winnicott, *International Journal of Psycho-Analysis*, 48, Part 1 (1967), 102-107.

941 Review of *Educated American Women: Self Portraits*, by Eli Ginzberg and Alice M. Yohalem, *Annals of the American Academy of Political and Social Science*, 373 (September, 1967), 291.

942 Review of *Religion: An Anthropological View*, by Anthony C. Wallace, *Zygon*, 2, No. 4 (December, 1967), 418-431.

1968

943 "Alternatives to War." In *War: The Anthropology of Armed Conflict and Aggression*, Morton Fried, Marvin Harris and Robert Murphy, eds. Garden City, New York: Natural History Press, 1968, 215-228.

944 "Anthropology and Education," *Papua and New Guinea Journal of Education*, 5, No. 4 (June, 1968), 12-15.

945 "Benedict, Ruth." In *International Encyclopedia of the Social Sciences*, 17 vols., ed. David L. Sills. New York: Macmillan and Free Press, 1968, 2, 48-52.

946 "The Case for Compulsory National Service," *Current History*, 55, No. 324 (August, 1968), 84-85, 106-107.

947 "Celebration: A Human Need," *Catechist*, 1, No. 6 (March, 1968), 7-9.

948 "Conferences." In *International Encyclopedia of the Social Sciences*,

17 vols., ed. Da\ d L. Sills. New York: Macmillan and Free Press, 1968, 3, 215-220.

949   "The Crucial Role of the Small City in Meeting the Urban Crisis." In *Man in the City of the Future*, Richard Eells and Clarence Walton, eds. New York: Macmillan, 1968, 29-57.

950   "Cybernetics of Cybernetics." In *Purposive Systems: Proceedings of the First Annual Symposium of the American Society for Cybernetics*, H. von Foerster and others, eds. New York and Washington: Spartan Books, 1968, 1-11.

951   "The Family Life Is Changing." In *The New Encyclopedia of Child Care and Guidance*, ed. Sidonie M. Gruenberg. Garden City, N. Y. : Doubleday, 1968, 675-682.

952   "The Importance of National Cultures." In *International Communication and the New Diplomacy*, ed. Arthur S. Hoffman. Bloomington and London: Indiana University Press, 1968, 89-105.

953   "Incest." In *International Encyclopedia of the Social Sciences*, 17 vols., ed. David L. Sills. New York: Macmillan and Free Press, 1968, 7, 115-122.

954   "Introductory Remarks," and "Concluding Remarks." In *Science and the Concept of Race*, Margaret Mead, Theodosius Dobzhansky, Ethel Tobach and Robert E. Light, eds. New York and London: Columbia University Press, 1968, 3-9, 169-177.

955   "Listening to the Young," *National Catholic Reporter*, 5, No. 1 (October, 1968), 1, 10.

956   "Man and Culture of Tomorrow." In *Science: The Achievement and the Promise. The New York Academy of Sciences, Sesquientennial Celebration 1817-1967*. ("Special Publications," Vol. 8.) New York: The New York Academy of Sciences, 1968, 60-66.

957   "Margaret Mead Replies to John T. Noonan, Jr. ," *National Catholic Reporter*, 5, No. 4 (November, 1968), 4. (Letter to the editors.)

958   "Problems and Progress in the Study of Personality." In *The Study of Personality*, Edward Norbeck and others, eds. New York: Holt, Rinehart and Winston, 1968, 373-381.

959   "The Right to Die," *Nursing Outlook*, 16, No. 10 (October, 1968), 20-21.

960   "The Road to Racial Irrelevance in America," *The New York Times*, April 20, 1968, 32.

961   "The Role of Women in the Next Half Century: An Address." (Delivered at the International Seminar in Honor of Dr. Helen Kim's Fifty Years of Service to Ewha, May 29, 1968.) Seoul, Korea:

138

Ewha Womans University, 1968, 1-11.

962   "Some Social Consequences of a Guaranteed Income." In
Committed Spending: A Route to Economic Security, ed. Robert
Theobald. Garden City, N. Y. : Doubleday, 1968, 93-116.

963   "Statement." In *Proposed White House Conference on Aging.
Hearings before the Special Subcommittee on Aging of the
Committee on Labor and Public Welfare, United States Senate,
Ninetieth Congress, Second Session on S. J. Res. 117, March 5-6,
1968*. Washington D. C. : US Government Printing Office, 1968,
70-72; discussion, 73-75; prepared statement, 75-83.

964   "Testimony on Hunger: Correction," *The New York Times*,
December 24, 1968, 22. (Letter to the editor.)

965   "This Changing World." Annual Report 1968, *International
Industries*, 1968, 3.

966   "We Must Learn to See What's Really New," *Life*, 65, No. 8
(August 23, 1968), 30-31, 34.

967   "What is a Culture? What is a Civilization? " In *Talks with Social
Scientists*, ed. Charles F. Madden. Carbondale and Edwardsville:
Southern Illinois University Press; London and Amsterdam:
Feffer and Simons, 1968, 3-17.

968   "The Wider Significance of the Columbia Upheaval," *Columbia
Forum*, 11, No. 3 (Fall, 1968), 5-8.

969   "Margaret Mead Replies," in "The Columbia Upheaval: an Exchange,"
Columbia Forum, 11, No. 4 (Winter, 1968), 41-42.

970   "Wolf Children." In *Encyclopaedia Britannica*, Warren E. Preece
and others, eds. Chicago: Benton, 1968, Vol. 1, 507.

971   (With Paul Byers.) *The Small Conference: An Innovation in
Communication*. ("Publications of the International Social Science
Council," 9.) Paris and The Hague: Mouton, 1968. Paperback
edition 1968.

972   Editor. (With Theodosius Dobzh?.sky, Ethel Tobach, and Robert
E. Light, eds.) *Science and the Concept of Race*. New York and
London: Columbia University Press, 1968. Paperback edition
1969.

973   (With Rudolf Modley.) "Communication among All People,
Everywhere," *Natural History*, 77, No. 7 (August-September,
1968), 56-63.

974   "Margaret Mead Answers: Should We Have Laws Banning the Use
of LSD? Are Women Basically Uncooperative? " *Redbook
Magazine*, 130, No. 3 (January, 1968), 30, 32, 34.

975   "A Summer in the Woodlands, a Summer by the Sea," *Redbook*

Magazine, 130, No. 4 (February, 1968), 38, 40, 42.

976   "Margaret Mead Answers: Are We Losing the War against Crime? Should We Award Diplomas for Homemaking? " *Redbook Magazine*, 130, No. 5 (March, 1968), 10, 12-13.

977   "A Continuing Dialogue on Marriage," *Redbook Magazine*, 130, No. 6 (April, 1968), 44, 46, 48, 50-52, 119.

978   "Double Talk about Divorce," *Redbook Magazine*, 131, No. 1 (May, 1968), 47-48, 50.

979   "Margaret Mead Answers: Do Primitive Tribes Practice Birth Control? Should Single Women Be Permitted to Adopt Children? " *Redbook Magazine*, 131, No. 2 (June, 1968), 33, 37.

980   "The Nudist Idea," *Redbook Magazine*, 131, No. 3 (July, 1968), 38, 40, 42-43.

981   "A Letter from Tambunam," *Redbook Magazine*, 131, No. 4 (August, 1968), 22, 24, 26.

982   "Margaret Mead Answers: Are Americans Less Sophisticated than Communists about Spying? As a Child Were You a Daydreamer? Are Women Bad Drivers? " *Redbook Magazine*, 131, No. 5 (September, 1968), 30, 33, 35.

983   "What We Can Learn from Sex Education in Sweden," *Redbook Magazine*, 131, No. 6 (October, 1968), 34, 36-38, 166.

984   "Filming Life and Death in a New Guinea Village," *Redbook Magazine*, 132, No. 1 (November, 1968), 46, 50-52, 54.

985   "Why Celebrate New Year's?" *Redbook Magazine*, 132, No. 2 (December, 1968), 31, 33-34.

986   Preface to The American Museum Science Book Edition of *The Mountain Arapesh*. American Museum Science Books B 19a. Garden City, N. Y. : Natural History Press, 1968, vii-ix.

987   Introduction to *Gardens of War*, Robert Gardner and Karl G. Heider, eds. New York: Random House, 1968, vii-x.

988   Introduction to *Reflections of Man*, Timothy Wall and others, eds. New York: Smithtown Central School District, 1968. (Mimeographed, not for publication.)

989   Review of *Holy Ghost People*. Filmed in 1966-67 by Peter Adair, produced by Blair Boyd, *American Anthropologist*, 70, No. 3 (June, 1968), 655.

990   Review of *Infancy in Uganda: Infant Care and the Growth of Love*, by Mary D. Salter Ainsworth, *Annals of the American Academy of Political and Social Science*, 380 (November, 1968), 208-209.

991   Review of *Dema: Description and Analysis of Marind-Anim Culture (South New Guinea)*, by J. Van Baal, *American Anthropol-*

ogist, 70, No. 2 (April, 1968), 381-382.

992   Review of *Culture and Aging: An Anthropological Study of Older Americans*, by M. Clark and B. G. Anderson, *Journal of Gerontology*, 23, No. 2 (April, 1968), 232-233.

993   Review of *Maori*, by Ans Westra and James Ritchie, *American Anthropologist*, 70, No. 6 (December, 1968), 1216-1217.

994   (Interviewed by Alumnus Staff.) "Questions and Answers," *DePauw Alumnus*, 32, No. 4 (March, 1968), 2-4, 7.

995   (Interviewed by Robert MacKenzie.) *The Listener*, No. 2046 (June 13, 1968), 765-767.

1969

996   "American Women Hung-Up on Success." In *World Book Science Service*. Houston: World Book Encyclopedia Science Service, 1969, 72-95.

997   "An Anthropologist Looks at the Generation Gap." In *A Search for the Meaning of the Generation Gap: A Symposium*. San Diego: Department of Education, 1969, 31-41. (Pamphlet.)

998   "Anthropology and Glyphs," *Print*, 23, No. 6 (November, 1969), 50-53.

999   "The Changing Status of Adolescents in the Modern World," *Maryland State Medical Journal*, 18, No. 11 (November, 1969), 61-64.

1000 "Character, Technology and Culture Change." In "U. S. Army National Junior Science and Humanities Symposium, 1-2 May 1969." West Point, N. Y. : United States Military Academy, Chief, Research and Development, 1969, 69-85.

1001 "Child Rearing and the Family," *Ekistics*, 28, No. 167 (October, 1969), 232-233.

1002 "Crossing Boundaries in Social Science Communication," *Social Science Information*, 8, No. 1 (February, 1969), 7-15.

1003 "From Intuition to Analysis in Communication Research," *Semiotica*, 1 (1969), 13-25.

1004 "The Generation Gap," *Science*, 164, No. 3876 (April, 1969), 135.

1005 "A Generation of Repetition," *Social Service Outlook*, 4, No. 6 (June, 1969), 1-3.

1006 "Is Sex Necessary? " *Siecus Newsletter*, 4, No. 3 (February, 1969), 1-3.

1007   "The Knowledgeable Young." In *Progress in Mental Health*, ed.
        Hugh Freeman. London: Churchill, 1969, 299-308.
1008   "Lawrence Kelso Frank 1890-1968," *American Sociologist*, 4,
        No. 1 (February, 1969), 57-58.
1009   "The Natural Ferocity of the Female," *This Week (Sunday
        Bulletin, Philadelphia)*, August 3, 1969, 4-5.
1010   "Note from Margaret Mead's Journal for October 12, 1968,"
        Haggis/Baggis (Miss Porter's School, Farmington, Conn.),
        Issue 3 (Winter, 1969), 22-23.
1011   "On the Politics of Aid," *Vista*, 5, No. 2 (September, 1969),
        40-43.
1012   "Our Leaders Do Not Understand Television," *TV Guide*,
        17, No. 49 (December, 1969), 10-15.
1013   "Postscript: The 1969 Demonstrations." In "The Hampton
        Institute Strike of 1927," by Edward K. Graham, *American Scholar*,
        38, No. 4 (Autumn, 1969), 682-683.
1014   "Population: The Need for an Ethic," *Journal of Medical
        Education*, 44, No. 11 (November, 1969), 30-35.
1015   "Prehistory and the Woman, Have There Been Changes? "
        Barnard Bulletin, Feminist Supplement, 73, No. 20 (April, 1969),
        S-1, S-7.
1016   "Preparedness for Participation in a Highly Differentiated Society,"
        Ekistics, 28, No. 167 (October, 1969), 243.
1017   "Public Policy and Behavioral Science," *Bulletin of the Atomic
        Scientists*, 25, No. 10 (December, 1969), 8-10.
1018   "The Rediscovery of Hunger in America." In *The Food Gap:
        Poverty and Malnutrition in the United States. Interim Report
        prepared by The Select Committee on Nutrition and Human
        Needs. United States Senate, August 1969*. Washington, D. C. :
        U. S. Government Printing Office, 1969, 1-3.
1019   "Reply to Does 'the Gap' Really Exist? " *Science*, 164, No. 3885
        (June, 1969), 1224-1225.
1020   "Research with Human Beings: A Model Derived from Anthropo-
        logical Field Practice," *Daedalus* (Spring, 1969), 361-386.
1021   "Secrecy and Dissemination in Science and Technology," *Science*,
        163 (February, 1969), 787-790.
1022   "Sex and Society," *Catechist*, 2, No. 6 (March, 1969), 9-11.
1023   "Tribute to Dr. Erickson," *News Letter (American Society of
        Clinical Hypnosis)*, 10, No. 4 (June, 1969), 1.
1024   "Violence and It's Regulation: How Do Children Learn to Govern
        Their Own Violent Impulses? " *American Journal of Orthopsychi-*

atry, 39, No. 2 (March, 1969), 227-229.

1025 "Where American Women Are Now," *Vogue*, 153, No. 9 (May, 1969), 176-178, 246-247.

1026 "A Working Paper for Man and Nature," *Natural History*, 78, No. 4 (April, 1969), 14-22.

1027 (With others.) "Voluntary Population Control? 3 Experts Debate Possibility," *Planned Parenthood News*, 1, No. 2 (May, 1969), 3.

1028 "Margaret Mead Answers: Questions about Are Children Born Loving and Taught to Hate? Why Do Some People Believe in Astrology? Do Prepared Foods Reduce a Woman's Importance as a Cook? etc.," *Redbook Magazine*, 132, No. 3 (January, 1969), 33, 35.

1029 "What Makes a Loving Marriage," *Redbook Magazine*, 132, No. 4 (February, 1969), 74-75, 113-115, 118-119.

1030 "President Nixon and the Two-Party System," *Redbook Magazine*, 132, No. 5 (March, 1969), 54, 56, 58, 59.

1031 "Why Students Are Angry," *Redbook Magazine*, 132, No. 6 (April, 1969), 50, 52, 54, 55.

1032 "A Radical New Plan for College Education," *Redbook Magazine*, 133, No. 1 (May, 1969), 55, 56, 58, 63.

1033 "The Police and the Community," *Redbook Magazine*, 133, No. 2 (June, 1969), 38, 40, 43, 44.

1034 "Man on the Moon," *Redbook Magazine*, 133, No. 3 (July, 1969), 70, 72, 74.

1035 "Why Save the Wilderness? " *Redbook Magazine*, 133, No. 4 (August, 1969), 38, 41, 43.

1036 "Sense—and Nonsense—About Race," *Redbook Magazine*, 133, No. 5 (September, 1969), 35, 37, 38, 42.

1037 "The Crisis of Our Overcrowded World," *Redbook Magazine*, 133, No. 6 (October, 1969), 40, 42.

1038 "A Theory of Male Superiority—Turned Upside Down," *Redbook Magazine*, 134, No. 1 (November, 1969), 62, 64, 67.

1039 "At Christmas I Remember...," *Redbook Magazine*, 134, No. 2 (December, 1969), 66, 68, 71.

1040 "Statement." In *Competitive Problems in the Drug Industry. Hearings before the Subcommittee on Monopoly of the Select Committee on Small Business, United States Senate, Ninety-First Congress, First Session on Present Status of Competition in the Pharmaceutical Industry, Part 13, Psychotropic Drugs, July 16, 29, 30, and October 27, 1969.* Washington: U. S. Government Printing Office, 1969, 5456-5477.

1041 "Statement." In *Environmental Quality. Hearings before the Subcommittee on Fisheries and Wildlife Conservation of the Committee on Merchant Marine and Fisheries, House of Representatives, Ninety-First Congress, First Session, H. R. 12143, Serial No. 91-6, May 7, 26, and June 13, 20, 23, 26, 27, 1969.* Washington: U. S. Government Printing Office, 1969, 26-38.

1042 "Statement." In *Nutrition and Human Needs. Hearings before the Select Committee on Nutrition and Human Needs of the United States Senate, Ninetieth Congress, Second Session. Part 1—Problems and Prospects. December 1968.* Washington, D. C. : U. S. Government Printing Office, 1969, 151-181.

1043 Comment on "Prize—or Lunacy? " *Newsweek*, 74, No. 1 (July, 1969), 61.

1044 (With others.) Comment on "Reaching into Space," *Wall Street Journal* (July 18, 1969), 1, 19.

1045 Introduction to the 1969 edition of *Social Organization of Manu'a. Bernice P. Bishop Museum Bulletin*, 76. Honolulu, Hawaii, 1969, xi-xxiii.

1046 Preface to *Reality and Dream: Psychotherapy of a Plains Indian*, by George Devereux. Anchor Books AO-7. Garden City, N. Y. : Doubleday, 1969, xi-xx.

1047 Foreword to *Sweet Pea*, by Jill Krementz. New York: Harcourt, Brace and World, 1969, 5.

1048 Foreword to *People in Pain*, by Mark Zborowski. San Francisco: Jossey-Bass, 1969, ix-xii.

1049 "Language in Diaspora," review of *The Joys of Yiddish*, by Leo Rosten, *Ararat*, 10, No. 1 (Winter, 1969), 41-42.

1050 Review of "Culture and Poverty: Critique and Counter-Proposals," by Charles A. Valentine, *Current Anthropology*, 10, Nos. 2-3 (April-June, 1969), 194.

1051 (Interviewed by Amy Stickney.) *News and Views*, April-May, 1969, 1-2, 20.

1970

1052 "Acceptance of the American Education Award," *AASA (American Association of School Administrators), Official Report*, 1970, 118-121.

1053 "Anomalies in American Postdivorce Relationships." In *Divorce and After*, ed. Paul Bohannan. Garden City, N. Y. : Doubleday,

1970, 97-112.

1054 "Anthropological Contributions to the Development of Rational Dietary Practices." In *VIIme Congrès International des Sciences Anthropologiques et Ethnologiques, Moscou, August 3-10, 1964, Vol. VIII.* Mockba: Hayka, 1970, 147-153.

1055 "The Art and Technology of Field Work." In *A Handbook of Method in Cultural Anthropology*, Raoul Naroll and Ronald Cohen, eds. Garden City, New York: Natural History Press, 1970, 246-265.

1056 "As Seen by a Social Scientist," *Pastoral Psychology*, 21, No. 201 (February, 1970), 8-15.

1057 "Bio-Social Components of Political Processes," *Journal of International Affairs*, 24, No. 1 (1970), 18-28.

1058 "Changing Family Styles," *American Red Cross Youth Journal*, 47, No. 3 (December, 1970), 4-7.

1059 "The Changing Significance of Food," *American Scientist*, 58, No. 2 (March, 1970), 176-181.

1060 "Community." In *No Deposit—No Return. Man and His Environment: A View Toward Survival*, ed. Huey D. Johnson. Reading, Mass. : Addison-Wesley, 1970, 89-91.

1061 "A Conversation with Margaret Mead and T. George Harris on the Anthropological Age," *Psychology Today*, 4, No. 2 (July, 1970), 58-68.

1062 "The Cultural Shaping of the Ethical Situation." In *Who Shall Live?* ed. Kenneth Vaux. Philedelphia: Fortress Press, 1970, 4-23.

1063 *Culture and Commitment: A Study of the Generation Gap.* Garden City, New York: Natural History Press/Doubleday, 1970. Paperback edition 1970.

—

English edition: *Culture and Commitment*. London: Bodley Head, 1970; London: Panther, 1972.
Argentinian edition: *Cúltŭra y Compromiso*. Buenos Aires: Granica, 1970.
Danish edition: *Kŭltŭr og Engagement*. Copenhagen: Schultz, 1970.
Finnish edition: *Ikäryhmien ristiriidat*. Helsinki: Kustannusosa-keyhtiö otava, 1971.
French edition: *Le Fossé des Générations*. Paris: Denoël, 1971.
German edition: *Der Konflikt der Generationen*. Munich and Stuttgart: Klett, 1970; Munich: Deutscher Taschenbuch Verlag,

1974.

Italian edition: *Generazioni in Conflitto*. Milan: Rizzoli, 1972.

Norwegian edition: *Broen over Generasjons Kløffen*. Oslo: Universitetsforlaget, 1971.

Swedish edition: *Kultur och engagemang*. Stockholm: Raben and Sjogren, 1970.

Swiss edition: *Der Konflikt der Generationen*. Olten: Walter, 1971.

Braille edition: *Culture and Commitment*. N. Y. : Recording for the Blind, 1970.

1064   "Earth People." In *Earth Day – The Beginning*. QZ 5822. New York: Bantam Books, 1970, 222-223.

1065   "Economic Growth and the Quality of Life." In *Scenario for Growth: International Two-Day Discourse at Toronto on Economic and Social Growth, May 27-28, 1970*. Toronto: Toronto Stock Exchange, 1970, 18-42.

1066   Editorial. "Question: 18 Year Old Vote - Answer: Dr. Margaret Mead," *Spectator (York Catholic High School)*, 27, No. 3 (December 22, 1970), 2.

1067   "Education for Humanity." In *The Place of Value in a World of Facts*, Nobel Symposium 14, Arne Tiselius and Sam Nilsson, eds. New York: Wiley Interscience Division, 1970, 419-427.

1068   "Establishment's Ranks Infiltrated by Dissent," *The New York Times / Annual Education Review*, January 12, 1970, 51.

1069   "Field Work in the Pacific Islands, 1925-1967." In *Women in the Field*, ed. Peggy Golde. Chicago: Aldine, 1970, 293-331.

1070   "Hunger, Food and the Environment." In *Hunger: A Scientists' Institute for Public Information Workbook*. New York: SIPI (Scientists' Institute for Public Information), 1970, 3-5.

1071   Introduction to "Synergy: Some Notes of Ruth Benedict," by Abraham H. Maslow and John J. Honigmann, *American Anthropologist*, 72, No. 2 (April, 1970), 320.

1072   "Introductory Remarks - Part III. Special Problems of Related Professions." In "New Dimensions in Legal and Ethical Concepts for Human Research," ed. Irving Ladimer. *Annals of the New York Academy of Sciences*, 169, Art. 2 (January, 1970), 397.

1073   "The Island Earth," *Natural History*, 79, No. 1 (January, 1970), 22, 102-103.

1074   "Margaret Mead Spoke Here," *Radcliffe Quarterly*, 54, No. 2 (June, 1970), 2-5.

1075   "More Parks Needed to Match Greater Densities of City Living,"

Los Angeles Times, January 11, 1970, 1, 3.

1076 "Museums in a Media-Saturated World," *Museum News*, 49, No. 1 (September, 1970), 23-25.

1077 "Neglected Books," *American Scholar*, 39, No. 2 (Spring, 1970), 332, 334.

1078 "Presenting: The Very Recent Past," *The New York Times Magazine*, March 15, 1970, 28-32.

1079 "Responsible Simplification of Consumption Patterns," *Ekistics*, 30, No. 179 (October, 1970), 324-326.

1080 "Some Considerations about Educational Issues in the 1970's." In *Needs of Elementary and Secondary Education for the Seventies, A Compendium of Policy Papers. Compiled by the General Subcommittee on Education of the Committee on Education and Labor. House of Representatives, Ninety-First Congress, First Session, March 1970*. Washington, D. C. : U. S. Government Printing Office, 1970, 588-591.

1081 "Some Cultural Anthropological Responses to Technical Assistance Experience," *Social Science Information*, 9, No. 6 (December, 1970), 49-59.

1082 "We Need a Religious System with Science at Its Very Core. . . ," *Look*, 34, No. 8 (April, 1970), 37.

1083 "Women in the Nineteen Seventies," transl. into Korean by Mrs. Seyoung Kim. Seoul, Korea: Korean Association of University Women (Twentieth Anniversary Issue), 1970, 56ff.

1084 "Women on Campus," in "Students in the Seventies," *Campus Call*, 10, No. 5 (January, 1970), 7-8.

1085 "Working Mothers and Their Children," *Manpower*, 2, No. 6 (June, 1970), 3-6.

1086 "Youth Revolt: The Future Is Now," *Saturday Review*, January 10, 1970, 23-25, 113.

1087 "Woodstock in Retrospect," *Redbook Magazine*, 134, No. 3 (January, 1970), 30, 32.

1088 "A Reasonable View of Vietnam," *Redbook Magazine*, 134, No. 4 (February, 1970), 48, 50.

1089 "Women: A Time for Change," *Redbook Magazine*, 134, No. 5 (March, 1970), 60, 62, 64, 67.

1090 "Women and Our Plundered Planet," *Redbook Magazine*, 134, No. 6 (April, 1970), 57, 59, 60, 64.

1091 "Women: A House Divided," *Redbook Magazine*, 135, No. 1 (May, 1970), 55, 59.

1092 "What Shall We Tell Our Children? " *Redbook Magazine*, 135,

No. 2 (June, 1970), 35, 37, 39, 41.

1093 "On Being a Grandmother," *Redbook Magazine*, 135, No. 3 (July, 1970), 70, 168, 169.

1094 "Communes: A Challenge to All of Us," *Redbook Magazine*, 135, No. 4 (August, 1970), 51, 52.

1095 "Can the Family Survive? " *Redbook Magazine*, 135, No. 5 (September, 1970), 52, 54, 57.

1096 "New Designs for Family Living," *Redbook Magazine*, 135, No. 6 (October, 1970), 22, 24, 25.

1097 "Women and Politics," *Redbook Magazine*, 136, No. 1 (November, 1970), 50, 52, 55.

1098 "Instinct and the Origins of Love," *Redbook Magazine*, 136, No. 2 (December, 1970), 39, 40.

1099 "Statement." In *Relating to Proposed Constitutional Amendments Lowering the Voting Age to 18. Hearing before the Subcommittee on Constitutional Amendments of the Committee on the Judiciary, United States Senate, Ninety-First Congress, Second Session, March 10, 1970*. Washington: U. S. Government Printing Office, 1970, 222-225, discussion 226-233.

1100 "Statement" in *All People and Drugs*, ed. H. E. Fraumann. Ann Arbor, Mich. : Specialty Books, 1970, 40.

1101 "Statement." In *Environmental Quality Education Act of 1970. Hearings before the Select Subcommittee on Education of the Committee on Education and Labor, House of Representatives, Ninety-First Congress, Second Session on H. R. 14753, April 8, 1970*. Washington: U. S. Government Printing Office, 1970, 185-190, discussion 191-206.

1102 "Statement." In "Peace on Campus Earth in 1971? " *Almater*, 37, No. 7 (December, 1970), 8.

1103 "Statement: Psychiatrists Should Use Skills Wisely," *Roche Report Frontiers of Clinical Psychiatry*, 7, No. 8 (April, 1970), 1, 2, 11.

1104 Moderator: Panel Discussion Part III "Special Problems of Related Professions." In *New Dimensions in Legal and Ethical Concepts for Human Research*, ed. Irving Ladimer. *Annals of the New York Academy of Sciences*, 169, Art. 2 (January, 1970), 452-460.

1105 Moderator: Discussion Part II "Feminine Life-Career and Personality in a Free-Choice Society: What Are the Most Desirable Models." In *The Impact of Fertility Limitation on Women's Life-Career and Personality*, ed. Esther Milner. *Annals of the New York Academy of Sciences*, 175, Art. 3 (October, 1970), 956-975.

1106 Participant in Discussions. In *New World or No World*, ed. Frank

Herbert. New York: Ace Books, 1970, 38-60.

1107 Comment for "Women: The New Sex," *Mademoiselle* (February, 1970), 162.

1108 Comment. In *From Here to Where? Technology Faith and the Future of Man*, by David M. Gill. Geneva: World Council of Churches, 1970, backcover.

1109 "Comment on Gluecks' Address," *Social Science*, 45, No. 2 (April, 1970), 82-83.

1110 Consultant. *The Social Sciences: Concepts and Values*, 2 vols. New York: Harcourt, Brace and World, 1970.

1111 Foreword to *The Netsilik Eskimo*, by Asen Balikci. Garden City, New York: Natural History Press, 1970, xi-xii.

1112 Foreword to *Traditional Balinese Culture*, by Jane Belo. New York, London: Columbia University Press, 1970, v.

1113 Preface to The American Museum Science Book Edition of *The Mountain Arapesh II*. American Museum Science Books B 19b. Garden City, N. Y. : Natural History Press, 1970, v-ix.

1114 Review of *Gifts and Nations*, by Wilton S. Dillon, *Teachers College Record*, 72, No. 1 (September, 1970), 150-153.

1115 Review of *Bedouin of the Negev*, by Emanuel Marx, *Jewish Social Studies*, 32, No. 1 (January, 1970), 83-84.

1116 Review of *The Making of a Counter Culture*, by Theodore Roszak, *Critic*, 28, No. 3 (January, 1970), 77-79.

1117 Review of *Race, Culture, and Evolution: Essays in the History of Anthropology*, by George W. Stocking, Jr. , *American Anthropologist*, 72, No. 2 (April, 1970), 374-378.

1118 (Interviewed by Lillian G. Genn.) "The New Morality," *Modern Maturity*, 13, No. 4 (August, 1970), 22-23.

1119 (Interviewed by Judy Tritz.) *Houston Post*, April 6, 1970, Sect. 4, 1, 4.

1120 (Interviewed by Lilian G. Genn.) "The New Morality," *Modern Morality*," *Star* (Kansas City), January 4, 1970, 46.

1971

1121 (With Ernst Bergmann, Henry R. Cassirer, and Erika Landau.) "Scientific Knowledge, Education, and Communication. Working Group Deliberations." In *Environment and Society in Transition*, Peter Albertson and Margery Barnett, eds. *Annals of the New York Academy of Sciences*, 184 (June, 1971), 566-594; Report of

        Working Group, 595-601.

1122   "Anthropology in 1970." In *Environment and Society in Transition*, Peter Albertson and Margery Barnett, eds. ("Annals of The New York Academy of Sciences," Vol. 184.) New York: The New York Academy of Sciences, 1971, 321-328.

1123   "Childbirth in a Changing World." In *Pregnancy, Birth and the Newborn Baby*. The Boston Children's Medical Center. Boston: Delacorte Press, 1971, 40-61.

1124   "Cross-Cultural Significances of Space," *Ekistics*, 32, No. 191 (October, 1971), 271-272.

1125   "Drugs and Us," *Bazaar*, No. 3112, (March, 1971), 130-131.

1126   "Early Childhood Experience and Later Education in Complex Cultures." In *Anthropological Perspectives on Education*, Murray L. Wax, Stanley Diamond and Fred O. Gearing, eds. New York and London: Basic Books, 1971, 67-90.

1127   "Future Family," *Transaction*, 8, No. 11 (September, 1971), 50-53.

1128   "Growing and Changing with America," *Volunteer (The Peace Corps)*, 9, No. 5-6 (Summer, 1971), 14.

1129   "Human Values and the Concept of an Optimal Level of Population." In *Is There an Optimum Level of Population?* S. Fred Singer, ed. New York: McGraw-Hill, 1971, 298-301.

1130   "Innate Behavior and Building New Cultures: A Commentary." In *Man and Beast: Comparative Social Behavior*, J. F. Eisenberg and W. S. Dillon, eds. Washington, D. C. : Smithsonian Institution Press, 1971, 369-381.

1131   "The Kalinga Prize," *Journal of World History*, 13, No. 4 (1971), 765-771.

1132   "Metaphors, Tools, and Man's Responsibilities," *Friends Journal*, 17, No. 14 (September, 1971), 424-425.

1133   "A New Style of Aging," *Christianity and Crisis*, 31, No. 19 (November, 1971), 240-243.

1134   "A Note on Contributions of Anthropology to the Science of the Future." In *Human Futuristics*, Magoroh Maruyama and James A. Dator, eds. Honolulu: Social Science Research Institute, University of Hawaii, 1971, 147-149.

1135   "Options Implicit in Developmental Styles." In *The Biopsychology of Development*, Ethel Tobach, Lester R. Aronson and Evelyn Shaw, eds. New York and London: Academic Press, 1971, 533-541.

1136   "Play in Cross-Cultural Perspectives." In *A College Looks at*

American Values, Vol. I, ed. Elwyn H. Odell. Ellensburg, Wash. : Central Washington State College, 1971, 246-255.

1137 "Rejoinder to Christopher Smith's Review of *Culture and Commitment*, by Margaret Mead," *Bulletin of the Menninger Clinic*, 35, No. 4 (July, 1971), 301.

1138 "Report of the Representative to the Council of the American Association for the Advancement of Science," *Bulletin of the American Anthropological Association*, 4, No. 1 (April, 1971), 37-39.

1139 "The Role of Sexuality in the Social Intergration of Children." In *Sex in Childhood, Third Annual Seminar, Tulsa-Oklahoma-1970*. Tulsa: Children's Medical Center, 1971, 85-104.

1140 Editor. "Traditional Rural Burma." In *Approaches to the Science of Socio-Economic Development*, ed. Peter Lengyel. Paris: UNESCO, 1971, 34-43.

1141 "What Kind of Fit? " *Ekistics*, 31, No. 186 (May, 1971), 329-330.

1142 "The Women Are Marching Again." In *Americana Annual 1971*, ed. S. J. Foderaro. New York: Americana, 1971, 15-18.

1143 "Women in National Service," *Teachers College Record*, 73, No. 1 (September, 1971), 59-63.

1144 (With James Baldwin.) *A Rap on Race*. Philadelphia and New York: Lippincott, 1971.
Reprinted in paperback 1972, Delta Book. New York: Dell; 1974, Laurel Edition. New York: Dell.

English edition: *A Rap on Race*. London: Joseph, 1971; London: Corgi, 1972.
Dutch edition: *Over ras*. Utrecht: Bruna Boeken, 1971.
French edition: *Le Racisme en Question*. Paris: Calmann-Lévy, 1972.
German edition: *Rassenkampf-Klassenkampf: Ein Streitgespräch*. Hamburg: Rowohlt, 1973.
Italian edition: *Dibattito Sulla Razza*. Milan: Rizzoli, 1973.
Japanese edition: Tokyo: Heibansha, 1973.
Mexican edition: *Un Golpe ti Racismo*. Mexico City: Extemporáneos, 1972.
Portüguese edition: *O Racismo au Vivo*. Lisbon: Don Quixote, 1973.

1145 (With Nicolas Calas.) "What is American in American Art," *Arts Magazine*, 45, No. 7 (May, 1971), 31-36.

1146 Editor. (With Preston McClanahan, ed.) "Peoples of the Pacific," *Natural History*, 80, No. 5 (May, 1971), 34-71.

1147   "Why Do We Overeat," *Redbook Magazine*, 136, No. 3 (January, 1971), 28, 30, 33.

1148   "Margaret Mead Answers: Do You Have a Need for Solitude? Do Men Have a Fathering Instinct? Do You Believe That 'Women Want More Children Than the Community Needs'? " *Redbook Magazine*, 136, No. 4 (February, 1971), 38, 40, 44.

1149   "Why We Go to the Movies," *Redbook Magazine*, 136, No. 5 (March, 1971), 48, 50, 52.

1150   "Margaret Mead Answers: Should Prostitution Be Legalized? Is Cooking a 'Feminine' Task? How Strong Will the Church Be 50 Years from Now? " *Redbook Magazine*, 136, No. 6 (April, 1971), 50, 53, 56.

1151   "Our New 'Hall of the Pacific': 45 Years in the Making," *Redbook Magazine*, 137, No. 1 (May, 1971), 54, 56, 58, 60.

1152   "Violence and Social Change," *Redbook Magazine*, 137, No. 2 (June, 1971), 60, 62, 64.

1153   "Margaret Mead Answers: What Changes Do You Foresee as a Result of the Liberalization of Abortion Laws? What Have You Most Wanted to Do in Life? What, if Anything, Has Stopped You? Do You Agree that Colleges Should Be Open to All? Wouldn't Such a Policy Make it Impossible to Provide a Proper Education for Those Who Are Academically Prepared? Do You Believe that Young People Today Are More Realistic About Love Than Their Parents? Or Are They More Idealistic? " *Redbook Magazine*, 137, No. 3 (July, 1971), 41, 44.

1154   "How Summer Camp Changes a Child," *Redbook Magazine*, 137, No. 4 (August, 1971), 45, 47, 49, 52.

1155   "*A Rap on Race*: How James Baldwin and I 'Talked' a Book," *Redbook Magazine*, 137, No. 5 (September, 1971), 70-72, 75.

1156   "What Have We Learned? Where Are We Going? " *Redbook Magazine*, 137, No. 6 (October, 1971), 12-13, 21, 24.

1157   "Why We Fear Witches," *Redbook Magazine*, 138, No. 1 (November, 1971), 49, 54, 56.

1158   "Can We Live Without Taboos? " *Redbook Magazine*, 138, No. 2 (December, 1971), 42, 46, 49.

1159   Comment on "The Community." In *46 National Leaders Speak Out on Options for Older Americans*, Margaret Abrams and Barry Robinson, eds. Washington: National Retired Teachers Association and the American Association of Retired Persons, 1971, 35.

1160   Comment. In *You, Your Child and Drugs*, by Staff of Child Study Association of America. New York: Child Study Press, 1971, backcover.

1161   "Statement." In *Attacks of Taste*, Evelyn B. Byrne and Otto M. Penzler, eds. New York: Gotham Book Mart, 1971, 29.

1162   Statement in "The Women's Movement: Aspects and Prospects," *Council Woman (National Council of Jewish Women)*, 33, No. 1 (Jan.- Mar. , 1971), 13-14.

1163   "Foreword," to *Seven Plus Seven*, by Katharane Edson Mershon. New York: Vantage Press, 1971, unpaged.

1164   Introduction to "Visual Anthropology," *Film Comment*, 7, No. 1 (Spring, 1971), 34.

1164a   Preface to The American Museum Science Book Edition of *The Mountain Arapesh III*. American Museum Science Books B 19c. Garden City, N. Y.: Natural History Press, 1971, vii-xiv.

1165   Review of *Yiwara: Foragers of the Australian Desert*, by Richard A. Gould, *Hemisphere*, 15, No. 10 (October, 1971), 40-41.

1166   Review of *Man's World, Woman's Place*, by Elizabeth Janeway, *The New York Times Book Review*, 76, No. 25 (June 20, 1971), 7, 18.

1167   Review of *Socialization: The Approach from Social Anthropology*, ed. Philip Mayer, *American Anthropologist*, 73, No. 2 (April, 1971), 327-328.

1168   (Interviewed by Pino Cimò.) "Intervista a Margaret Mead l'Antropologa più Famosa del Mondo," *Nova*, 31, No. 5 (March, 1971), 36-42.

1169   (Interviewed by Robin Darling, Jane Touzalin, and Linda Stevens.) *The Bullet (Mary Washington College)*, May 10, 1971, 3-6.

1170   (Interviewed by John Kronenberger.) "Is the Family Obsolete? " *Look*, 35, No. 2 (January 26, 1971), 36.

1171   (Interviewed by Steve Latz.) "Following Their Footsteps," *Seventeen*, January, 1971, 94-95, 121.

1172   (Interviewed by Judith Mizell.) "No Step Need Be Fatal," *The Graduate*, 1971, 7-19.

1173   (Interviewed by Doris R. Peters.) "Little Conflict Between Religion and Science," *Advocate* (*National Catholic News Service*), July 1, 1971, 3.

1174   (Interviewed by Claude Servan-Schreiber.) "L'Avenir du Couple et de la Famille," *Elle*, No. 1310 (January 25, 1971), 6-12.

1175   (Interviewed by Staff editor.) "Are Any School Administrators Listening? " *Nation's Schools*, 87, No. 6 (June, 1971), 41-45.

1176   (Interviewed by Staff.) "Governments Aren't That Dumb," *World Peace News*, 2, No. 6 (August, 1971), 3.

1972

1177   Editor. (With J. Edward Carothers, Daniel D. MacCracken, and
         Roger L. Shinn, eds.) *To Love or to Perish: The Technological
         Crisis and the Churches*. New York: Friendship Press, 1972.
         Paperback edition 1972.
1178   *Blackberry Winter: My Earlier Years*. New York: Morrow, 1972.
         Reprinted in paperback 1972, Touchstone Edition. New York:
         Simon and Schuster; 1975, New York: Pocket Books.
         —
         English edition: *Blackberry Winter*. London: Angus and Robertson,
         1973.
         Italian edition: Milan: Mondadori, 1975.
         Japanese edition: Tokyo: Heibon Sha Ltd. , 1975.
1179   "Changes in Life Style," *Briarcliff Alumnae Magazine* (Spring,
         1972), 1-3. (Excerpts of Address.)
1180   "Changing Life Patterns and the Consciousness of the Individual."
         In *The Challange of Life: Biomedical Progress and Human Values,
         Roche Anniversary Symposium*, Robert M. Kunz and Hans Fehr,
         eds. Basel and Stuttgart: Birkhäuser, 1972, 304-315.
1181   "Changing the Requirements in Anthropological Education,"
         Western Canadian Journal of Anthropology, 3, No. 3 (1972),
         19-23.
1182   "Response," to Comments on "Changing the Requirements in
         Anthropological Education," *Western Canadian Journal of
         Anthropology*, 3, No. 3 (1972), 80-85.
1183   "Conflict in Fellowship: A RISK Discussion," *RISK* (WCC), 8,
         No. 3 (1972), 37-47.
1184   "Emotional Aspects of Physical Illness." In *Regional Seminar*,
         November 4, 1970. New York: Council for Interdisciplinary
         Communication in Medicine, 1972, 4-9; discussion 21-23.
1185   "Family Life and Communal Participation," *Ekistics*, 33, No.
         197 (April, 1972), 271-273.
1186   "Field Work in High Cultures." In *Crossing Cultural Boundaries*,
         Solon T. Kimball and James B. Watson, eds. San Francisco:
         Chandler, 1972, 120-132.
1187   "From Plight to Power." In *Human Resources and Economic Wel-
         fare, Essays in Honor of Eli Ginzberg*, ed. Ivar Berg. New York
         and London: Columbia University Press; 1972, 241-256.
1188   "A Loyalty to the Whole World," *Yale Alumni Magazine*, 36,
         No. 2 (November, 1972), 16-17.
1189   "Mental Health in Our Changing Culture," *MH (Mental Hygiene)*,
         56, No. 3 (Summer, 1972), 6-8. (Compilation of Address.)

1190   "New Generation Coming of Age," *Spectator*, 5, No. 5 (April, 1972), 4-5.

1191   "On Growing Old in America: Health: Should an Individual's Life Be Prolonged Indefinitely When He and His Family Wish Life to Be Terminated? " *AAUW Journal*, 65, No. 5 (April, 1972), 22-23.

1192   "Our Shared Atmosphere: Commencement Address," Twenty-Fifth Anniversary 1947-1972. University of Maryland, University College, 1972, 4-12.

1193   "Philip Mosely Memorial Service, February 5, 1972." In *Philip E. Mosely In Memoriam*. New York: Columbia University, Institute on Western Europe, 1972.

1194   "Revolution-Evolution: Impact on the Family," Acceptance Speech of Wilder Penfield Award. Toronto, Canada: Vanier Institute, 1972. (Mimeographed.)

1195   "The Shared Atmosphere of This Planet," *Teilhard Review*, 7, No. 2 (June, 1972), 34-35.

1196   "Symbols Speak Their Own Language," review of *An Authoritative Guide to International Graphic Symbols*, by Henry Dreyfuss, *Smithsonian*, 3, No. 1 (April, 1972), 56-59.

1197   "Thailand Controversy: Response to the Board's Response to the Discussion," *Newsletter of the American Anthropological Association*, 13, No. 2 (February, 1972), 1, 6.

1198   "Toward an Open Society with Cultural Diversity," *Ekistics*, 33, No. 197 (April, 1972), 306-307.

1199   "Two Possible Answers for Women," *The Tablet*, 65, No. 46 (December, 1972), 2M.

1200   (With Roger Shinn.) "Dialogue on the Future," *Youth*, 23, No. 12 (December, 1972), 2-15.

1201   "A New Understanding of Childhood," *Redbook Magazine*, 138, No. 3 (January, 1972), 49, 54.

1202   "Margaret Mead Answers: Are You Optimistic About Mankind? Should Fathers Share the Kitchen Chores? How Can Parents Prepare Their Children for the Future? " *Redbook Magazine*, 138, No. 4 (February, 1972), 45, 47-49.

1203   "Can We Protect Children from Pornography? " *Redbook Magazine*, 138, No. 5 (March, 1972), 74, 76, 79, 80.

1204   (With Benjamin Spock.) "A Redbook Dialogue," *Redbook Magazine*, 138, No. 6 (April, 1972), 80-81, 138-141.

1205   "Letter to a First-Time Voter," *Redbook Magazine*, 139, No. 2 (June, 1972), 31, 33.

1206   "Return to Samoa," *Redbook Magazine*, 139, No. 3 (July, 1972), 29-30, 32, 34.

1207   "The Legacy of Rachel Carson," *Redbook Magazine*, 139, No. 4 (August, 1972), 41, 43, 44.

1208   "Margaret Mead Answers: What Has Happened to the 'Generation Gap'? Must Men Be Violent? Should Parents Limit Their Families to Two Children? *Redbook Magazine*, 139, No. 5 (September, 1972), 70, 72, 76.

1209   "The Candid Memoirs of a Remarkable Woman: Margaret Mead's Personal Story," *Redbook Magazine*, 139, No. 6 (October, 1972), 97-99, 180, 182, 184.

1210   "My First Marriage," *Redbook Magazine*, 140, No. 1 (November, 1972), 50-52, 54.

1211   "The Islands Named Samoa, A Man Named Reo," *Redbook Magazine*, 140, No. 2 (December, 1972), 24, 28, 31, 33.

1212   Discussant: "Session II: Impact of Biomedical Progress on Society and the Individual." In *The Challenge of Life: Biomedical Progress and Human Values, Roche Anniversary Symposium*, Robert M. Kunz and Hans Fehr, eds. Basel and Stuttgart: Birkhäuser, 1972, 89-92, 99-115.

1213   Discussant: "Session III: The Right to Health." In *The Challenge of Life: Biomedical Progress and Human Values, Roche Anniversary Symposium*, Robert M. Kunz and Hans Fehr, eds. Basel and Stuttgart: Birkhäuser, 1972, 136-139, 164-182, 194-215.

1214   Discussant of "Split-off Male and Female Elements Found Clinically in Men and Women: Theoretical Inferences," by D. W. Winnicott. In *The Psychoanalytic Forum*, Vol. 4, ed. John A. Lindon. New York: International Universities Press, 1972, 380-384.

1215   Participant in "A Dialogue: The Role of the Churches Now." In *To Love or to Perish: The Technological Crisis and the Churches*, J. Edward Carothers, Margaret Mead, Daniel D. McCracken and Roger L. Shinn, eds. New York: Friendship Press, 1972, 107-136.

1216   Participant in Symposium: *Biology and the History of the Future*, ed. C. H. Waddington. Edinburgh: Edinburgh University Press; Chicago: Aldine-Atherton, 1972.

1217   "Statements," in "Human Settlements: From Knowledge of the Past to Action for the Future—The 1972 Athens Ekistics Month," *Ekistics*, 34, No. 203 (October, 1972), 246, 247, 254, 260-261, 267, 269, 271, 281, 295, 296.

1218   "Statement." In "Twelve of Today's Women Look Ahead," *Chicago Tribune Magazine*, Sec. 7, November 26, 1972, 93-94.

1219   Foreword to *Introduction to Socialization: Human Culture Transmitted*, by Thomas Rhys Williams. St. Louis: Mosby, 1972, ix-xi.

1220   Foreword to *The Women's Movement*, Helen Wortis and Clara Rabinowitz, eds. New York: AMS Press, 1972, xi-xv.

1221   Introduction to *Rumanian Culture and Behavior*, by Ruth Benedict. Fort Collins: Anthropology Club and Anthropology Faculty, Colorado State University, 1972, unpaged. (First published 1943.)

1222   Introduction to *Sexual Life Between Blacks and Whites*, by Beth Day. New York: World Publishing, 1972, ix-xv.

1223   Introduction to *Psychiatry and Ethics*, by Maurice Levine. New York: Braziller, 1972, xi-xvi.

1224   Introduction to HIM. Exhibit January-February, 1973. New York: Cordier and Ekstrom, 1972, unpaged.

1225   Review of *The Culture of Childhood: Child's-Eye Views of Society and Culture*, by Mary Ellen Goodman, *American Anthropologist*, 74, Nos. 1-2 (February, 1972), 167-168.

1226   Review of *The Human Aviary*, by George Holton and Kenneth E. Read, *Natural History*, 81, No. 3 (March, 1972), 99.

1227   "The Society That Fell Apart," review of *The Mountain People*, by Colin Turnbull, *Newsday*, Long Island, New York, November 5, 1972, 40, 37.

1228   (Interviewed by C&UB Staff.) "Education Needs an Open System," *College and University Business*, 52, No. 2 (February, 1972), 30.

1229   (Interviewed by Colloquy Staff.) "Religion," *Colloquy*, 5, No. 8 (September, 1972), 29-31.

1230   (Interviewed by F. P.) "Est-Il Masculin de Faire la Guerre et Féminin de Faire la Cuisine? " *Femme Pratique*, No. 107 (May, 1972), 52-58.

1231   (Interviewed by Roger Alan Jones.) "Machine-Made Ecology," *East West Journal*, 11, No. 15 (October, 1972), 22-23.

1232   (Interviewed by Ward Kaiser.) "Natives of This Age," *Face to Face*, 4, No. 6 (February, 1972), 1-4.

1233   (Interviewed by John R. Unwin.) "Youth and Culture." In *Youth: Problems and Approaches*, by S. J. Shamsie. Philadelphia: Lea and Febiger, 1972, 11-42.

1973

1234   "The American Indian as a Significant Determinant of Anthropological Style." In *Anthropology and the American Indian:*

A Symposium. San Francisco: Indian Historian Press, 1973, 68-74.

1235   "Background: An American Family," *TV Guide*, 21, No. 1 (January, 1973), 21-23.

1236   "Can the Socialization of Children Lead to Greater Acceptance of Diversity? " *Young Children*, 28, No. 6 (August, 1973), 322-329.

1237   "Changing Styles of Anthropological Work." In *Annual Review of Anthropology, Vol. 2*, ed. Bernard J. Siegel. Palo Alto: Annual Reviews, 1973, 1-26.

1238   "A Crisis, a Challenge," *Washington Post*, December 30, 1973, C6.

1239   "The Direction of Future Research in Papua New Guinea," *Man in New Guinea*, 5, No. 2 (June, 1973), 7-8.

1240   "The Kind of City We Want," *Ekistics*, 35, No. 209 (April, 1973), 204-207.

1241   "Letter to the New York Times: Margaret Mead Thumps Times on Coverage of Environment," *World Peace News*, 4, No. 4 (April, 1973), 1.

1242   "Models and Systems Analyses as Metacommunication." In *The World System: Models, Norms, Applications*, ed. Ervin Laszlo. New York: Braziller, 1973, 19-28.

1243   "New Towns to Set New Life Styles." In *New Towns: Why and for Whom?* Harvey S. Perloff and Neil C. Sandberg, eds. New York: Praeger, 1973, 117-129.

1244   "The Oldest Post-War People," *The New York Times*, January 21, 1973, 17.

1245   "Population Control: For and Against." In *Population Control: For and Against*. New York: Hart, 1973, 52-68.

1246   "Preface 1973 edition" to *Coming of Age in Samoa*. New York: Morrow, 1973, unpaged.

1247   "Prospects for World Harmony," *Indian and Foreign Review*, 11, No. 5 (December, 1973), 20-21.

1248   "Rights to Life," *Christianity and Crisis*, 32, No. 23 (January, 1973), 288-292.

1249   "Ritual and the Conscious Creation of New Rituals." In "Ritual: Reconciliation in Change," Symposium No. 59, Burg Wartenstein, July 21-29, 1973. New York: Wenner-Gren Foundation for Anthropological Research, 1973, 1-33.

1250   "Ritual and Social Crisis." In *The Roots of Ritual*, ed. James D. Shaughnessy. Grand Rapids: Eerdmans, 1973, 87-101.

1251   "Ruth Benedict." In *McGraw-Hill Encyclopedia of World Biography*, ed. David I. Eggenberger. New York: McGraw-Hill, 1973, 494-495.

1252   "She is no Doomsday Prophetes," *Philadelphia Inquirer*, January 10, 1973, 10-A. (Letter to the editor.)

1253   "The Social Responsibility of Anthropologists," *Scientia (International Review of Scientific Synthesis)*, 108, Nos. 9-12 (1973), 685-691.

1254   "2073 A. D.–An Expanded Role for Anthropology," *Sunday News, Detroit*, September 16, 1973, Sect. E, Sunday Viewpoint.

1255   "World Community as an Alternative to War," *Fellowship*, 39, No. 1 (Winter, 1973), 10.

1256   "What I Learned from Three Cultures: The Lost, the Gentle and the Fierce," *Redbook Magazine*, 140, No. 3 (January, 1973), 40, 42, 47.

1257   "A Perfect Partnership," *Redbook Magazine*, 140, No. 4 (February, 1973), 31, 32, 34, 38.

1258   "My Grandmother, My Mother and Me," *Redbook Magazine*, 140, No. 5 (March, 1973), 38, 40, 42, 44.

1259   "Snapshots From My Family Album," *Redbook Magazine*, 140, No. 6 (April, 1973), 38, 40, 42.

1260   "Cathy, Born in Wartime," *Redbook Magazine*, 141, No. 1 (May, 1973), 38, 40, 43, 44, 47, 49.

1261   "Trial Parenthood," *Redbook Magazine*, 141, No. 2 (June, 1973), 26, 29, 30.

1262   "Margaret Mead Answers: Are Women Stronger than Men? Do We Cheat our Children of Childhood? Are You in Favor of Mercy Deaths?" *Redbook Magazine*, 141, No. 3 (July, 1973), 33-34.

1263   "A Next Step in Being a Woman," *Redbook Magazine*, 141, No. 4 (August, 1973), 38, 40, 41.

1264   "Reducing the Need for Abortions," *Redbook Magazine*, 141, No. 5 (September, 1973), 62, 65, 71.

1265   "Does the World Belong to Men–Or to Women?" *Redbook Magazine*, 141, No. 6 (October, 1973), 46, 48, 52.

1266   "What Singles and Married Couples Should Know about Each Other," *Redbook Magazine*, 142, No. 1 (November, 1973), 62, 72, 74.

1267   "Can Christmas Bring the Generations Together?" *Redbook Magazine*, 142, No. 2 (December, 1973), 27-28.

1268   Comment in "Points to Ponder," *Reader's Digest*, June, 1973, 196.

1269   "Statement." In "How Will We Raise Our Children in the Year 2000?" *Saturday Review of Education*, 1, No. 2 (February, 1973), 36-37.

1270   Foreword to *The Tender Gift: Breastfeeding*, by Dana Raphael.
              Englewood Cliffs, N. J. : Prentice-Hall, 1973, 5.

1271   Review of *The Coming of Age*, by Simone de Beauvoir, *American
              Journal of Orthopsychiatry*, 43, No. 3 (April, 1973), 470-474.

1272   (Interviewed by Anil Agarwal.) "Education and Sex," *Hindustan
              Times, New Delhi*, February 11, 1973, 7.

1273   (Interviewed by Robert R. Dye.) "Perspectives for Social Relevance
              in Long-range Planning," *YMCA*, 1973, 42-43.

1274   (Interviewed by David Ehrlich.) "Election of President AAAS,"
              Bulletin AAAS, 18, No. 4 (September, 1973), 1, 4, 24.

1275   (Interviewed by Peter Joseph.) "On Women." In *Good Times*,
              by Peter Joseph. New York: Charterhouse, 1973, 52-54.

1276   (Interviewed by Paul H. Sherry.) "A Twentieth Century Faith,"
              Journal of Current Social Issues, 11, No. 2 (Spring, 1973), 4-11.

1974

1277   "Adolescence in a Changing World," *UNICEF News*, 79, No. 1
              (1974), 3-11.

1278   "Aggression and Violence in Modern Society," *Rivista IBM*, 10,
              No. 2 (June, 1974), 20, 22-23, 25. (In Italian.)

1279   "Answer to Anne Roe's Review of *Blackberry Winter*," *Reviews
              in Anthropology*, 1, No. 4 (November, 1974), 614-615.

1280   "Changing Perspectives on Modernization." In *Rethinking
              Modernization: Anthropological Perspectives*, John J. Poggie, Jr.
              and Robert N. Lynch, eds. Westport and London: Greenwood
              Press, 1974, 21-36.

1281   "The Crisis of Self: America's Secret War," *Parks and Recreation*,
              9, No. 3 (March, 1974), 24-28, 48-51.

1282   "Grandparents as Educators," *Teachers College Record*, 76, No. 2
              (December, 1974), 240-249.

1283   "On Freud's View of Female Psychology." In *Women and Analysis*,
              ed. Jean Strouse. New York: Grossman (Division of Viking Press),
              1974, 95-106.

1284   "How Anthropology Can Become a Component in a Liberal Arts
              Education." In *Essays on the Teaching of Culture. A Festschrift
              to Honor Howard Lee Nostrand*, Howard B. Altman and Victor
              E. Hanzeli, eds. Detroit: Advancement Press of America, 1974,
              1-19.

1285   "I Think of Farmers," *19NU*, 10, No. 1 (January, 1974), 16.

1286 "Islands as Ethnologically Special Environments." In *11th and 12th Annual Reports 1972-74, Thomas Burke Memorial Washington State Museum*. Seattle: University of Washington, 1974, 108-131. (Mimeographed.)

1287 "Margaret Mead." In *A History of Psychology in Autobiography*, Vol. VI, ed. Gardner Lindzey. New York: Prentice-Hall, 1974, 293-326.

1288 "The Next Billion Years," *PSA*, 9, No. 5 (May, 1974), 72-73, 78.

1289 "A Note on the Evocative Character of the Rorschach Test." In *Toward a Discovery of the Person: The First Bruno Klopfer Memorial Symposium, and Carl G. Jung Centennial Symposium*, ed. Robert Wm. Davis. Burbank, Cal.: The Society for Personality Assessment, 1974, 62-67. (Special Monograph.)

1290 "Opening Address." In *Advances in Cybernetics and Systems Research*, F. de P. Hanika and others, eds. London: Transcripta Books, 1974, 1-4.

1291 *Ruth Benedict*. New York and London: Columbia University Press, 1974. Paperback edition 1974.

1292 "Tamu-Tamu," 17th Festival of Two Worlds, Spoleto, June 14-July 7, 1974. Spoleto: Festival Foundation, 1974, unpaged (3 pp.).

1293 "This Time There Is No Enemy," *AAUW Journal*, 67, No. 6 (April, 1974), 6-8.

1294 "Uniqueness and Universality," *Childhood Education*, 51, No. 2 (November-December, 1974), 58-63.

1295 "Ways to Deal with the Current Social Transformation," *Futurist*, 8, No. 3 (June, 1974), 122-123.

1296 "I. What I Think I Have Learned about Education 1923-1973; II. Selected Reprints; III. Epilogue," *Education*, 94, No. 4 (April-May, 1974), 289-406.

1297 "World Population: World Responsibility," *Science*, 185, No. 4157 (September, 1974), 1113. (Editorial.)

1298 "The Danger Point in Marriage," *Redbook Magazine*, 142, No. 3 (January, 1974), 42, 47.

1299 "Too Many Divorces, Too Soon," *Redbook Magazine*, 142, No. 4 (February, 1974), 72, 74.

1300 "Divorce Insurance: A New Idea," *Redbook Magazine*, 142, No. 5 (March, 1974), 38, 41.

1301 "The Energy Crisis—Why Our World Will Never Again Be the Same," *Redbook Magazine*, 142, No. 6 (April, 1974), 54, 56, 58.

1302 "Pollution: The Need to Think Clearly about Clear Water,"

Redbook Magazine, 143, No. 1 (May, 1974), 38, 41-42, 46.

1303   "Margaret Mead Answers: How Does Your Daughter Feel about Being an Only Child? Are You a Cautious Person or a Risk Taker? Can You See an End to the Kinds of Violence—the Muggings, the Rapes, the Murders—That are so Much a Part of Life Today in American Cities? In Other Cultures to What Degree Are Women Valued for—and Judged by—their Appearance? Some Time Ago a Plane Crashed in South America. In Order to Stay Alive the Survivors Ate the Flesh of Their Dead Companions. What Is Your Feeling about Their Action? " *Redbook Magazine*, 143, No. 2 (June, 1974), 33, 37.

1304   "Margaret Mead Answers: Is Jealousy Innate? Has It Ever Played a Part in Your Life? As an Anthropologist, a Mother and a Grandmother, What Do You Think Are the Qualities Most Valuable to a Mother in Helping her Children toward Maturity? Do You Believe that Some People are 'Born to Kill' Because of a Faulty Chromosome Balance? Do Children Owe Their Parents Anything in the Way of Concern and Consideration to Say Nothing of Understanding that the Parents Need to Feel the Children Care About Them? Does the Recent Popularity of Fundamentalist Forms of Religion Indicate that Society in General is Becoming More Conservative? " *Redbook Magazine*, 143, No. 3 (July, 1974), 33, 34, 37.

1305   (Interviewed by Irene Kubota.) "On Women," *Redbook Magazine*, 143, No. 4 (August, 1974), 31, 33-34.

1306   "UFOs—Visitors from Outer Space? " *Redbook Magazine*, 143, No. 5 (September, 1974), 57-58, 61.

1307   "Margaret Mead Answers: Is True Sexual Equality Possibel? Do Children's Games Have Hidden Meaning? Should Individuals Be Free to Choose Death? " *Redbook Magazine*, 143, No. 6 (October, 1974), 72, 74.

1308   "Our Lives May Be at Stake," *Redbook Magazine*, 144, No. 1 (November, 1974), 52, 54-55, 57.

1309   "The Gift of Celebrating Christmas," *Redbook Magazine*, 144, No. 2 (December, 1974), 4, 153, 155.

1310   "Statement." In "1984 Minus 10," *Museum News*, 52, No. 9 (June, 1974), 51.

1311   "Statement." In *Science, Technology, and the Economy. Hearings before the Subcommittee on Science, Research and Development of the Committee on Science and Astronautics, U. S. House of Representatives, Ninety-Third Congress, Second*

Session, No. 33, February 19, 20, 21, 1974. Washington: U. S. Government Printing Office, 1974, 27-43.

1312 "Statement." In "Controlling the Population," *Development Forum (UN)*, 2, No. 7 (September-October, 1974), 4.

1313 "Statement," *The Reading Teacher*, 28, No. 1 (October, 1974), inside cover.

1314 "Statement." In "Ask Them Yourself: Do Most People Have Extra Brain Power They Don't Use? " *Family Weekly*, June 23, 1974, 2.

1315 "Statement." In *American Families: Trends and Pressures, 1973. Hearings before the Subcommittee on Children and Youth of the Committee on Labor and Public Welfare, United States Senate, Ninety-Third Congress, First Session Examination of the Influence that Governmental Policies have on American Families, September 24, 25 and 26, 1973.* Washington: U. S. Government Printing Office, 1974, 121-127; prepared statement 128-133.

1316 "Statement." In "Block Parties," *The New York Times*, June 2, 1974, 25.

1317 Participant in *What Makes Some People Travel—And Others Stay at Home?* New York: Ziff-Davis, 1974. (Mimeographed.) 1972. New York: United Nations (ST/ECA/192), 1974.

1318 Participant in *Earth Talk: Independent Voices on the Environment*, ed. Tom Artin. New York: Grossman, 1973.

1319 Participant in *What Makes Some People Travel- And Others Stay at Home?* New York: Ziff-Davis, 1974. (Mimeographed.)

1320 Preface to *Culture and Psychotherapy*, by Theodora M. Abel and Rhoda Metraux. New Haven: College and University Press, 1974, unpaged (6 pp.).

1321 Introduction to *Transformation and Identity: The Face and Plastic Surgery*, by Frances Cooke Macgregor. New York: Quadrangle, 1974, xi-xvii.

1322 Review of *Cultural Relativism: Perspectives in Cultural Pluralism*, by Melville J. Herskovits, *American Journal of Sociology*, 79, No. 5 (March, 1974), 1326-1330.

1323 Review of *Soviet and American Society: A Comparison*, by Paul Hollander, *Russian Review*, 33, No. 2 (April, 1974), 225-226.

1324 Review of *Tahitians: Mind and Experience in the Society Islands*, by Robert I. Levy, *American Anthropologist*, 76, No. 4 (December, 1974), 907-909.

1325 Review of *The Politics of Nonviolent Action*, by Gene Sharp, *American Journal of Orthopsychiatry*, 44, No. 3 (April, 1974),

459-460.

1326   (Interviewed by Wilton Dillon.) "Outlook for Space." Washington, D. C. : NASA (National Aeronautics and Space Administration), 1974. (Pamphlet.)

1327   (Interviewed by B. Epstein and W. Hironaka.) "Women in Modern Society," *Taihaku Renge*, 4, No. 276 (April, 1974), 48-55. (In Japanese.)

1328   "On Growth, an Interviwe." In *On Growth: The Crisis of Exploding Population and Resource Depletion,* ed. Willem L. Oltmans. New York: Capricorn Books/Putnam, 1974, 18-25.

1329   (Interviewed by Maryanne Raphael and Charlotte Hastings.) "Margaret Meat Speaks Out," *Chatelaine*, 47, No. 7 (July, 1974), 21, 52-53.

1330   (Interviewed by Staff.) "Current Scene," *Foundation*, 1 (Summer, 1974), 15-17.

1331   (Interviewed by Gregory A. Vitiello.) "On Men and Women," *Pegasus (Mobil Services)*, 1974, unpaged.

1975

1332   "Agriculture: Men's Work, Women's Work? " *RF Illustrated (Rockefeller Foundation)*, 2, No. 3 (August, 1975), 12

1333   "Children's Play Style: Potentialities and Limitations of its Use as a Cultural Indicator," *Anthropological Quarterly*, 48, No. 3 (July, 1975), 157-181.

1334   Essay: "On the Quality of Life." In *Voices for Life: Reflections on the Human Condition*, ed. Dom Moraes. New York: Praeger, 1975, 124-132.

1335   "Ethnicity and Anthropology in America." In *Ethnic Identity*, George de Vos and Lola Romanucci-Ross, eds. Palo Alto: Mayfield, 1975, 173-197.

1336   "The Family – How to Protect it." Los Angeles: Women's Division, Reiss-Davis Child Study Center, April 28, 1975. (Mimeographed pamphlet.)

1337

1338   "The Heritage of Children in the United States," *Journal of Current Social Issues*, 12, No. 3 (Summer, 1975), 4-8.

1339   "Is Big Business Biting into the World Food Supply? " *Cincinnati Horizons*, 4, No. 5 (April, 1975), 15-17; discussion 17-18

1340   "Learning for Friendship." In *Other Choices for Becoming a Woman*, by Joyce Slayton Mitchell. Pittsburgh: Know, 1975, 31-38.

1341   "Liberation Liberates," *World Health (WHO)*, January, 1975, 33

1342   "Margaret Lowenfeld 1890-1973," *Journal of Clinical Child Psychology*, 3, No. 2 (Summer, 1974), 56-57. (Published Summer 1974, received in 1975.)

1343   "Of Muggers, Bystanders, Courage and Skill," *The New York Times*, March 10, 1975, 28. (Letter to the editor.)

1344   "Needed: Full Partnership for Women," *Saturday Review*, June 14, 1975, 26-27.

1345   "The Relationship of the Bucharest Seminar to the Main Currents at the United Nations Conference on Population." In *The Cultural Consequences of Population Change. Report on a Seminar held in Bucharest, Romania, August 14-17, 1974.* Washington, D. C. : The Center for the Study of Man, Smithsonian Institution, 1975, 1-6. (Mimeographed.)

1346   "Seniors' Needs and Rights," *Senior Summary*, 1, No. 3 (Summer, 1975), 2. (Letter to the editor.)

1347   "Sex Differences: Innate, Learned, or Situational? " *Quarterly Journal of the Library of Congress*, 32, No. 4 (October, 1975), 260-267.

1348   "Social and Cultural Needs of Settlements in Different Societies," In *Planning and Administration*, ed. E. M. Harloff. The Hague: International Union of Local Authorities and the International Federation for Housing and Planning, 1975-1, 17-24.

1349   "The Social Significance of Theories of Human Aggression," *Newsletter (World Federation for Mental Health)*, 2 (may, 1975), 3-4.

1350   "Summit V: One is the Human Spirit," in "One Woman's Voice," *Anderson-Moberg Syndicates*, New York, October, 1975.

1351   "Toward an Educational Protocracy," *New York University Education Quarterly*, 6, No. 3 (Spring, 1975), 2-7.

1352   "Visual Anthropology in a Discipline of Words." In *Principles of Visual Anthropology*, ed. Paul Hockings. The Hague and Paris: Mouton, 1975, 3-10.

1353   "Why Do We Speak of Feminine Intuition? " *Anima*, 1 (Spring, 1975), 44-49.

1354   "Why We Should Celebrate the Bicentennial in Vermont," *The Hazen Road Dispatch*, 1, No. 2 (March, 1975), 1.

1355   "Women and the Future of Mankind," *Prospects*, 5, No. 3 (1975), 342.

1356   (With Walter Fairservis.) "Kulturelle Verhaltensweisen und die Umwelt des Menschen" ("Cultural Attitudes Toward the Human Environment"). In *Umwelt Strategie*, ed. Hans D. Engelhardt. Gütersloh, Germany: Mohn, 1975, 15-32.

1357 "Bisexuality: What's It All About? " *Redbook Magazine*, 144, No. 3 (January, 1975), 29, 31.

1358 "How Women Can Help Other Women Who Drink," *Redbook Magazine*, 144, No. 4 (February, 1975), 49-50, 52.

1359 "How Can We Help the World's Hungry People? " *Redbook Magazine*, 144, No. 5 (March, 1975), 33, 38, 40.

1360 "Celebrating the Bicentennial – Family Style," *Redbook Magazine*, 144, No. 6 (April, 1975), 31, 33, 37.

1361 "Margaret Mead Answers: What makes Marriage Such a Special Relationship? Who were the Women That Most Influenced You, Both Personally and Professionally? What Can We Do to Curb the Escalating Violence in Our Country? " *Redbook Magazine*, 145, No. 1 (May, 1975), 64, 66.

1362 "Women as Priests: A New Challenge," *Redbook Magazine*, 145, No. 2 (June, 1975), 31-32, 36.

1363 "Our 200th Birthday: What We Have to Celebrate," *Redbook Magazine*, 145, No. 3 (July, 1975), 38, 40.

1364 "Margaret Mead Answers: Hostility Between Male Chauvinists and Female Liberationists; Men Who Feel Threatened by a Woman's Need to Grow; Female Role Models for Little Girls," *Redbook Magazine*, 145, No. 4 (August, 1975), 10, 14.

1365 "Do We Really Need Volunteers? " *Redbook Magazine*, 145, No. 5 (September, 1975), 60, 62, 65-66.

1366 "Halloween: Where Has All the Mischief Gone? " *Redbook Magazine*, 145, No. 6 (October, 1975), 31, 33-34.

1367 "Lexington and Concord – A Meeting of Christmas Past and Present," *Redbook Magazine*, 146, No. 2 (December, 1975), 61, 63.

1368 "Statement." In "The American Family," *U. S. News & World Report*, 79, No. 17 (October, 1975), 30-31.

1369 "Statement." In "Famine," *Our World/World Review (American Field Service)*, 27 (March, 1975), 7.

1370 "Statement." In "Elizabeth L. Post Column: Doing the Right Thing," *Chicago Tribune-New York News Syndicate*, April 21, 1975.

1371 "Statement." In "Ask Them Yourself: Do You Believe in UFO's? " *Family Weekly*, May 18, 1975, 2.

1372 "Statement on Equality." In *Souvenir Book 15th Annual United Nations Concert and Dinner, 25th of October, 1975*. Washington, D. C. : Concert Hall John F. Kennedy Center for Performing Arts, 1975, 22.

1373 "Statement." In *Listen to the Women . . . for a Change*, ed. Kay Camp. Geneva: 60th Anniversary Publication of the Women's

International League for Peace and Freedom, 1975, 30.

1374 Discussant: "Anthropology and Education," by Elliot L. Richardson.
In *Anthropology and Society*, ed. Bela C. Maday. Washington,
D. C. : Anthropological Society, 1975, 109-111.

1375 Discussant: "Anthropology in Law and Civic Action," by Ralph
Nader. In *Anthropology and Society*, ed. Bela C. Maday.
Washington, D. C.: Anthropological Society, 1975, 41-45.

1376 Discussant: "The Role of Anthropology in International Relations,"
by Glen H. Fisher. In *Anthropology and Society*, ed. Bela C. Maday.
Washington, D. C.: Anthropological Society, 1975, 13-18.

1377 Preface to *Kyra's Story*, by Kyra Karadja. New York: Morrow,
1975, 7-8.

1378 Preface to the 1975 edition of *Growing Up in New Guinea*.
New York: Morrow, 1975, iii-x.

1379 Preface to the 1975 edition of *New Lives for Old*. New York:
Morrow, 1975, x-xv.

1380 Preface to *Population: Dynamics, Ethics and Policy*, Priscilla
Reining and Irene Tinker, eds. Washington, D. C. : AAAS,
1975, v-vi.

1381 Preface to Psi Lines: A Documentation of the Psi Search
Exhibition. Los Angeles: California Museum of Science and
Industry, 1975, 7.

1382 Introduction to *Five Families*, by Oscar Lewis. New York:
Basic Books, 1975, vii-ix.

1383 Review of *Darwin and Facial Expression: A Century of Research
in Review*, ed. Paul Ekman. *Journal of Communication*, 25, No. 1
(Winter, 1975), 209-213.

1384 Review of *The Individual in Cultural Adaption: A Study of Four
East African Peoples*, by Robert B. Edgerton. *American Anthropologist*, 77, No. 3 (September, 1975), 638-639.

1385 (Interviewed by Judy Lessing.) "From Poetry to Racism," *Thursday*
(Aukland, N. Z.), June 12, 1975, 22-23.

1386 (Interviewed by Joan Wixen.) "I've Always Been a Woman. . . I've
Never Been an Imitation Man," *The Sunday News Magazine* (Detroit),
June 22, 1975, 12-13, 15-16, 18.

1387 (Interviewed by Staff.) "Men Have Always Stuck By Us," *News
Advertiser* (New Zealand), June, 24, 1975, 1.

1388 (Interviewed by Staff.) "Men Have Always Stuck by Us," *News
Cultural Identity," *Revista Interamericana*, 5, No. 1 (Spring,
1975), 5-10.

1389 (Interviewed by Bill Thompson.) "Problems of Puerto Rican
Cultural Identity – Comments on Dr. Mead's Interview,"
Revista Interamericana, 5, No. 2 (Summer, 1975), 171-181.

ADDENDUM

1969

1390   "Statement." In *Psychological Aspects of Foreign Policy.* Hearings before the Committee on Foreign Relations, United States Senate, Ninety-first Congress, First Session, June 20, 1969. Washington, D.C.: U.S. Government Printing Office, 1969, 87-138.

1972

1391   "Statement." In *U.N. Conference on Human Environment: Preparations and Prospects.* Hearings before the Committee on Foreign Relations, United States Senate, Ninety-second Congress, Second Session, May 5, 1972. Washington, D.C.: U.S. Government Printing Office, 1972, 125-145.

1975

1392   "Comments on Working Paper No. 1 of Goals for a Global Society," *Forum for Correspondence and Contact*, 7, No. 3 (October, 1975), 25-26.

1393   "We need to Know More about Traditional Snacks," *Nutrition and Development*, 1, No. 3 (1975), 58-60.

1394   "Women and the Balance of Hope and Fear," In *Hunger, Politics and Markets*, ed. Sartaj Aziz. New York: New York University Press, 1975, 67-69.

1395   (With Ken Heyman.) *World Enough: Rethinking the Future.* Boston: Little, Brown, 1975.

1396   Review of *Trough Navajo Eyes: An Exploration of Film Communication and Anthropology,* by Sol Worth and John Adair. *Studies in the Anthropology of Visual Communication*, 2, No. 2 (Fall, 1975), 122-124.

1397   (Interviewed by Joyce Mullins.) "Anthropology and Man," *Delaware Today Magazine* (January 1973), 18-19.

RECORDS

1953

1   *This I Believe*, interviewed by Edward R. Murrow for CBS-Radio. New York: Columbia Records, 1953. 2 Records No. SL192A.

1954

2   Participant in *Invitation to Learning*, for WABC-TV. White Plains, New York: TV-Time-Off-The-Air Recordings, 1954. 2 Records.

1957

3   (With Max Lerner.) Participant in *The Open Mind*, moderated by Richard D. Heffner for NBC-TV. White Plains, New York: TV-Time-Off-The-Air Recordings, 1957. Record.

4   *Counterpoint*, interviewed by William Kunstler for WNEW-Radio. New York: Gotham Recording, 1957. Record.

1959

5   *Social Anthropology, American Character and Primitive Societies: An Interview*. New York: Folkways Records, 1959. Record No. FC7354.

6   Participant in *The Business of Sex*, interviewed by Edward R. Murrow for CBS-Radio. New York: Gotham Recording, 1959. 2 Records.

1960

7   Participant in *The Revolution in Diet*, interviewed by Ned Calmer for CBS-Radio. New York: Rockhill Recordings, 1960. Record.

1970

8   Participant in *2001: Science Fiction or Man's Future*. WKCR-

Columbia University Radio. New York: Erwin Frankel Productions, 1970. Record.

1972

9   (With James Baldwin.) *A Rap on Race: A Recorded Dialog.* New York: CMS Records, 1972. Record No. 641/2.

10   *Marriage and the Family*, interviewed by Selma Greenberg. Great Neck, New York: Classroom Materials, 1972. Record.

TAPES AND CASSETTES

1966

11   *An Overview of Approaches to Personality*, 36 min. Rice
University Symposium on the Study of Personality. New York:
Norton, 1966. Cassette and Tape No. 29183.

1969

12   Participant in *The Changing Significance of Food*, 3 hours. In
Hunger and Malnutrition Symposium. Washington, D. C. : AAAS,
1969. Cassette and Tape No. 1/69-VII.

13   *The Communication Gap*, 90 min. Talk at Spencer Memorial
Church, Brooklyn, New York. Port Chester, New York: Noumedia,
1969. Cassette and Tape No. 6946.

1970

14   *The Irreversibility of Parenthood*, 90 min. Talk to Single Parent
Group, St. Luke Chapel, New York City. Port Chester, New York:
Noumedia, 1970. Cassette and Tape No. 7011.

15   Participant in *Is There a Generation Gap in Science?* 3 hours.
Washington, D. C. : AAAS, 1970. Cassette and Tape No. 75-70.

16   Participant in *The Revolution in Values: An Overview*, 30 min.
Speech given at Regency House, Atlanta, Georgia. Pittsburgh:
Thesis Theological Cassettes, 1970. Cassette.

17   Participant in *2001: Science Fiction or Man's Future*, 55 min.
WKCR-Columbia University Rauio. New York: Erwin Frankel
Productions, 1970. Tape and Record.

18   *Shaping the Future*, 30 min. Commencement Address at Northern
Virginia Community College, Annandale, Virginia. Port Chester,
New York: Noumedia, 1970. Cassette and Tape No. N7042.

1971

19   Participant in *Biological and Cultural Bases of Sex Role Differen-*

tiation, 3 hours. Washington, D. C. : AAAS, 1971. Cassette and Tape No. 102-71.

1972

20   Discussion: *Can the Socialization Process of Children Lead to Greater Acceptance of Diversity?* 90 min. Speech given to the National Association for the Education of Young Children. Hampton, Va. : Child Care Information Center, 1972. Cassette.

21   *On the Family and Growing Up*, 21 min. , interviewed by Joan Burke for CBS News. Vital History Cassettes. New York: Grolier Educational, 1972. Cassette No. 2, Side B.

22   Participant in *Public Speaking of Science*, 30 min. , interviewed by Edward Edelson. In *Speaking of Science*, Vol. 1. Washington, D. C. : AAAS, 1972. Cassette.

23   *That Each Child May Learn What It is to Be Completely Human*, 45 min. Opening Session, Annual Meeting National Council of Teachers of English. Waukegan, Illinois: Comtrom, 1972. Cassette No. ET-2.

1973

24   *The Crisis of Self: America's Secret War*, 40 min. Talk to General Session of the Congress for Recreation and Parks. Arlington, Virginia: National Recreation and Park Association, 1973. Cassette.

25   Participant in Discussion of *Why People Hate: The Origins of Discrimination*, 45 min. Westport, Conn. : Mass Communications, 1973. Cassette No. 1.

26   (With René Dubos.) Press Conference AAAS Meeting *The World System*, 30 min. Toronto: Canadian Broadcasting System, 1973. Cassette and Tape No. 932.

1974

27   Discussion of Ralph Nader's Lecture: *Anthropology in Law and Civic Action*, 90 min. Anthropology in Society Series. Washington, D. C. : Anthropological Society of Washington, 1974. Cassette and Tape.

1975

28   *In Conversation with David Watmough*, 25 min. Vancouver,
B. C. : Canadian Broadcasting System, 1975. Tape 7".

29   *The Child in Society*, 120 min. Conference on Child Advocacy,
Madison, Wisconsin. Chicago: Audio Archives, 1975. 2 Cassettes
No. CCA1-16A/B.

30   Participant in *Women Today: Options, Obstacles, Opportunities*,
20 min. Westport, Conn. : Mass Communications, 1975. Cassette
No. 1 Side A.

FILMS

1952

31   (With Gregory Bateson.) Character Formation in Different Cultures:
A Balinese Family, 17 min. ,
Bathing Babies in Three Cultures, 9 min. ,
Childhood Rivalry in Bali and New Guinea, 20 min. ,
First Days in the Life of a New Guinea Baby, 19 min. ,
Karba's First Years, 20 min.
Distributor: New York: New York University Film Library;
London: British Universities Film Council, 1952. 16 mm, black and white, sound.

32   (With Gregory Bateson and Jane Belo.) Character Formation in Different Cultures:
Trance and Dance in Bali, 20 min.
Distributor: New York: New York University Film Library;
London: British Universities Film Council, 1952. 16 mm, black and white, sound.

1958

33   Narrator and Consultant: *Bali Today*, 17 min. , produced by Elda Hartley. Great Minds of Our Times Series.
Distributor: Cos Cob, Conn. : Hartley Productions, 1958. 16 mm, color, sound.

1959

34   Narrator and Consultant: *Four Families*, 2 parts, 60 min. , written, produced and directed by Ian McNeill.
Distributor: Toronto: National Film Board of Canada; New York: McGraw-Hill Films, 1959. 16 mm, black and white, sound.

35   *A Conversation with Margaret Mead*, 30 min. , interviewed by Donald B. Hyatt.
Distributor: Wilmette, Ill. : Films Inc. , 1959. 16 mm, black and white, sound.

1960

36   *New Lives for Old*, 20 min. , produced and directed by Robert E.
Dierbeck with Theodore and Lenore Schwartz. Horizons of Science
Series Vol. 1, No. 6.
Distributor: Princeton, N. J. : Educational Testing Service, 1960.
16 mm, color, sound.

1968

37   *Margaret Mead's New Guinea Journal*, 90 min. , written, produced
and directed by Craig Gilbert.
Distributor: Bloomington, Ind. : National Educational Television
Film Service, Indiana University Audio-Visual Center, 1968. 16 mm,
color, sound.

1969

38   *An Interview by Robert McKenzie on Natives in the Pacific during
World War II*, 27 min. , produced by Vernon Sproxton for BBC-TV.
Distributor: New York: Time and Life Films, 1969. 16 mm, black
and white, sound.

1971

39   *What is Marriage?* Pleasantville, New York: Guidance Associates-
Harcourt, Brace, Jovanovich, 1971. 2 Color Filmstrips, 2 Records.

1973

40   Participant in *Lifestyle 2000: What Will We Take to the Future?*
10 min. (Pt. 2, Segm. 1). Chicago: Denoyer-Geppert Audio Visuals,
1973. 2 Color Filmstrips and 2 Records or 2 Cassettes No. 69726.

1975

41   *Reflections: Margaret Mead*, 58 min. Producer and Distributor:
Washington, D. C. : USIA (United States Information Agency),
1975. 16 mm, color, sound.

VIDEOTAPES

1973

42   *Our Open Ended Future*, 60 min. Talk in NASA Lecture Series
at San Francisco State College *The Next Billion Years: Our Future
in a Cosmic Perspective*. Distributed by National Aeronautic Space
Administration (NASA), Moffett Field, California: AMES Research
Center, 1973. Black and white, standard ½", sound.

1975

43   Participant in *The Thin Edge: Guilt*, 60 min. WNET. New York:
MedCom, 1975. ¾" Video Cassette.

INDEX OF NAMES

INDEX OF SUBJECTS